# THE
# PHYSICIANS
# OF
# MYDDFAI

## IMPORTANT NOTICE

# THE

# PHYSICIANS OF MYDDVAI;

## Meddygon Myddfai,

OR THE MEDICAL PRACTICE OF THE CELEBRATED RHIWALLON AND HIS SONS, OF MYDDVAI, IN CAERMARTHENSHIRE, PHYSICIANS TO RHYS GRYG, LORD OF DYNEVOR AND YSTRAD TOWY, ABOUT THE MIDDLE OF THE THIRTEENTH CENTURY. FROM ANCIENT MSS. IN THE LIBRARIES OF JESUS COLLEGE, OXFORD, LLANOVER, AND TONN; WITH AN ENGLISH TRANSLATION: AND THE LEGEND OF THE LADY OF LLYN Y VAN.

TRANSLATED BY

JOHN PUGHE, ESQ. F.R.C.S. OF PENHELYG, ABERDOVEY,

AND EDITED BY

THE REV. JOHN WILLIAMS AB ITHEL, M.A.

RECTOR OF LLANYMOWDDWY.

PUBLISHED FOR

## The Welsh MSS. Society.

Facsimile reprint of the English translation by Llanerch Publishers, Felinfach, 1993. ISBN 1 897853 15 7.

LLANDOVERY,

PUBLISHED BY D. J. RODERIC;—LONDON, LONGMAN & CO.

MDCCCLXI.

# CONTENTS

Note the pagination follows that of the original edition
of the Physicians of Myddfai. The gaps in pagination
represent the Welsh text which the publishers intend to
reprint as a separate paperback. Retaining the original
pagination avoids confusion where page references are
given in the literature.

# PREFACE.

MEDDYGINIAETH, or medicine, numbers as one of "the nine rural arts, known and practised by the ancient Cymry before they became possessed of cities and a sovereignty;"[*] that is, before the time of Prydain ab Aedd Mawr, which is generally dated about a thousand years anterior to the Christian era. In that remote period the priests and teachers of the people were the GWYDDONIAID, or men of knowledge, obviously so called from their being looked upon as the chief sources and channels of wisdom in the land. It is to these men that the art of healing is attributed, which they seem to have practised mainly, if not wholly, by means of herbs. Indeed Botanology, or a knowledge of the nature and properties of plants, is enumerated as one of the three sciences, which primarily engaged their attention—the other two being Theology and Astronomy, as appears from the following Triad:—

"The three pillars of knowledge, with which the Gwyddoniaid were acquainted, and which they bore in memory from the beginning: the first, a knowledge of Divine things, and of such matters as appertain to the worship of God, and the homage due to goodness; the second, a knowledge of the course of the stars, their names and kinds, and the order of times: the third, a knowledge of the names and use of the herbs of the field, and of their application in practice, in medicine, and in religious worship. These were preserved in the memorials of vocal song, and in the memorials of times, before there were Bards of degree and chair."[+]

[*] Myv. Arch. iii. p. 129.   [+] Llanover MS.

Most of the nations of antiquity pretended to derive the medical art immediately from their gods. It does not appear, however, that the Cymry went so far as to claim for it a divine origin, except in regard to its elementary principles, though the practice of it was confined to the priesthood. In this latter respect also they differed from many old and powerful races. The most ancient physicians we read of in history were those who embalmed the patriarch Jacob by order of his son Joseph.* Moses styles these physicians servants to Joseph, whence we are sure they were not priests, for in that age the Egyptian priests were in such high favour, that they retained their liberty, when, through a public calamity, all the rest of the people became slaves to the king. In Egypt, then, religion and medicine were not combined together. That the Jewish physicians as a class were absolutely distinct from the priests, is also very certain; for when king Asa was diseased in his feet, " he sought not to the Lord, but to the physicians."† It would appear that such, likewise, was the case with the heathens, who dwelt near the Jews, as may be inferred from what is recorded of Ahaziah, king of Judah; when he sent messengers to enquire of Baalzebub, god of Ekron, concerning his disease, he did not desire any remedy from him or his priest, but only to know whether he should recover or not.‡

But among the Cymry all branches of knowledge were centered indiscriminately in the Gwyddoniaid until the time of Prydain. These in his reign were divided into three orders, Bards, Druids, and Ovates,

---

* Gen. l. 2.        † 2 Chron. xvi. 12.        ‡ 2 Kings i. 2.

each having its peculiar duties as well as privileges. It was to the Ovate more especially that the studies and application of terrestrial and natural sciences, such as the one which now engages our attention, were entrusted.

In the Laws of Dyvnwal Moelmud "medicine, commerce, and navigation," are styled "the three civil arts," each having "a peculiar corporate privilege," which privilege is stated to be "by the grant and creation of the lord of the territory, authenticated by the judicature, and distinct from the general privileges of a country and kindred."*

The great legislator is said to have flourished about the year 430 before Christ. At that time, then, supposing the clause in question to be authentic, the art of medicine was protected and encouraged by the state—a fact which, whilst it indicates some progress in medical knowledge, tells much in favour of the humanity and peaceful habits of the people in general.

Soon after the era usually assigned to Dyvnwal Moelmud—about B.C. 400, Hippocrates lived, who is very generally considered as the father of physic, inasmuch as from his time medicine seems to have assumed the form of science among the Greeks. Whether any of the British Ovates became acquainted with his system in the interval between this and the Roman invasion, we are, of course, unable to say. It is possible that they might have derived some information of his medical skill and treatment through the Phoceans, who traded between Marseilles and Britain; and we are certain that they were not men

---

* Ancient Laws and Institutions of Wales, Vol. ii. p. 515.

to despise any opportunity that fell in their way of adding to the store of their general knowledge.

In after times, however, we find that Hippocrates was much esteemed by the medical profession in this country, and the Physicians of Myddvai quote him with admiration.* But their acquaintance with him was, no doubt, derived from a perusal of his works, rather than by tradition.

Some people there may be who are unwilling to admit the authority of our native memorials as to the Druidic antiquity of the art of medicine among the Cymry. But there exists not the slightest reason for any incredulity or doubt on the subject. On the contrary, the classical writers of Greece and Rome, as soon as they are in a position to address us, bear witness in a greater or less degree to the same fact, and support the general correctness of our traditions. The physical researches of the Bards and Druids seem to have caught their especial attention. "The soothsayers," says Strabo, "are sacrificers and physiologists (φυσιολογοι.) The Druids in addition to *physiology* practise ethic philosophy." Nature both external and human—causes and effects—diseases and their antidotes—all came under their cognizance, and in their hands underwent a complete and practical investigation. Cicero informs us that he was personally acquainted with one of the Gallic Druids, Divitiacus the Æduan, a man of quality in his country, who professed to have a thorough knowledge of the laws of nature including, as we may well suppose the science of medicine.

* See § 176.

Pliny enumerates some of the plants most in
repute among the Britons for their medicinal properties. He mentions the mistletoe, and observes that
in Druidical language it signified "All heal," *omnia
sanantem*—a name indicative of the efficacy which it
was supposed to possess; and it is remarkable, as
corroborative of his assertion, that *Oll iach* is to this
very day one of the names by which the plant in
question is known to the Cymry. Nor does it appear
that its virtues, real or traditionary, were forgotten
in comparatively recent times. In the Book of
Howel Veddyg, a descendant of the celebrated physicians of Myddvai, and which forms the second part
of the present volume, we are informed that the
mistletoe was efficacious in cases of general debility—
nervous complaints—brain fever—rheumatism—affection of the heart, liver, bowels, kidneys, spine—
epilepsy—paralysis—insanity. It will strengthen the
sight and hearing, and all the bodily senses—prevent
barreness—and "whosoever takes a spoonful of the
powder in his ordinary drink once a day, shall have uninterrupted health, strength of body, and manly vigour."

Another plant mentioned by Pliny, is the selago,*
a kind of club moss, resembling savine, which,
according to him, the Druids much admired for its
medicinal qualities, particularly in diseases of the eyes.

The samolus,† or marshwort, is said also to have
been greatly used by them to cure their oxen and swine.

Welsh Botanology comprehends several plants,
which either by name or tradition, are associated
with the art of healing, and may be referred purely

' Lycopodium Selago, or Upright Fir Moss.
† Samolus Valerandi, or Water Pimpernel.

to Druidical times, or at least to times when the
Bardic College enjoyed the protection of the state.
Such are the Derwen Vendigaid, or Vervain, the
symbol of Alban Hevin, as the Mistletoe was of
Alban Arthan—Arian Cor—Arian Gwion—Berwr
Taliesin—Bogail Gwener—Boled Olwen—Bronwen—
Cerddinen—Clych Enid—Erbin—Eirin Gwion—Ffa-
en Taliesin— Golch Enid—Llys y Dryw—Llys Tal-
iesin—Meillionen Olwen—Pumbys yr Alban—Ys-
pyddaden, with many others.

We do not know to what extent British medicine
was influenced one way or other by the Roman domina-
tion.   It is very certain that the masters of the world
did not generally regard with a favourable eye our
native institutions; and as in the matter of medicine
they themselves were not particularly celebrated, we
are warranted in supposing that the medical college
received no very great advantage from their rule.
The Bards, however, though pre-eminently conser-
vative, would not reject any real improvements which
the Romans might propose to their notice, as we
infer from their conduct in other matters, such as
their reception of the Roman mode of making parch-
ment and books.

Soon after the departure of the Romans, partiality
for medical or physical pursuits becomes once more
characteristic of our Cymric ancestors.  The following
constituents of man are attributed to the "Chief of
Bards" in the 6th century.

### "THE ELEMENTS OF MAN BY TALIESIN."

"Man consists of eight parts :—the first is the *earth*, which is
sluggish and heavy, whence is the flesh.  The second is the *stones*,
which are hard, and these are the materials of the bones.  The third
is *water*, which is moist and cold, and is the substance of the blood.

The fourth is *salt*, which is briny and sharp, whence are the passions and the faculties of feeling in respect of corporeal sense and perception. The fifth is the *air*, or *wind*, whence is the breath. The sixth is the *sun*, which is clear and fair, whence is the fire, or corporeal warmth, and the light and colour. The seventh is the *Holy Spirit*, whence are the soul and life. The eighth is *Christ*, that is, the intellect and wisdom, and the light of the soul and life.

If the part of man that preponderates be of the *earth*, he will prove unwise, sluggish and very heavy, and will be a little, short, thin dwarf, according as the preponderance may be, whether great or small. If it be of the *air*, the man will be light, unsteady, garrulous, and given to gossip. If of the *stones*, he will be hard of heart, understanding and judgment—a miser and a thief. If of the *sun*, he will be a man of genius, affectionate, active, docile, and poetical. If of the *Holy Spirit*, he will be godly, amiable, and compassionate, of a just and tender judgment, and fond of the arts and sciences; and this cannot otherwise than equiponderate with *Christ* and divine sonship."*

Taliesin has likewise the credit of being the propounder of the following medical Triads;—

"There are three intractable substantial organs : the liver; the kidney ; and the heart.

There are three intractable membranes: the dura mater ; the peritoneum ; and the urinary bladder.

There are three tedious complaints : disease of the knee joint : disease of the substance of a rib, and phthysis ; for when purulent matter has formed in one of these, it is not known when it will get well."†

The period between the 6th and 10th centuries, being especially occupied with national troubles, does not seem to have been favourable to the study of the arts and sciences in Wales ;—at any rate the literary remains of that interval are extremely scanty, and furnish us with no information as to the state of medical science, or the estimation in which the physician was held in the country.

Not so, however, the era of Howel Dda, (or the Good.) In his laws, which were compiled about A.D. 930, several particulars are noticed in connexion with

* Llanover MS. † Llanover MS.

these points, and more especially the mediciner of
the Royal Court.   Of him it is thus stated :—

" Of the mediciner of the household, his office, his privilege, and his
duty, this treats,

1. The twelfth is the mediciner of the household.

2. He is to have his land free ; his horse in attendance ; and his
linen clothing from the queen, and his woollen clothing from the king.

3. His seat in the hall within the palace is at the base of the pillar
to which the screen is attached, near which the king sits.

4. His lodging is with the chief of the household.

5. His protection is, from the time the king shall command him to
visit a wounded or sick person, whether the person be in the palace
or out of it, until he quit him, to convey away an offender.—

6. He is to administer medicine gratuitously to all within the
palace, and to the chief of the household ; and he is to have nothing
from them except their bloody clothes, unless it be for one of the
three dangerous wounds, as mentioned before : these are a stroke on
the head unto the brain ; a stroke in the body unto the bowels ; and
the breaking of one of the four limbs ; for every one of these three
dangerous wounds the mediciner is to have nine score pence and his
food, or one pound without his food, and also the bloody clothes.

7. The mediciner is to have, when he shall apply a tent, twenty
four pence.

8. For an application of red ointment, twelve pence.

9. For an application of herbs to a swelling, four legal pence.

10. For letting blood, four pence.

11. His food daily is worth one penny halfpenny.

12. His light every night is worth one legal penny.

13. The worth of a medical pan is one penny .

14. The mediciner is to take an indemnification from the kindred
of the wounded person, in case he die from the remedy he may use, and
if he do not take it, let him answer for the deed.

15. He is to accompany the armies.

16. He is never to leave the palace, but with the king's permission.

17. His saraad is six kine, and six score of silver, to be augmented.

18. His worth is six score and six kine, to be augmented."

Elsewhere we meet with the following particulars :—

" Of the three conspicuous scars this is—

There are three conspicuous scars : one upon the face ; another
upon the foot ; and another upon the hand ; thirty pence on the foot ;
three score pence on the hand ; six score pence on the face.

Every unexposed scar, four pence.

The cranium, four pence.*

For every broken bone, twenty pence: unless there be a dispute as to its diminutivness; and if there be a dispute as to the size let the mediciner take a brass basin, and let him place his elbow upon the ground, and his hand over the basin, and if its sound be heard, let four legal pence be paid; and if it be not heard, nothing is due."†

This singular test is made more clear in another place :—thus

"Four curt pennies are to be paid to a person for every bone, taken from the upper part of the cranium, which shall sound on falling into a copper basin."‡

If the mediciner was insulted while inebriated he was not entitled to saraad, as " he knew not at what time the king might want his assistance."

He was " free to travel the road, and out of the road—along with the messenger of the sick," and, as stated in legal fragments entitled " Elucidation," any one might take another's horse to procure a medical man for a person in danger without being required to make amends.

We have no reason to suppose that there was any material difference either in the position of the physicians, or in the attention paid to the study of medicine during the succeeding ages, until we come to the era of Rhys Gryg, when the Physicians of Myddvai flourished.

Rhys Gryg‖ was the son of Rhys ab Gruffydd, prince of South Wales, and lived in the former part of the 13th century. He was a distinguished warrior, and fought with varied success in the wars which were carried on in Wales almost without intermission during his life. According to old usage he had his domestic

---

* Ancient Laws and Institutes of Wales, vol. 1. p. 41, &c.    † Ib. p. 315.    ‡ p. 507.

‖ i.e. Rhys the Hoarse.   This surname would seem to indicate that Rhys was afflicted with some disease of the Larynx, or his hoarseness may have been the result of a wound in that part.

Physician, namely Rhiwallon, who was assisted by his three sons, Cadwgan, Gruffydd, and Einion, from a place called Myddvai, in the present county of Caermarthen, whose rights and privileges, as enjoined by law were worthily maintained and upheld by the prince. Under his patronage these men made a collection of valuable medicinal recipes applicable to the various disorders to which the human body was then subject. But though this collection bears their name, we are not to suppose that all the prescriptions contained therein were the result of the studies and experience of the Physicians of Myddvai. Some no doubt had been in the *materia medica* of Wales long before; a few indeed may perhaps be traced up to the time of Howel the Good, if not to the sixth century. Such, however, do not seem to have been reduced to writing, until the Physicians of Myddvai took the matter in hand, and produced the work, which is now for the first time printed. The original manuscript is supposed to be the one lately transferred from the library of the Welsh Charity School, in London, to the British Museum. Of this there are several copies; the one adopted as the basis of the present volume is from the Red Book, in Jesus College, Oxford, which was carefully collated by the Rev. Robert Owen, B.D., Fellow of the said College, with a transcript made by the late Mr. Saunders, from Mr. Rees of Tonn's copy; which MS. was, moreover, copied about 1766, by William Bona, of Llanpumsant, from another belonging to Iago ap Dewi of Llanllawddog. The various readings of the Tonn copy are all arranged at the foot of each page, and referred to under the letter T.

A knowledge of medicine was preserved in the
descendants of this family, and they continued to
practice as physicians at Myddvai, without intermission, until the middle of the last century.

The second portion of this volume purports to
have been compiled by Howel the Physician, son of
Rhys, son of Llewelyn, son of Philip the Physician,
a lineal descendant of Einion, the son of Rhiwallon,
from the Books of the first Physicians of Myddvai.
William Bona made a transcript from the Book of
John Jones, Physician of Myddvai, the last lineal
decendant of the family, A.D. 1743. The late Iolo
Morganwg took a copy of this MS. in 1801, and it is
his copy, now in Llanover Library, that forms the
text of our volume.

Besides these collections, several fragments, some
indeed of considerable lengths, but of uncertain date,
may be often met with in MSS. having for the most
part, perhaps, been made by individual practitioners
for their own private use, before the art of printing
became general. Some medical prescriptions assumed
a proverbial shape, and in that form clung firmly to
the public mind. We subjoin a few of these; and as
proverbs loose much of their point when translated,
we give them first in their original form.

### DIARHEBION MEDDYGOL,
(O Lyfr Iaco ab Dewi.)

A gysgo'n ddigwynos, nid rhaid iddo wrth Rhiwallon Myddfai.
Cwynos o afalau, boreufwyd o gnau.
Genau oer a thraed gwresog fydd byw'n hir.
I farchnad y pysgod y boreu, a'r gigfa brydnhawn.
Dwr oer a bara twym a wnant fol afiachus.
Tair cynneddf dwr; ni ddug afiechyd, dyled, na gweddwdod.
Bwytta wyau heb halen a bair afiechyd.
Nid sarhad dwyn cwynos hen wr.
Llysowen mewn pastai, a llamprai yn yr halen.

Cryd neu dwymyn ar gwympad y dail sydd bob amser yn hir,
neu'n farwol.

Mynn mis, oen tri mis.

Traed sychion, genau ir.

Gleisiad a phregeth y Grawys.

Fe ladd cwynos fwy nac a wellhawyd erioed gan Feddygon Myddfai.

Prydnawnfwyd ysgafn, cwynos lai, cwsg da, hir oes.

Na flysia laeth wedi pysgod.

Iechyd ieuengctyd, afiechyd henaint, yw cysgu llawer.

Hir iechyd ieuengctyd a fyrha'r einioes.

Iachach arogli twym na'i fwytta.

Clefyd byr i'r corph, a rhew byr i'r ddaear, a iachant, ac a gryfhant ;
pob un o'r ddau yn hir a ddinystriant.

Tra phiswyf yn loyw, cardotted y meddyg.

Gwell yw blys na glothineb.

Digon o fara, ychydig o ddiod.

Y bara ddoe, y cig heddyw, a'r gwin y llynedd, a bair iechyd.

Torr dy syched lle cyrcho golchyddes ei dwr.

Tri dyn a fyddant hiroesoeg, aradwr sychdir, hafottwr mynydd, a
physgottwr môr.

Tair gwledd iechyd, llaeth, bara, a halen.

Tair meddyginiaeth Meddygon Myddfai, dwr, mel, a llafur.

Iechyd yw llafur cymhedrol.

Tri chymhedroldeb a barant hir oes, ymborth, llafur, a myfyrdod.

Ni thorro ei gythlwng ym Mai, cyfrifed ei hun gyda'r meirw.

Yr hwn a welo ffunegl a'r nis casglo, nid dyn namyn diafol yw.

O mynni farw, bwytta ddeilcawl yn Awst.

Na pha faint a fwytteych, yf deirgwaith.

E ddenfyn Duw fwyd i ddwylo wedi eu golchi.

Yf ddwr fal ych, a gwin fal brenin.

Cynhildeb yw un wr, bonheddigeiddrwydd yw dau, glewder yw tri,
a dirhidra yw'r pedwerydd.

Pei gwypei rai ddaed iar yn Ionawr, ni adewid un ar y glwyd.

Caws defaid, llaeth geifr, menyn gwartheg, sydd oreu.

Tri enllyn iechyd, mel, ymenyn, a llaeth.

Tri enllyn afiechyd, cig, cwrw, ac aesel.

Na ddiosg dy bais cyn y Derchafael.

Os mynni fyned yn glaf, golch dy ben, a dos i gysgu.

Nid oes mewn cawl heb lysiau na daioni, na maeth.

O mynni farw, bwytta gig maharen, rhost, a chwsg yn fuan.

Os bwyttai beth drwg, bwytta ysgyfarnog rost.

Mwstard wedi bwyd.

A gartho ei ddanedd â blaen ei gyllell, gall eu carthu cyn bo hir
i'r carn.

Udgorn angau yw peswch sych.

## MEDICAL MAXIMS,

(From the Book of Iago ab Dewi.)

He who goes to sleep supperless will have no need of Rhiwallon of Myddvai.

A supper of apples—breakfast of nuts.

A cold mouth and warm feet will live long.

To the fish market in the morning, to the butcher's shop in the afternoon.

Cold water and warm bread will make an unhealthy stomach.

The three qualities of water : it will produce no sickness, no debt, and no widowhood.

To eat eggs without salt will bring on sickness.

It is no insult to deprive an old man of his supper.

An eel in a pie, lampreys in salt.

An ague or fever at the fall of the leaf is always of long continuance, or else is fatal.

A kid a month old—a lamb three months.

Dry feet, moist tongue.

A salmon and sermon in Lent.

Supper will kill more than were ever cured by the Physicians of Myddvai.

A light dinner, a less supper, sound sleep, long life.

Do not wish for milk after fish.

To sleep much is the health of youth, the sickness of old age.

Long health in youth will shorten life.

It is more wholesome to smell warm bread than to eat it.

A short sickness for the body, and short frost for the earth, will heal ; either of them long will destroy.

Whilst the urine is clear, let the physician beg.

Better is appetite than gluttony.

Enough of bread, little of drink.

The bread of yesterday, the meat of to-day, and the wine of last year will produce health.

Quench thy thirst where the washerwoman goes for water.

Three men that are long-lived, the ploughman of dry land, a mountain dairyman, and a fisherman of the sea.

The three feasts of health, milk, bread, and salt.

The three medicines of the Physicians of Myddvai, water, honey, and labour.

Moderate exercise is health.

Three moderations will produce long life ; in food, labour, and meditation.

Whoso breaks not his fast in May, let him consider himself with the dead.

He who sees fennel and gathers it not—is not a man, but a devil.

If thou desirest to die, eat cabbage in August.

Whatever quantity thou eatest drink thrice.
God will send food to washed hands.
Drink water like an ox, and wine like a king.
One egg is economy, two is gentility, three is greediness, and the
fourth is wastefulness.
If persons knew how good a hen is in January, none would be left on
the roost.
The cheese of sheep, the milk of goats, and the butter of cows are
the best.
The three victuals of health, honey, butter, and milk.
The three victuals of sickness, flesh meat, ale, and vinegar.
Take not thy coat off before Ascension day.
If thou wilt become unwell, wash thy head, and go to sleep.
In pottage without herbs there is neither goodness, nor nourishment.
If thou wilt die, eat roast mutton, and sleep soon after it.
If thou wilt eat a bad thing, eat roast hare.
Mustard after food.
He who cleans his teeth with the point of his knife, may soon clean
them with the haft.
A dry cough is the trumpet of death."

In conclusion, we beg to congratulate the Welsh
MSS. Society, under whose auspices the present
volume is published, upon its selection of a Translator.
Mr. Pughe, himself a member of the medical profession
and a good Welsh Scholar, has done full justice to a
work, the execution of which required skill and
judgment of no ordinary kind. We are sure that the
country will appreciate his labours.

Our thanks are greatly due to Lord Llanover for
the liberal use of his MS., likewise to the Rev. Robert
Owen, B.D., Jesus College, Oxford, for the very kind
and careful manner in which he collated the Tonn MS.
with the Red Book version; also to Mr. Rees of
Tonn, for his kindness in lending his MS. for that
purpose, and for the pains with which he compiled the
Myddvai Legend; when gratuitous aids of such a kind
are so rare, they deserve special acknowledgment.

*Llanymowddwy,*
*Feast of St. David,* 1861.                THE EDITOR.

THE

# LEGEND OF LLYN-Y-VAN-VACH,

### OR THE ORIGIN OF

## Che Meddygon Myddfai,

### COLLECTED FROM VARIOUS SOURCES,* IN THE YEAR 1841.†

WHEN the eventful struggle made by the Princes of South Wales
to preserve the independence of their country was drawing to
its close in the twelvth century, there lived at Blaensawdde‡
near Llanddeusant, Carmarthenshire, a widowed woman, the relict
of a farmer who had fallen in those disastrous troubles.

The widow had an only son to bring up, and Providence smiled
upon her, and, despite her forlorn condition, her live stock had so
increased in course of time that she could not well depasture them
upon her farm, so she sent a portion of her cattle to graze on the
adjoining Black Mountain, and their most favourite place was
near the small lake called Llyn-y-Van-Vach, on the North Western
side of the Carmarthenshire Vans.

* Written down by Mr. William Rees, of Tonn, near Llandovery, from the
oral recitations of the late Mr. John Evans, Tiler, Myddvai; Mr. David
Williams, Mason, Morfa, Myddvai; (about 90 years old) and Mrs. Elizabeth
Morgan, of Henllys Lodge, near Llandovery, a native of Myddvai.

† Mr. Rees begs to acknowledge his obligations to J. Joseph, Esq. F.S.A.
Brecon, for collecting several particulars and incidents of the Legend from
amongst the old inhabitants of the Parish of Llanddeusant.

‡ Blaensawdde, or the upper end of the river Sawdde—is situate about three
quarters of a mile S. E. from the village of Llanddeusant. It gives its name to
one of the hamlets of that parish. The Sawdde has its source in Llyn y Van-
Vach, which is nearly two miles distant from Blaensawdde house.

The son grew up to manhood, and was generally sent by his mother to look after the cattle on the mountain. One day in his peregrinations along the margin of the lake, to his great astonishment, he beheld, sitting on the unruffled surface of the water, a Lady; one of the most beautiful creatures that mortal eyes ever beheld, her hair flowed gracefully in ringlets over her shoulders, the tresses of which she arranged with a comb, whilst the glassy surface of her watery couch served for the purpose of a mirror, reflecting back her own image. Suddenly she beheld the young man standing on the brink of the lake, with his eyes rivetted on her, and unconsciously offering to herself the provision of barley bread and cheese with which he had been provided when he left his home.

Bewildered by a feeling of love and admiration for the object before him, he continued to hold out his hand towards the lady, who imperceptibly glided near to him, but gently refused the offer of his provisions. He attempted to touch her, but she eluded his grasp, saying

> " Cras dy fara !
> Nid hawdd fy nala."

> Hard baked is thy bread !
> 'Tis not easy to catch me ;

and immediately dived under the water, and disappeared, leaving the love stricken youth to return home, a prey to disappointment and regret that he had been unable to make further acquaintance with one, in comparison with whom the whole of the fair maidens of Llanddeusant and Myddvai,* whom he had ever seen were as nothing.

* Myddvai parish was, in former times, celebrated for its fair maidens, but whether they were descendants of the Lady of the Lake or otherwise cannot be determined. An old pennill records the fact of their beauty thus :—

> " Mae eira gwyn
> Ar ben y bryn,
> A'r glasgoed yn y Ferdre,
> Mae bedw mân
> Ynghoed Cwm-brân,
> A merched glân yn Myddfe,"

Which may be translated,

> There is white snow
> On the mountain's brow,
> And greenwood at the Verdre,
> Young birch so good
> In Cwm-brân wood,
> And lovely girls in Myddve.

On his return home the young man communicated to his mother the extraordinary vision he had beheld. She advised him to take some unbaked dough or " toes " the next time in his pocket, as there must have been some spell connected with the hard baked bread, or " Bara cras," which prevented his catching the lady.

Next morning, before the sun had gilded with its rays the peaks of the Vans, the young man was at the lake, not for the purpose of looking after his mother's cattle, but seeking for the same enchanting vision he had witnessed the day before ; but all in vain did he anxiously strain his eye-balls and glance over the surface of the lake, as only the ripples occasioned by a stiff breeze met his view, and a cloud hung heavily on the summit of the Van, which imparted an additional gloom to his already distracted mind.

Hours passed on, the wind was hushed, and the clouds which had enveloped the mountain had vanished into thin air, before the powerful beams of the sun, when the youth was startled by seeing some of his mother's cattle on the precipitous side of the acclivity, nearly on the opposite side of the lake. His duty impelled him to attempt to rescue them from their perilous position, for which purpose he was hastening away, when, to his inexpressible delight, the object of his search again appeared to him as before, and seemed much more beautiful than when he first beheld her. His hand was again held out to her, full of unbaked bread, which he offered with an urgent proffer of his heart also, and vows of eternal attachment. All of which were refused by her, saying

" Llaith dy fara !
Ti ni frnna'."

Unbaked is thy bread!
I-will not have thee.

But the smiles that played upon her features as the lady vanished beneath the waters raised within the young man a hope that forbade him to despair by her refusal of him, and the recollection of which cheered him on his way home. His aged parent was made acquainted with his ill-success, and she suggested that his bread should next time be but slightly baked, as most likely to please the mysterious being, of whom he had become enamoured.

Impelled by an irresistible feeling, the youth left his mother's house early next morning, and with rapid steps he passed over the

mountain.  He was soon near the margin of the lake, and with
all the impatience of an ardent lover, did he wait with a feverish
anxiety for the re-appearance of the mysterious lady.

The sheep and goats browsed on the precipitous sides of the
Van ; the cattle strayed amongst the rocks and large stones, some
of which were occasionally loosened from their beds and suddenly
rolled down into the lake; rain and sunshine alike came and
passed away, but all were unheeded by the youth, so wrapped up
was he in looking for the appearance of the lady.

The freshness of the early morning had disappeared before the
sultry rays of the noon-day sun, which in its turn was fast verging
towards the west as the evening was dying away and making
room for the shades of night ; and hope had well nigh abated of
beholding once more the Lady of the Lake.  The young man cast a
sad and last farewell look over the waters, and, to his astonishment beheld several cows walking along its surface.  The sight of
these animals caused hope to revive that they would be followed
by another object far more pleasing, nor was he disappointed, for
the maiden re-appeared, and to his enraptured sight, even lovelier
than ever.  She approached the land, and he rushed to meet her
in the water.  A smile encouraged him to sieze her hand ; neither
did she refuse the moderately baked bread he offered her ; and
after some persuasion she consented  to become his bride, on condition that they should only live together until she received from
him three blows without a cause

"Tri ergyd diachos."

Three causeless blows.

And if he ever should happen to strike her three such blows, she
would leave him for ever.  To such conditions he readily consented, and would have consented to any other stipulation, had
it been proposed, as he was only intent on then securing such a
lovely creature for his wife.

Thus the lady of the lake engaged to become the young man's
wife, and having loosed her hand for a moment, she darted away
and dived into the lake.  His chagrin and grief were such that he
determined to cast himself headlong into the deepest water, so as
to end his life in the element that had contained in its unfathomed
depths the only one for whom he cared to live on earth.  As he
was on the point of committing this rash act, there emerged out

of the lake *two* most beautiful ladies accompanied by a hoary headed man of noble mien and extraordinary stature, but having otherwise all the force and strength of youth. This man addressed the almost bewildered youth, in accents calculated to soothe his troubled mind, saying that as he proposed to marry one of his daughters, he consented to the union provided the young man could distinguish which of the two ladies before him was the object of his affections. This was no easy task as the maidens were such perfect counterparts of each other, that it seemed quite impossible for him to choose his bride, and if perchance he fixed upon the wrong one, all would be for ever lost.

Whilst the young man narrowly scanned the two ladies, he could not perceive the least difference betwixt the two, and was almost giving up the task in despair, when one of them thrust her foot a slight degree forward. The motion, simple as it was, did not escape the observation of the youth, and he discovered a trifling variation in the mode with which their sandals were tied, this at once put an end to the dilemma, for he, who had on previous occasions, been so taken up with the general appearance of the Lady of the Lake, had also noticed the beauty of her feet and ankles, and on now recognizing the peculiarity of her shoe-tie he boldly took hold of her hand.

"Thou hast chosen rightly" said her father, "be to her a kind and faithful husband, and I will give her, as a dowry, as many sheep, cattle, goats, and horses, as she can count of each, without heaving or drawing in her breath. But remember that if you prove unkind to her at any time, and strike her three times without a cause, she shall return to me and shall bring all her stock back with her."

Such was the verbal marriage settlement, to which the young man gladly assented, and his bride was desired to count the number of sheep she was to have. She immediately adopted the mode of counting by *fives*, thus :—One, two, three, four, five—One, two, three, four, five ; as many times as possible in rapid succession, till her breath was exhausted. The same process of reckoning had to determine the number of goats, cattle, and horses respectively ; and, in an instant the full number of each came out of the lake when called upon by the Father.

The young couple were then married, by what ceremony was not stated, and afterwards went to reside at a farm called Esgair

Llaethdy, somewhat more than a mile from the village of Myddvai, where they lived in prosperity and happiness for several years, and became the parents of three sons, who were beautiful children.

Once upon a time there was a christening to take place in the neighbourhood, to which the parents were specially invited. When the day arrived the wife appeared very reluctant to attend the christening, alledging that the distance was too great for her to walk. Her husband told her to fetch one of the horses which were grazing in an adjoining field. "I will" said she, "if you will bring me my gloves which I left in our house." He went to the house and returned with the gloves, and finding that she had not gone for the horse, jocularly slapped her shoulder with one of them, saying "go ! go ! (dos, dos) when she reminded him of the understanding upon which she consented to marry him :—That he was not to strike her without a cause ; and warned him to be more cautious for the future.

On another occasion when they were together at a wedding ; in the midst of the mirth and hilarity of the assembled guests, who had gathered together from all the surrounding country, she burst into tears and sobbed most piteously. Her husband touched her on her shoulder and enquired the cause of her weeping ? she said " now people are entering into trouble, and your troubles are likely to commence as you have the second time stricken me without a cause."

Years passed on, and their children had grown up, and were particularly clever young men. In the midst of so many worldly blessings at home the husband almost forgot that there remained only one causeless blow to be given to destroy the whole of his prosperity. Still he was watchful lest any trivial occurence should take place, which his wife must regard as a breach of their marriage contract. She told him, as her affection for him was unabated, to be careful that he would not, through some inadvertence give the last and only blow, which, by an unalterable destiny, over which she had no control, would separate them for ever.

It however so happened that one day they were together at a funeral, where, in the midst of the mourning and grief at the house of the deceased, she appeared in the highest and gayest spirits, and indulged in immoderate fits of laughter, which so shocked her husband that he touched her saying " Hush ! Hush ! dont laugh." She said that she laughed " because people when they die go out of trouble," and, rising up, she went out of the house, saying, "The last blow has been struck, our marriage contract is broken, and at an end! Farewell!" Then she started off towards Esgair Llaethdy, where she called her cattle and other stock together, each by name. The cattle she called thus:—

> " Mu wlfrech, Moelfrech,
> Mu olfrech, Gwynfrech,
> Pedair cae tonn-frech,
> Yr hen wynebwen
> A'r las Geigen,
> Gyda'r Tarw Gwyn
> O lys y Brenin ;
>  A'r llo du bach,
>  Sydd ar y bach,
> Dere dithau, yn iach adre ! "

> Brindled cow, white speckled,
> Spotted cow, bold freckled,
> The four field sward mottled,
> The old white-faced,
> And the grey Geingon,
> With the white Bull,
> From the court of the King ;
>  And the little black calf
>  Tho' suspended on the hook,
> Come thou also, quite well home !

They all immediately obeyed the summons of their mistress, the "little black calf" although it had been slaughtered, became alive again and walked off with the rest of the stock at the command of the Lady. This happened in the spring of the year, and there were four oxen ploughing in one of the fields, to these she cried,

> " Pedwar eidion glas
> Sydd ar y maes,
> Deuwch chwithau
> Yn iach adre ! "

> The four grey oxen,
> That are on the field,
> Come you also.
> Quite well home!

Away the whole of the live stock went with the Lady across Myddvai Mountain, towards the lake from whence they came, a distance of above six miles, where they disappeared beneath its waters, leaving no trace behind except a well marked furrow, which was made by the plough the oxen drew after them into the lake, and which remains to this day as a testimony to the truth of this story.

What became of the affrighted ploughman—whether he was left on the field when the oxen set off, or whether he followed them to the lake has not been handed down by tradition; neither has the fate of the disconsolate and half-ruined husband been kept in remembrance. But of the sons it is stated that they often wandered about the lake and its vicinity, hoping that their mother might be permitted to visit the face of the earth once more, as they had been apprised of her mysterious origin, her first appearance to their father, and the untoward circumstances which so unhappily deprived them of her maternal care.

In one of their rambles, at a place near Dôl Howel, at the Mountain Gate, still called "Llidiad y Meddygon" The Pysicians' Gate, the mother appeared suddenly, and accosted her eldest son, whose name was Rhiwallon, and told him that his mission on earth, was to be a benefactor to mankind by relieving them from pain and misery, through healing all manner of their diseases ; for which purpose she furnished him with a bag full of Medical Prescriptions and instructions for the preservation of health. That by strict attention thereto, he and his family would become for many generations the most skilful Physicians in the country. Then promising to meet him when her counsel was most needed, she vanished. But on several occasions she met her sons near the banks of the lake, and once she even accompanied them on their return home as far as a place still called "Pant-y-Meddygon" The dingle of the Physicians, where she pointed out to them the various plants and herbs which grew in the dingle, and revealed to them their medicinal qualities or virtues, and the knowledge she imparted to them, together with their unrivalled skill soon caused them to attain such celebrity that none ever possessed before them. And in order that their knowledge should not be lost, they wisely committed the same to writing, for the benefit of mankind throughout all ages.

And so ends the story of the Physicians of Myddvai, which has been handed down from one generation to another, thus :—

> "Yr hén wr llwyd o'r cornel,
> Gan ei dad a glywodd chwedel,
> A chan ei dad fe glywodd yntau
> Ac ar ei ôl mi gofiais innau."

> The grey old man in the corner,
> Of his father heard a story,
> Which from his father he had heard,
> And after them I have remembered.

As stated in the Introduction of the present Work, Rhiwallon and his sons became Physicians to Rhys Gryg, Lord of Llandovery and Dynevor Castles, "who gave them rank, lands, and privileges at Myddvai for their maintenance in the practice of their art and science, and the healing and benefit of those who should seek their help," thus affording to those who could not afford to pay, the best medical advice and treatment, gratuitously.   Such a truly Royal Foundation could not fail to produce corresponding effects. So the fame of the Physicians of Myddvai was soon established over the whole country, and continued for centuries among their descendants.

The celebrated Welsh Bard, Dafydd ap Gwilym, who flourished in the following century, and was buried at the Abbey of Tal-y-llychau, in Caermarthenshire, about the year 1368, says in one of his Poems, as quoted in Dr. Davies' Dictionary.

> " Meddyg ni wnai modd y gwnaeth
> Myddfai, o chai ddyn meddfaeth."
>
> A Physician he would not make
> As Myddvai made, if he had a mead fostered man.

Of the above lands bestowed upon the Meddygon, there are two farms in Myddvai parish still called "Llwyn Ifan Feddyg," the Grove of Evan the Physician; and "Llwyn Meredydd Feddyg" the Grove of Meredith the Physician.   Esgaer Llaethdy, mentioned in the foregoing Legend, was formerly in the possession of the above descendants, and so was Ty newydd, near Myddvai, which was purchased by Mr. Holford, of Cilgwyn, from the Rev. Charles Lloyd, Vicar of Llandefalle, Breconshire, who married a daughter of one of the Meddygon, and had the living of Llandefalle from a Mr. Vaughan, who presented him to the same out of gratitude, because Mr. Lloyd's wife's father had cured him of a disease in the eye.   As Mr. Lloyd succeeded to the above living in 1748, and died in 1800, it is probable that the skilful occulist was John Jones, who is mentioned in the following inscription on a tombstone at present fixed against the west end of Myddvai Church.

### HERE

Lieth the body of Mr. David Jones, of Mothvey, Surgeon,
who was an honest, charitable, and skilful man.
He died Septemder 14th, Anno Dom 1719, aged 61.

### JOHN JONES, Surgeon,

Eldest son of the said David Jones, departed this life
the 25th of November, 1739, in the 44th year
of his Age, and also lyes interred hereunder.

These appear to have been the last of the Physicians who practised at Myddvai. The above John Jones resided for some time at Llandovery, and was a very eminent surgeon. One of his descendants named John Lewis, lived at Cwmbran, Myddvai, at which place his great grandson Mr. John Jones, now resides.

Dr. Morgan Owen, Bishop of Llandaff, who died at Glasallt, parish of Myddvai, in 1645, was a descendant of the Meddygon, and an inheritor of much of their landed property in that parish, the bulk of which he bequeathed to his nephew, Morgan Owen, who died in 1667, and was succeeded by his son, Henry Owen; and at the decease of the last of whose descendants, Robert Lewis, Esq. the estates became through the will of one of the family, the property of the late D. A. S. Davies, Esq. M.P. for Caermarthenshire.

Bishop Owen bequeathed to another nephew, Morgan ap Rees, son of Rees ap John, a descendant of the Meddygon, the farm of Rhyblid, and some other property. Morgan ap Rees' son, Samuel Rice, resided at Loughor, in Gower, Glamorganshire, and had a son, Morgan Rice, who was a merchant in London, and became Lord of the Manor of Tooting Graveney, and High Sheriff in the year, 1772. and Deputy Lieutenant of the County of Surrey, 1776. He resided at Hill House, which he built. At his death the whole of his property passed to his only child, John Rice, Esq. whose eldest son, the Rev. John Morgan Rice, inherited the greater portion of his estates. The head of the family is now the Rev. Horatio Morgan Rice, Rector of South Hill, with Callington, Cornwall, and J.P. for the County, who inherited with other property, a small estate at Loughor. The above Morgan Rice had landed property in Llanmadock and Llangenith, as well as Loughor, in Gower, but whether he had any connexion with Howel the Physician, (ap Rhys ap Llywelyn ap Philip the Physician, and lineal descendant from Einion ap Rhiwallon,) who resided at Cilgwryd in Gower is not known.

Amongst other families who claim descent from the Physicians were the Bowens of Cwmydw, Myddvai; and Jones of Dollgarreg and Penrhock, in the same parish; the latter of whom are represented by Charles Bishop, of Dollgareg, Esq. Clerk of the Peace for Caermarthensbire, and Thomas Bishop, of Brecon, Esq.

Rees Williams of Myddvai is recorded as one of the Meddygon. His great grandson was the late Rice Williams, M.D. of Aberystwyth, who died May 16th, 1842, aged 85, and appears to have been the last, although not the least eminent, of the Physicians descended from the mysterious Lady of Llyn-y-Van.

THE

# Physicians of Myddvai.

§ 1.  HERE by the help of God, the supreme chief Sovereign,
are shewn the most notable and principal methods of healing
the human body, the persons who caused them to be written
after this fashion being Rhiwallon the Physician, and his
sons, even Kadwgan, Griffith, and Einion.  For they were
the ablest and most eminent of the physicians of their time,
and of the time of Rhys Gryg [1] their lord, and the lord of
Dinevor, the nobleman who maintained their rights and
privileges, in all integrity and honour, as was meet.  The
reason why they thus caused a record of their skill to be
committed to writing was, lest no one should be found after
them so endowed with the requisite knowledge as they were.

### THE HEAD.

§ 2.  The head is the first and the most important portion
of man's body, which God formed, for therein are the five
corporeal senses.

---

[1] Rhys Gryg, " arwr Dinefwr," was the son of Rhys ab Gruffydd, Prince of
South Wales.  He married the daughter of the Earl of Clare, A.D. 1219, died
at Llandeilo Vawr in 1233, and was buried in the Cathedral of St. David's,
where his monumental effigy still remains in a good state of preservation.  Rhys
Gryg was a distinguished warrior, and fought with various success in the wars
which were carried on in Wales, almost without intermission, during his life.
Several odes are preserved in the first volume of the Myvyrian Archaiology,
which were addressed to him by the poets, Llywarch ab Llywelyn, Phylip Bryd-
ydd, and Dewi Mynyw, the two latter of whom also wrote elegies upon him.

## ORIGIN OF DISEASES IN THE HEAD.

§ 3. Diseases originate in three places in the head ; one is the pericranium, the second is the cranium, and the third is the dura mater.

### PRESERVATION OF THE CRANIUM AND SCALP.

§ 4. By an incision in the scalp, extending to the cranium, and giving exit to the venom, is the cranium preserved. By phlebotomy and cauterization is the scalp preserved.

### DURA MATER.—TREATMENT.

§ 5. By exposing the dura mater, taking two parts of wood betony, and three parts of the violet, with salt butter, pounded together, and applying them thereto, the venom is removed from the dura mater. It will extract any inflammation and pain existing therein.

### DURATION OF TREATMENT.

§ 6. From the time the scalp is laid open to the end of nine days, shall this issue remain on the bone : that is to say, this plan should be followed in an old standing complaint of the head.

### WOUND ON THE HEAD.—TREATMENT. PHYSICIAN'S FEE.

§ 7. As to a recent blow or fresh wound on the head, the sooner it is dressed the better, lest there should be extravasated blood upon the dura mater, and that it should become concocted there. When the bone and the dura mater are exposed, take the violet and fresh butter, and pound together. If the violet cannot be gotten, take the white of eggs and linseed, pounding them together ; or fresh butter and linseed, and apply thereto till (the pain is) assuaged. Then an ointment should be prepared of herbs, butter and tallow, and applied thereto until it is cured.   A pound is the physician's fee for this treatment as regards the deed of mercy simply, without victuals : or nine score (pence) with victuals.[1]

### PAIN IN THE EYE.  CAUTERY.

§ 8.  For pain in the eye.   The actual cautery applied to the hollow of the eyebrow, and another in the nape of the neck, is beneficial for rheum of the head.

### WATERY EYE.—TREATMENT.

§ 9.  For a red watery eye (ophthalmia tarsi cum epiphora) insert a seaton under the jaw, and apply the actual cautery in the nape of the neck, and this is beneficial for rheum of the head.

### DISEASED EYELIDS.—REMEDY.

§ 10.  For a dry scurfy condition of the eye (lids.)  Take the juice of the strawberry, a hen's fat, and May butter.  Pound them well together, and keep in a horn (box.)  When going to bed, anoint (about) thine eye and eyelids well, and they will be cured.

### PNEUMONIA.—TREATMENT.

§ 11.  There are three kinds of lung disease ;—simple pneumonia, white pneumonia, (bronchitis) and black pneumonia, (phthysis) which is marked by pain below the mammæ, under the armpit, and in the top of the shoulders, with (hectic) redness of the cheeks.   And thus are they

---

[1] The same fee is ordered in the Venedotian Code of Hywel Dda ;—" The compensation for the medicaments is this.   For each, [a stroke on the head unto the brain ; a stroke in the body unto the bowels ; and the breaking of one of the four limbs,] the person wounded is to receive three pounds from the one who shall have so wounded him ; the amount likewise due from the person who shall wound him, for his medical treatment, is a pound, without food : or nine score pence, with his food, and the bloody clothes."—Ancient Laws and Institutes of Wales, v. i. p. 313.   See also p. 391.

treated. Let (the patient) take, for three successive days, of the following herbs; hemlock, agrimony, herb Robert, and asarabacca, then let him undergo a three day's course of aperients. When the disease is thus removed from the bronchial tubes, an emetic should be given him (daily) to the end of nine days. Afterwards let a medicine be prepared, by digesting the following herbs in wheat ale or red wine : madder, sharp dock, anise, agrimony, daisy, round birth-wort, meadow sweet, yellow goat's beard, heath, water avens, woodruff, crake berry, the corn cockle, caraway, and such other herbs as will seem good to the physician.

Thus is the blessed confection prepared. Take of May butter, a she-goat's suet or a doe's fat, the shepherd's needle, and as many as may be desired of such herbs as may be suitable for the purpose. A wounded lung is the physician's third difficulty, for he cannot controul it, but must wait for the will of God. By means of the herbs just mentioned, a medicine may be prepared for any one who has a pulmonary abcess (empyema.) He should let out (the matter) and support (the patient) as in the case of a wounded lung, till he is recovered. But most usually, he will have died within eleven years (al. one year.)

### FEVERS.

§ 12. There are four kinds of fevers, deriving their origin from the summer, viz. latent fever, intermittent fever, ephemeral fever, and inflammatory fever. The fifth fever is typhus, and this kind proceeds from the brain. A latent fever is relieved by an emetic, a cordial, and cauteries. Thus it originates ; from the over generating of tough humor in the stomach, from which results a distaste for food, and lassitude during summer. The mugwort, madder, meadow sweet, milfoil, hemp, red cabbage, and the tutsan, all these seven herbs enter into the composition of the medicine required. Whosoever obtains them all, will not languish long from a wounded lung, or need fear for his life. Any of the following herbs may be added thereto, butcher's broom, agrimony, tutsan, dwarf elder, amphibious persicaria, centaury, round birth wort, field scabious, pepper mint, daisy, knap weed, roots of the red nettle, crake berry, St. John's wort, privet, wood betony, the roots of the yellow goat's beard, heath, water avens, woodruff, leaves of the earth nut, agrimony, wormwood, the bastard balm, small burdock, and the orpine.

### INTERMITTENT FEVERS. TREATMENT.

§ 13. For intermittent fevers. Take dandelion and fumatory, infused in water, the first thing in the morning. Then about noon take wormwood infused in water likewise, drinking it as often as ten times, the draught being rendered tepid. Let bread made with pounded wheat be also taken, or oaten cakes, goat's whey, the flesh of a young fowl, husky porridge in water, milk being abstained from, and indeed every kind of milk diet. If the ague does not then terminate, the patient must be put in a bath, when the paroxysm comes on, and an emetic given him whilst in the bath, as it will then act more powerfully.

### COOLING DRINKS.

§ 14. The three best cooling drinks are apple water, goat's whey, and spring water.

### INTERMITTENT FEVERS.

§ 15. Another treatment for an intermittent fever. Take the mugwort, dwarf elder, tutsan, amphibious persicaria, pimpernel, butcher's broom, elder bark, and the mallow, and boiling them together as well as possible in a pot, or cauldron. Then take the water and herbs, and add them to

G

the bath.   The following is a good medicine for this class of
diseases : take moss, ground ivy, or elder, if obtainable,
(if not obtainable, caraway,) and boil these two vegetable
substances well together.   Then take the mallow, fennel,
pimpernel, butcher's broom, borage, and the young leaves
of the earth nut, and bruise them as well as possible, putting them on the fire with the two herbs before mentioned,
and boiling them well.   This being done, let elder bark be
taken from that portion of the tree which is in the ground,
let it be scraped and washed thoroughly, and bruised well in
a mortar.   Then take the liquor prepared from the fore-
mentioned herbs, and mix the said bark therein assiduously
between both hands, and set it to drain into a vessel to
acidify, fermenting it with goat's whey, or cow's whey.   Let
a good cupful thereof be drank every morning as long as it
lasts, a portion of raw honey, apple or wood sorrel, being
taken subsequently in order to remove the taste from the
mouth, after the draught. .  This liquor is beneficial to every
man who requires to purge his body.

HEMORRHOIDS.—EXCITING CAUSE.   TREATMENT—SURGI-
CAL.   ANOTHER METHOD.—MEDICAL.   FORBIDDEN FOOD.

§ 16.  There are two kinds of hemorrhoids, humoral
hemorrhoids and inflamed hemorrhoids, the latter produced by summer heat, the former by summer moisture,
when either condition prevails.   It is in this manner that it
comes.   Four veins proceed from the liver to the anus ;
therefore, thus it may be cured.   Secure three of these by
means of a ligature, and let the fourth be left free.   The
cautery also should be applied to the ancles, and about the
knees and hams.   Thus the blood will be habitually diverted
to the lower extremities, when the cauteries shall have discharged all the humor from the vein.

The second plan of treatment is as follows. Take the mallow, and boil it in wheat ale, or in spring water. Then take that which grows in the earth of the elder (bark,) bruise well in a mortar, and mix it, crude as it is, with the above mentioned decoction, and administer it quickly to the patient, so as to act upon his bowels. Let him afterwards be forbidden beef, cheese, leeks, large fish, salmon, eels, ducks, garlic, and all kinds of milk diet, except whey made with warm milk (from the cow.)

### ABDOMINAL COMPLAINTS.—ASCITES, PERITONITIS, ABDOMINAL TUMOR, TYMPANITIS. TREATMENT OF PERITONITIS. EMETIC. EXTRACT OF STINKING HELLEBORE. INTERNAL ABDOMINAL TUMOR.—TREATMENT.

§ 17. There are four kinds of abdominal complaints. ascites, peritonitis, abdominal tumor, and tympanitis. Ascites cannot be cured. Tympanitis also is a disease from which there is no escape, though it is not soon fatal. Peritonitis is treated by means of an emetic, the blue confection and a medicine. These are the herbs required (for the medicine;) the sweet gale, bay leaves, pimpernel, male speedwell, river startip, borage, moss, liverwort, the young leaves of the earth nut, and the mallow. The before-mentioned emetic should be thus prepared. Take the stinking hellebore (dug fresh) from the ground, from the root, washing it well, slicing it thin, then bruising it in a mortar, as well as can be done, the refuse being thrown away (after the juice is expressed.) The juice should then be put in a pan on the fire (and boiled) whilst there is any ebullition (till nearly solid,) keeping it by you as long as you wish, making small pills thereof when you administer it to the sick. Abdominal tumor is cured by means of cauteries, issues, a cordial, and an emetic.

## ANAL WARTS.

§ 18. Certain warts will often form about the anus. The best way to remove them, is to dig them out with cold iron, afterwards cauterizing their seat, and anointing the same with honey.

THREE KINDS OF URINARY DISORDERS. STRANGURY. HOT AIR BATH. CALCULUS—OPERATION. SUBSEQUENT TREATMENT. PREPARATORY TREATMENT. GRAVEL—TREATMENT.

§ 19. There are three kinds of painful urinary disorders. Strangury. It is cured by means of an emetic, a cordial, cauteries, and a dry (hot air) bath. A hard vesical calculus is thus extracted by operation. Take a staff and place it in the bend of the knee; then fix both arms within the knees, doubling them up over the staff, and securing both wrists with a fillet, over the nape of the neck, the patient (being placed on the back,) his stomach up, with some support under both thighs, and the calculus cut for on the left side of the urethra. Let him be subsequently put in a water bath that same day, also the day following early, and after this he should be put in the kyffeith. Then he should be removed to his bed, and laid there on his back, his wound being cleaned, and dressed with flax and salt butter. He should be kept in the same temperature, until it be known whether he shall escape (the effects of the operation.) He should be kept without food or drink for a day and a night previous to the operation, and should have a bath.

If the disease be gravel, make a medicine of the following herbs, mascerated in strong clear wheat ale, viz. water pimpernel, tutsan, meadow sweet, St. John's wort, ground ivy, agrimony, milfoil, birch, common burnet, columbine, motherwort, laurel, gromwel, betony, borage, dandelion, little field madder, amphibious persicaria, liverwort.

## STERILITY.—TREATMENT.

§ 20. A sterile woman may have a potion prepared for her by means of the following herbs, viz :—St. John's wort, yew, agrimony, amphibious persicaria, creeping cinque foil, mountain club moss, orpine and pimpernel, taking an emetic in addition.

## PROFUSE MENSTRUATION.—TREATMENT.

§ 21. A woman who is subject to profuse menstruation, should take the reddish bastard balm, small burdock, orpine, stinking goose foot, pimpernel, water avens, with the ashes of a hart's horns, that has been killed with his antlers on, boiling them, as well as possible in red wine, straining the liquor carefully, and drinking it daily, till it is finished, abstaining (the while) from stimulating food. Being restrained by the above means, the blood will be habitually diverted to the thighs and ancles.

## QUINSEY.

§ 22. The roots of the corn bell flower, will break the quinsey, being digested in cold water, drank and retained in the mouth.

## EXFOLIATION OF DEAD BONE FROM THE SKULL.

§ 23. Dandelion digested in cold water, and drank, will promote the exfoliation of the skull in aged men.

## ISSUES AND SEATONS.

§ 24. Viper's garlic, and shepherd's needle. The juice of the roots will form an issue, that of the leaves a seaton.

## ISSUES AND WORMS.

§ 25. The roots of the mugwort boiled in wine, will form an issue also ; the leaves treated in like manner will destroy worms.

### AN IMPOSTUME.

§ 26.  Comfrey root, dock root, valerian root, butter, old lard, and sulphur, pounded well together, and expressed through a cloth, are useful for an impostume.

### MILK.  YOUNG PORK, AND MUTTON.

§ 27.  From the time of calving up to fifteen days, cow's milk will be heating, and from thence until she is in calf, as long as she remains in profit, the milk will be heating. The flesh of a sow, under a year, and sheep flesh are watery, and for the man whose flesh is flabby in consequence of disease, such meat is not proper.

### WHOLESOME MEATS.—VENISON AND PORK, PARTRDIGE AND THE HEN, FLATFISH, BASS, AND TROUT.

§ 28.  The most wholesome wild beast's flesh is venison.[1] The most wholesome domestic animal's flesh is pork.[2]  The most wholesome wild fowl's flesh is partridge.  The most wholesome domestic bird's flesh is that of the hen.  The most wholesome sea fish is the flatfish.[3]  The most wholesome fresh water fish is the bass and the trout.[4]

### ECZEMA OR HUMID TETTER.

§ 29.  For a humid tetter: honey of ivy, fox marrow, and white rosin.

### TOOTHACHE.—TREATMENT.

§ 30.  For the toothache.  Take the inner bark of the ivy, and the leaves of the honeysuckle, bruising them well together in a mortar, expressing them through a linen cloth into both nostrils, the patient lying on his back, and it will relieve him.

---

[1] " The best hunted flesh is venison."  Prov.
[2] " The best animal meat is mutton."  Prov.
[3] " The best sea fish are the flounders."  Prov.
[4] " The best fresh water fish is trout."  Prov.

### DEAFNESS. DROPS. CAUTERY.

§ 31. For deafness.  Take a ram's urine, and eel's bile, and the juice of ash, expressing the same into the ear, and about the tooth.  The actual cautery should also be applied behind the ear and angle of the jaw, a nut being inserted therein.  This is a good plan.

### A VIPER'S BITE.  STRANGE PROPOSAL FOR EXTRACTING THE VENOM BY MEANS OF FOWLS.

§ 32. For the bite of a viper.  If the patient be a male, let a living cock be procured, and let the anal extremity be applied to the wound, and so held.  This is a good plan. If the patient be a woman, let a living hen be procured and applied in the same way.  This will extract the venom.

### CRUSTED SCALL, OR IMPETIGO CAPITIS.

§ 33. For a crusted scall.  Take goat's dung, barley meal and red wine, boil together into a poultice, and apply to the part.  This is the remedy, when the sore is not opened (by the forcible removal of the crust.)

### HEADACHE, AND PAIN OF JOINTS.  TREATMENT BY COUNTER IRRITATION.

§ 34. For headache or pain in the joints.  Take cakes of pounded wheat, and grind into fine meal.  Then take wood sorrel, dandelion, betony, and red wine, bruising them together in a mortar well, then mixing them throughly together on the fire, adding ox tallow and salt thereto freely. Let this plaster, spread on thick cloth, be then applied to the shaven scalp.  This will induce the breaking forth of boils, thereby extracting the venom, and relieving the patient.

### BITE OF A SPIDER. REMEDY.

§ 35. The bite of the spider, will not be found venomous, save from the feast of the nativity of the Virgin Mary, to that of her purification, and then by applying the yellow bed straw thereto bruised, the venom will be extracted therefrom.

### WORMS. TREATMENT. FASTING.

§ 36. For worms. Take elder bark, wallnut bark, white thorn bark, bitter sweet, and boil them together in water. Let a cupful be drank thereof daily fasting, and let the patient abstain from food till it is almost evening. This should be repeated nine times.

### A PUNCTURED WOUND.

§ 37. For a punctured wound. Take the dung[1] of a-bull, apply thereto, and it will be healed.

### CARBUNCLE. SEVERAL PLANS OF TREATMENT.

§ 38. For a carbuncle. Take St. John's wort, and apply it thereto, when first observed. Another plan is to take the flower of the knap weed or the leaves, pounding with the yolk of an egg and fine salt, then applying thereto, and this will disperse it. Another is to take the self heal, bruising it with rancid lard, and applying it thereto. Another is to take the roots of the purple dead nettle, the roots of the mugwort, and the speedwell, boiling well together in goat's milk whey, adding butter to the scum thereof, and drinking it day and night.

### TREATMENT WHEN A SLOUGH IS REMOVED AFTER CARBUNCLE AND CAUTERY.

§ 39. The treatment of a carbuncle, when the slough has been removed, or a burn (cauterization) in like circumstance.

---

[1] " Warm dung " in the Book of Harri Sion of Pontypool.

Take the wild chamomile, bake it well and powder, anointing the wound regularly, and sprinkling the powdered herbs upon it. This will produce a good and fair cicatrix. We judge that every kind of wound is benefited by milk whey.

### ACTIVE HEMORRHAGE.

§ 40. To restrain an active hemorrhage. Take meadowsweet, digest in cold water, and drink thereof, and this will stop it by the help of God.

### HOARSENESS.

§ 41. For hoarseness. Take the water avens, and St. John's wort, boil in pure milk, mixing butter therewith when boiling. Boil a portion thereof briskly every morning and drink.

### TOOTHACHE. SEVERAL REMEDIES.

§ 42. For the toothache. Take betony and lay it under the head, in an unbleached linen cloth, and it will cure it. Another method is to take self heal, put it in a dock leaf under the tooth, or on a hot stone, and place it hot in a cloth under the painful tooth. Another is to take the round birthwort, bruise it well, and apply it to the patient's tooth for a night. Another is to take the thorn apple and apply it well.

### IMFLAMMATION OF THE MAMMA.

§ 43. For inflammation of the mamma. Take the round birthwort and lard, apply them thereto, and they will cure it.

### WORMS. REMEDY.

§ 44. For intestinal worms. Take wine and natron, mix together and drink every morning fasting.

H

BITE OF A VIPER.—REMEDY.  OPPROBRIUM MEDICI.

§ 45.  For the bite of a viper.  Take the round birthwort, knapweed, and field scabious ;  mix with water and drink.

The Physician's three master difficulties are, a wounded lung, a wounded mammary gland, and a wounded knee joint.[1]

### RING WORM.

§ 46.  For the ring worm, (favus.)  Take white rosin, warm it, and when soft apply it to the part.  This will cure it.

SEVEN THINGS INJURIOUS TO THE EYES.

§ 47.  There are seven things hostile to the eye : weeping, watching, feasting, drunkenness, impurity, a dry film, and smoke.

THREE BONES WHICH WILL NOT UNITE WHEN FRACTURED.

§ 48.  There are three bones in a man's body, which when fractured, will never unite again, and neither of them exists when a man is born, viz, a tooth, the knee pan, and the fontenelle (or os frontis.)

TO INDUCE SLEEP.

§ 49.  Poppy heads bruised in wine, will induce a man to sleep soundly.[2]

IMPOTENCY.

§ 50.  For impotency.  Take some birch, digest in water, and drink.

INTERMITTENT FEVER.  TREATMENT.

§ 51.  For intermittent fever.  Take the mugwort, the purple dead nettle, and the round birthwort, as much as you

---

[1] " The three imminent dangers to a man are ;—a stroke on the head, unto the brain ; a stroke in the body, unto the bowels ; and the breaking of one of the four limbs of the body."—Welsh Laws, Venedotian Code.

[2] This is practically identical with Sydenham's " Liquid Laudanum," so that our Meddygon may be said to have anticipated the discovery of that preparation.

like of each, bruising them well in stale goat's milk whey, and
boiling afterwards. Let the patient drink some thereof every
morning, and it will cure him.

### TOOTHACHE. A STRANGE REMEDY, AND STRANGER PATHOLOGY.

§ 52. For the toothache. Take a candle of sheep's suet,
(some eringo seed being mixed therewith,) and burn it as near
the tooth as possible, some cold water being held under the
candle. The worms (destroying the tooth) will drop into
the water, in order to escape from the heat of the candle.

### A TUMOR OF THE ABDOMEN.—POULTICE. TUMOR OF THE ABDOMEN AGAIN.

§ 53. For a tumor of the abdomen. Take sheep's suet,
oatmeal, foxglove, and pimpernel, making a poultice of
them, and apply it thereto. If it contains matter this
will bring it to a head.

For a tumor of the abdomen again. Take goat's milk
whey, being fresh, mix ramsons therewith, and drink
of it for three days, and the swelling will disappear.

### FALLING FITS. TREATMENT, ROUGH, BUT READY.

§ 54. For falling fits. Burn a goat's horn, directing the
smoke upon the patient, and in consequence of the smell he
will forthwith arise. Before he has risen from the ground,
apply dog's gall upon his head, and that disease will not
attack him any more.

### INTERMITTENTS OR AGUES. A STRANGE MODE OF PROGNOSTIC.

§ 55. For all sorts of agues, write in three apples, on
three separate days. In the first apple ✠ o nagla pater.
In the second apple ✠ o nagla. filius. In the third apple ✠ o
nagla spiritus sanctus. And on the third day he will recover.

If you would know how it will happen to a man who sickens, whether he will live or die of his disease, take the herb called violet, bruise it, and bind a portion to both legs, and if the patient will live, he will sleep, and if he cannot sleep, he will die.

### TO PREVENT INTOXICATION.   TO PREVENT WEARINESS.

§ 56. If you would not be drunk, drink in the morning as much as will fill an egg-shell of the juice of the hemp agrimony.

If you would not be weary on a journey, drink in the morning an egg-shell full of the juice of mugwort and garlic, and you will neither be hurt nor tired, whatever distance you may walk that day.

### DRUNKENNESS.   TO REMOVE.

§ 57. If you would remove a man's drunkenness, let him eat bruised saffron with spring water.

### HOW TO BE MERRY.

§ 58. If you would be at all times merry, eat saffron in meat or drink, and you will never be sad : but beware of eating over much, lest you should die of excessive joy.

### TO CURE ENVY.

§ 59. If you would never be in an envious mood, drink as much as would fill an egg shell of the juice of the herb called wild clary, and you will not after fall into an evil temper. If you would be always in good health, drink a spoonful of the juice of the herb mallows, and you will always be so.

### TO PRESERVE CHASTITY.

§ 60. If you would always be chaste, eat daily some of the herb called hart's tongue, and you will never assent to the suggestions of impurity.

## PROLAPSUS UTERI. TREATMENT.

§ 61. For prolapsus of the womb (that is an extrusion thereof.) The best remedy is to take wheaten flour, and knead it with the yolks of nine eggs[1] and honey, working into it the breast fur of two hares; then bake it under ashes, and (making a potion thereof) drink it till the organ returns.

## TOOTHACHE. TO PREVENT.

§ 62. If you would always be free from toothache, whenever you wash, rub the inside of your ears with your fingers.

## SMALL TUMOR. A FOWL APPLICATION.

§ 63. For a small tumor. Take a cock or hen, (as the patient may be a man or a woman,) and apply the rump feathered, to the part, till the bird dies. This will extract the venom.

## WARTS. TO REMOVE.

§ 64. Whosoever would remove warts, let him apply daisy bruised in dog's urine thereto, and they will all disappear.

## FLEAS. TO DESTROY.

§ 65. Whosoever would destroy fleas, let him steep wormwood in the sea for an hour, and afterwards dry it in the sun. When sufficiently dry, any fleas coming in contact therewith will die.

## FLIES. TO DESTROY.

§ 66. To destroy flies, let the mugwort be put in the place where they frequent, and such of them as shall come in contact with the herb will die.

## BITE OF A VIPER.

§ 67. For the bite of a snake. Let the juice of the elder be drank, and it will disperse all the poison.

---

[1] Or as it may be also read, simply " the yolks of eggs."

### LOSS OF REASON OR SPEECH.

§ 68. Whosoever shall have lost his reason or his speech, let him drink of the juice of the primrose, within two months afterwards, and he will indeed recover.

### STRANGE DIAGNOSTIC OF PREGNANCY.

§ 69. Whosoever would know whether a woman be *enceinte* with a boy or girl, let him observe her sitting and standing, and if she moves the right foot first it signifies a son, but if the left, a daughter.

### STRANGE DIAGNOSTIC OF VIRGINITY.

§ 70. If you would distinguish between a wife and a virgin, scrape some jet into water, and give it her to drink. If she be a wife, she will without fail pass water, but if a virgin she will not have a more urgent call than usual.

### TO SILENCE A COCK.

§ 71. If you should wish that a cock should not crow, anoint his crest with oil, and he will be mute.

### OPACITY OF THE EYE.

§ 72. For an opacity of the eye. Let some ground ivy juice be put therein, and the opacity will be removed, the eye becoming spotless and clear.

### A WEEPING CHILD.

§ 73. Let the two lower extremities of the babe, much given to weeping, be anointed with hart's marrow, and he will weep the less.

### TO REMOVE A SMALL TUMOR.

§. 74. Should a man have a small tumor in a dangerous part of his body, and you should wish to remove it, your object can thus be accomplished. Take the leaves of the foxglove, and press them well on any part (of the tumor,) and it will remove it an inch and a half from the herb.

### HYGEIAN OF THE YEAR. JANUARY.

§ 75. Month of January. Do not bleed. Drink three cupfuls of wine, fasting. Take a potion. Let your diet be goat's flesh and wholesome vegetables.

### FEBRUARY.

§ 76. Month of February. Bleed from the thumb of the left hand. Obtain a confection and a potion, which will render your eyes healthy.

### MARCH.

§ 77. Month of March. Use enemata, the roots of vegetables, and the bath. Do not bleed frequently. Do not take an emetic, as it generates cold within. Drink sweet wine, fasting.

### APRIL.

§ 78. Month of April. Bleed. Take a gentle emetic, eat fresh meat, use warm drink. Eat two mouthfuls of hart's tongue twice a day. Avoid the roots of vegetables, as they will occasion an obstruction. Drink hemp agrimony.

### MAY.

§ 79. Month of May. Do not eat sheep's head or trotters, use warm drink. Eat twice daily of hart's tongue, fasting. Take a gentle emetic. Use cold whey. Drink of the juice of fennel and wormwood.

### JUNE.

§ 80. Month of June. Take a cupful of cold water, fasting daily. Do not drink ale or mead. Drink milk warm, and eat lettuce.

## JULY.

§ 81. Month of July. Do not bleed. Take an emetic. Make use of flowers and wholesome vegetables. Avoid impurity.

## AUGUST.

§ 82. Month of August. Make use of soups and vegetables. Drink neither ale nor mead. Take white pepper in gruel.

## SEPTEMBER.

§ 83. Month of September. Take three draughts of milk the first thing in the morning daily. You may after this take what you wish, for vegetables and fruit are then ripe, and bread apt to be mouldy.

## OCTOBER.

§ 84. Month of October. Make use of new wine. Eat minnows. Take an emetic. Let your diet consist of fresh meat and vegetables of a wholesome nature.

## NOVEMBER.

§ 85. Month of November. Do not take butter, as at this time (of the year,) the blood of all men has a tendency to coagulation, which is dangerous. At this time also the heads of beasts and all vegetables are to be avoided, being unwholesome.

## DECEMBER.

§ 86. Month of December. Do not drink soup or eat the red cabbage in the soup, nor trotters (sheep's,) and reduce your blood.

## A GOOD DAY TO BLEED.

§ 87. Whoever is bled on the 17th of March, will not be liable to intermittents or cough in that year.

## SAME.

§ 88. Whosoever is bled on the 3rd day of April, will not suffer from disease, from the head to the coccyx, in that same year, unless he is subjected to (undue) abstinence.[1]

## SAME.

§ 89. The 11th day of the same month is also a good time to be bled, so also is the 4th and 5th day of May.

## SAME.

§ 90. Whosoever is bled on the 17th day of September, will not be attacked by colic, ague, nor cough that year.

## DANGEROUS DAYS TO BLEED.

§ 91. Whosoever is bled on the third Monday in January, the first Monday in February, and the second Monday of October, will be in danger of death. There are three days in the year in which no bleeding should take place, nor any medicinal potion taken, even the last day of April, the first Monday of August, and the last Monday in September.

## THINGS TO BE AVOIDED.

§ 92. Whosoever is bled on those days, will die by the 15th or 7th day. And this is the reason. The veins will be full in those days, and if any medicinal potion is taken, it will be dangerous. And if he eats of the flesh of a goose, he will die on the third day, or else will be an invalid in a fortnight, or else he will die in the days mentioned of sudden death.[2]

[1] Lit. " Unless he doeth abstinence."

[2] In a manuscript, apparently written by Llywelyn Sion, about 1580, the following are enumerated as good days or times for letting blood :—

| | |
|---|---|
| The first day after the golden number in each month, before noon. | The fourth, before anterth, i. e. before 6 in the morning. |
| The second, at noon. | The fifth, before anterth. |
| The third, in the forenoon and after. | The seventh, any part of the day. |

I

## DANGEROUS DAYS IN THE YEAR.

§ 93. Sound teachers have discovered and written as follows, namely, that thirty two days in the year are dangerous. Know that whosoever is born on one of those days, will not live long, and whosoever is married on one of them, will die ere long, or will only exist in pain and poverty. And whosoever shall begin business on one of them, will not complete it satisfactorily; and those days are :—

In JANUARY there are seven, even 1st, 2nd, 4th, 5th, 10th, 15th, 17th.

In FEBRUARY there are three,—16th, 17th, 18th.

In MARCH there are three,—15th, 16th, 18th.

In APRIL there are two,—3rd and 16th.

In MAY there are four,—15th, 16th, 17th, 20th.

In JUNE there is one,—2nd.

In JULY there are two,—15th and 17th.

In AUGUST there are two,—18th and 20th.

In SEPTEMBER there are two,—16th and 18th.

In OCTOBER there is one,—6th.

In NOVEMBER there are two,—15th and 20th.

In DECEMBER there are three,—16th, 17th, 18th.[1]

The eighth, at noon.
The ninth, at all times.
The tenth.
The eleventh, in the evening.
The twelfth, at all times.
The thirteenth, at all times.
The fourteenth, at all times.
The sixteenth, in the morning.
The seventeenth.
The eighteenth, at the third hour.

The twentieth, after dusk.
The twenty third.
The twenty fourth, before noon.
The twenty fifth, at vesper time.
The twenty sixth, at all times.
The twenty seventh.
The twenty eighth, in the evening.
The twenty ninth.
The thirtieth.

[1] In the MS. just quoted, the following are reckoned as the unlucky or dangerous days.

January, 1st, 2nd, 4th, 5th, 10th, 12th, 19th.
February, 7th, 14th, 18th.
March, 15th, 16th, 18th.
April, 6th, 11th.
May, 5th, 6th, 16th, 20th.
June, 12th.

July, 15th, 20th.
August, 2nd, 12th, 19th.
September, 16th, 17th.
October, 5th.
November, 7th, 16th, 20th.
December, 6th, 8th, 15th.

Whosoever doubts these sayings, let him know that he is wiser than those who obtained this knowledge first.[1]

## SWELLING OF STOMACH.

§ 94. For swelling or hardness of the stomach. Boil duckweed in goat's milk, and foment it therewith frequently.

## SWELLING AND PAIN IN THE LOWER EXTREMITIES.

§ 95. For swelling or pain in the lower extremities. Take the roots of tutsan and the bark thereof, boiling them in water, and when boiled pour off the supernatant liquor, and take the residuum and mix with old lard. Then spread on a cloth or a handkerchief, and apply to the swollen feet or legs, and it will be dispersed.

## SWELLING AND PAIN IN THE NAPE OF THE NECK.— TREATMENT.

§ 96. For swelling or pain in the nape of the neck. Pound the roots of celandine in a mortar, with fennel, garlic, vinegar or wine, and butter, binding the same about your neck, and it will remove the pain and disperse the swelling.

## EPISTAXIS.

§ 97. For bleeding of the nose. Boil garlic in milk and water and drink it. It is proved.

[1] The intelligent reader hardly needs being told, that all this statement relative to good and bad seasons for bleeding has no foundation in fact, and the equivocal structure of this sentence seems to indicate that our ancient mediciners were quite aware of this, and must have indited it with a laughing twinkling eye; we must be guided in the use of the lancet by more certain indications, even the actual condition of the patient carefully and skilfully ascertained. Nevertheless it is curious to observe, that the type of disease seems to change in the course of an uncertain cycle of years, from a sthenic to an asthenic form and *vice versa*. Thus 25 years ago the sthenic constitution prevailed, and the lancet was freely employed, but of late years in consequence of the markedly asthenic tendency of all complaints, this characteristic implement of our art is rarely used, certainly not once where then it would have been used fifty times. From Sydenham to the present, this fact has from time to time, attracted the attention of medical observers, that father of English medicine having been the first to call attention to it.

## BURNS. A CAPITAL PLASTER. ANOTHER GOOD ONE. ANOTHER AGAIN.

§ 98. For burns occurring in any part of the body. Take the root of the white lily, and wash clean, boiling it briskly in water. Then reduce to a pulp, and mix with oil, and a little white of eggs, spreading it on lint. Let this be applied night and morning. The more plaster you apply the better. .

Another mode. Burn ivy in a clean place, and cover the burn with the ashes of the same, and it will heal it presently.

Another way is to burn fern, and mix the ashes with the white of eggs ; or else oil, anointing the burn with it, and it will heal it quickly and wonderfully.

## NETTLE RASH, OR ERYSEPELATOUS ERETHEMA. TREATMENT.

§ 99. A medicine for nettle rash, (when indicating a bad constitution,) so that it may disappear in three days. Take good cheese and pound it briskly in a mortar. Mix honey with it till it is transparent. Anoint the part therewith frequently, laying a cabbage leaf thereon, and it will have disappeared in three days.

## BITE OF A MAD DOG. TREATMENT.

§ 100. For the bite of a mad dog. Pound ground ivy well in a mortar with lard, or pound leeks and vinegar, or fennel seed, and honey together, and apply thereto.

## INFLAMMATION OF MAMMÆ.

§ 101. For inflammation of the mammæ. Pound the roots of the tutsan with rancid lard, and apply thereto.

## INSANITY.—TO CURE.

§ 102. When a man becomes insane, take daisy, field southernwood and sage, digesting it in wine, and let the patient drink it for fifteen days.

### OBSTINATE CONSTIPATION.—TO OVERCOME.

§ 103. If the bowels become so constipated that they cannot be moved, take duckweed, boiling it briskly in a pot, then cast it into a pan, and fry with a quantity of blood and butter, eating it hot.

### PALSY.—TO CURE.

§ 104. For the palsy. Take the field southernwood, pound it in a mortar, and strain the juice to about a small cupful, and give it the patient to drink, on the dawn of God's day of Christmas.

### BLEEDING OF THE NOSE.—REMEDY.

§ 105. For bleeding of the nose. Take as much as you can hold between your three fingers of the betony, being briskly powdered with salt, and put it in your nostrils, which will stop it quickly.

### ADHESION OF THE LIVER.—TREATMENT.

§ 106. If a man's liver should adhere to his ribs, take in the morning at sun rise, (chanting thy pater noster,) some river star tip. Digest it in new ale, and give it the patient to drink (whilst in a bath,) for nine days.

### COUGH.—REMEDY. ANOTHER METHOD.

§ 107. For a cough. Bruise hemp agrimony, in a mortar, and mix the juice with boiling milk, strain and use.

Another method. Boil a potful of water until it is wasted to the half. Then mix rye meal therewith, and add butter, eating it hot.

### WORMS.—TO DESTROY. ANOTHER METHOD.

§ 108. To destroy worms in the stomach or bowels. Take the juice of turnips, foment therewith, and they will come out.

Another method is to take a handful of the bark of the peach tree, growing in dry ground, drinking it fasting with goat's milk, and they will all come out.

### CONSTIPATION.—TO OVERCOME.—SUPPOSITORY.

§ 109. To overcome constipation. Take salt and second milk, equal parts of each, put on the fire in an evaporating dish, leaving it there until it is reduced into a soft waxlike mass. Then make cakes (suppositories) of the same, and pass them into the patient's rectum.

### BITE OF A SNAKE.—ANTIDOTES FOR. ANOTHER WAY.

§ 110. For the bite of a snake. Drink the juice of the greater plantain, with oil and salt. The juice of the mugwort also, when bruised and strained will neutralize poison.

Another way is to take the brains of a red cock and rue; mix with sweet milk, curdled milk or wine, and drink. Take also of the flesh of the breast whilst warm, (the cock being alive,) and apply to the wound. It will extract the venom.

### WORMS.—A CATAPLASM.—A REMEDY. ANOTHER.

§ 111. For worms. Take the milk of a cow, that has a bull calf sucking her, with barley meal and honey. Boil it in a pan after the manner of porridge, and apply hot to the stomach.

Another method is to make bread of barley and the kernels of nuts, (shelled,) eating it.

Another plan is to bruise fresh rue and mugwort in a mortar, and drink the juice thereof.

### DIFFICULT PARTURITION.—TO HELP.

§ 112. If a woman be unable to give birth to her child, let the mugwort be bound to her left thigh. Let it be instantly removed when she has been delivered, lest there should be hemorrhage.

### SWELLING AND PAIN OF LEGS.—AN APPLICATION FOR.

§ 113. For swelling and pain in the thighs. Bruise rue, honey, and salt, apply thereto, and it will disperse the swelling.

### PAIN IN THE KIDNEYS.—A REMEDY.

§ 114. For pain in the kidneys. Take the centaury, infused in cold water, and give it to the patient to drink.

### EXTREME THIRST.—TO HELP.

§ 115. For extreme thirst. Drink the centaury infused in hot water. This will quench thirst, and clear the breast and stomach.

### SMALL POX.—AN APPLICATION.

§ 116. For the small pox. Take the ashes of heath, balm or smallage, and the ashes of hartshorn, with honey, and anoint therewith.

### A SURFEIT.—TO RELIEVE.

§ 117. For a surfeit. Take turnip, boil in goat's milk, and let the patient drink thereof, and he will be relieved.

### A BURN OR SCALD.—A FOMENTATION FOR.

§ 118. For a burn or scald. Put the leaves of the lily, in boiling milk, and apply to the part till it is well.

### RETENTION OF URINE.—A STRANGE REMEDY.

§ 119. For retention of urine. Take the brains of a hare, and mix the same with wine. Let the patient smell it for an hour and then drink it.

### BITE OF A VIPER.—REMEDY.

§ 120. For the bite of an adder. Mix the juice of the fennel, of radish, rue or wormwood, with oil, let the patient drink the same, or eat it.

### VOMITING OF BLOOD.—REMEDIES.

§ 121. For vomiting of blood. Boil the milfoil with wine or milk, and drink, as this will stop it. Or boil the betonica in goat's milk, or wine, and this will restrain it.

### CONSTIPATION.—REMEDY FOR.

§ 122. For constipation. Boil roots of the small thistles, growing in woods, and give the water to the patient to drink

### FATNESS.—TO REDUCE.

§ 123. Whosoever is over fat, let him drink of the juice of the fennel, and it will reduce him.

### IRRITABILITY OF MIND.—TO CALM.

§ 124. If a man be irritable of mind, let him drink of the juice of the apinm, (celery) frequently, as it will relieve him of his irritability, and produce joy.

### REPTILES IN THE STOMACH.—TO EXPEL THEM.

§ 125. If a snake should enter a person's mouth, or there should be any other living reptiles in him, let him take wild camomile, (in powder,) in wine, till it is thickned, and drink the same, as it will relieve him of them.

### WORMS IN MAN OR BEAST.—TO KILL. ANOTHER PLAN.

§ 126. If worms be generated in man or beast, apply to (his stomach,) the roots of the taragon, and the worm will die forthwith.

Another way is to mix the leaves of the dittany with strong wine, and let the patient drink it fasting.

INTESTINAL WORMS.—REMEDY. ANOTHER.

§ 127. For intestinal worms. Let the patient drink a cupful of the juice of the plantain, and apply the same herb to the navel.

Another way is to take milfoil in wine, once whilst fasting, and they will be expelled that day.

AGUE.—A REMEDY WITH A PATER NOSTER. ANOTHER REMEDY.

§ 128. For the ague. Drink the juice of rue in wine, swallow three grains of coriander, drink celery (apium) in water, (sweetened,) and collect plantain whilst saying your pater noster, and drink it infused in wine and pepper.

Take the juice of the mugwort bruised, the juice of the wormwood, and tepid oil. Then anoint your whole body on one side three days successively, and it will cure the ague for you cheaply.

AN OBSTINATE AGUE.—TREATMENT.

§ 129. But if a man has indeed an obstinate ague, cause him to go into a bath, and let him avoid touching the water with his arms. Let him also take ground ivy, boiling it briskly, and apply hot to his head. He must also be bled in his arm, and he will be cured by the help of God.

VOMITING AND SIGHING.—A REMEDY.

§ 130. For vomiting and sighing. Mix a handful and a half of betony in warm water, and drink it.

To cure vomiting, take betonica, and boil in honey, pounding in a mortar, and form into four balls, and administer to him one daily as a drink, in a warm potion.

POISON.—ANTIDOTE.

§ 101. If a man has taken poison let him take of the juice of the dittany, and wine.

K

### BLEEDING FROM THE NOSE.—REMEDY. ANOTHER.

§ 132. To stop bleeding from the nose, take the tops of three nettles, pounding them together. Put this cataplasm on the nape of your neck, and if possible in your nostrils.

Another method is to pound the milfoil with vinegar in a mortar. Plug the nostrils therewith, and it will stay the bleeding.

### VOMITING.—STRANGE TREATMENT.

§ 133. For vomiting. Drink milfoil digested in warm wine, till a cure is obtained.

Another plan is to immerse the scrotum in vinegar.

### DEAFNESS AFTER FEVER.

§ 134. For deafness succeeding a fever ; take a cow's gall, a woman's milk, and honey, putting it in your ears warm. This is a cure that will not fail.

### MANIFOLD VIRTUES OF THE LEEK.

§ 135. The following are the virtues of the leek. It is good to drink the juice against vomiting of blood. It is good for women who desire children to eat leeks. It is good to take leeks and wine for the bite of an adder, or other (venomous) beast. It is good to apply a plaster of leeks and wine to ulcers. The juice of leeks and woman's milk is a good remedy for a chronic whooping cough, or pneumonia. The juice of leeks, goat's gall, and honey, mixed in three equal parts, are useful for deafness. It should be put warm in the ears and nostrils. It is good for headache. Leeks are good to promote the union of bones, and maturing of boils. If leeks and salt are applied to ulcers, it will heal them rapidly. If leeks are eaten raw, they will occasion intoxication. They will strengthen men who have suffered from hemorrhage. They will relieve flatulency of the stomach. They are oppressive to the stomach, whether boiled or raw, as they will destroy the nervous energy thereof, and their fumes rising to the head, injure the sight.   They produce terrific dreams.   Unless the lettuce or the poppy, or the like are eaten first to temperate them, such is their tendency.   They kill the worms that are generated in the stomach or bowels.

### VOMITING.—TO STAY.

§ 136. Those that cannot retain food or drink, but vomit it, the milfoil digested in warm wine, should be given them to drink.

### ANTIDOTE TO POISON.

§ 137. As an antidote for poison, mix two nuts, three dry figs, and a handful of rue, and thirty grains of salt, giving it to the patient, fasting.

### PROUD FLESH.—APPLICATION.

§ 138. The following is useful when proud flesh forms in a wound, namely, white alum, reduced to powder, the same powder being applied thereon.

Another for the same purpose.   Take a toad that can scarcely creep, beat it with a rod, till irritated, it smells, and dies.   Then put it in an earthen pot, closing the same so that no smoke can come out, or air enter in.   Then burn it till it is reduced to ashes, and apply the same to the part.

### ANOTHER WAY.

Another plan is to take a mole, (al. raven,) and burn it in the same way, applying the ashes upon the part.

### ANOTHER.

In like manner, make ashes of human flesh, taken if possible from a corresponding part of the body to that in which the disease is situated.

### PROUD FLESH.—ANOTHER APPLICATION.

In like manner you may take the ashes of the ermine, burnt in the way above mentioned, and apply thereto.

### ANOTHER.

Another plan is to take as many as you please of the cloves of garlick, burning them on a clean floor; when they are incinerated, quench (the fire) with drops of honey, make a powder thereof, and apply. Bind it over with a plaster, and in three days afterwards let it be washed. Boil rye meal and a sow's blood together, applying it thereon when it is worked; over that a plaster of boiling honey, and a third part of salt should be applied. Do this daily.

### ANOTHER.

Another plan is to take the jaw of a horse, with all the teeth remaining therein. Burn a cupful thereof (in powder,) and mix with pepper and lard: anoint the part with this, tempering with sage. Continue to apply this plaster daily, for a fortnight.

### ANOTHER.

Another is to take honey, the yolk of an egg, good milk, and fine confectioner's meal, mix together and apply to the part twice daily. This is proved.

### VIRTUES OF MUSTARD.

§ 139. Mustard. . It is useful to expel cold humors. It is good with vinegar for the bite of an adder or toad. It is good for the toothache. It will purify the brain. It will restrain profuse menstruation. It will provoke the appetite, and strengthen digestion. It is good for colic, loss of hair, noise in the ears, and dimness of sight, cutaneous eruptions, palsy, and many other things.

URINAL PATHOLOGY.—FOUR URINARY ELEMENTS.*

§ 140. From the condition of a man's urine, may be distinguished his defects, dangers, fevers (plagues,) and diseases, whether he be present or absent. However, we should first show what is the composition of the urine. It contains four radical elements.

FIRST. The humor of the blood which circulates in the reproductive organs.

* The following is the translation of an extract upon the same subject, purporting to have been made from the Book of " Hywel ddu Feddyg," a descendant of Einion ab Rhiwallon, by "Ieinē ap Wm. ap ff," A.D. A thousand,
∇ ϛ ⸰° ρ υ ɯ

" The following are the elementary rules of urinoscopy. If the urine exhibits a yellow colour of a faint golden hue, or if it has the hue of refined gold ; it indicates that food and drink are perfectly digested in the stomach.

If of a fiery red, like the sunset in the west—if red like oriental saffron—if a fiery red like a vanishing flame—if red like a portion of consuming fire ; these four colours indicate that the food and drink have left the stomach in order that their digestion may be completed.

If urine is deep coloured like human liver, or the hue of (blushing) cheeks, like racked red wine, or greenish like the mane of oxen ; these three colours concur in indicating that food and drink are properly digested in the stomach.

If water has a leaden hue, or an intensely black colour like black ink, or a dead black, like black horn ; these three colours indicate the death of a man.

If it has the colour of clear spring water, if an opaline colour like transparent horn, or the colour of plain milk, or the hue of camel hair ; these four colours indicate the nondigestion of the food in the stomach.

If it has a greenish blue colour, this indicates that less food and drink should be allowed the patient.

If the colour of ill bled meat, it indicates that the digestion of food has commenced in the stomach.

If a greenish hue like an unripe apple,—if the hue of a ripe apple ; these two colours indicate that the food and drink are half digested in the stomach. And thus it terminates."

These extracts as well as the teaching of our " Meddygon " on the same subject, are of but slight value indeed, farther than as they show how rude and empiric was the urinary diagnosis and pathology of our fathers. The first writer on urinoscopy was Theophilus, called Philaretus, a monk, who was Physician to Heraclius, who reigned in the first half of the 7th century. His treatise on the urine has little originality, farther than as being the first of a class of writings, distinguished above all others for chicanery and humbug. After him we find a succession of authors (particularly the urinoscopists of the middle ages,) pursuing dreamy speculations to a greater pitch of absurdity than can be readily conceived by those whose curiosity has notled them to pay visits of discovery to the bve paths of medicine. In nothing has modern medical research made greater advances than urinary diagnosis and pathology, thanks to the microscopist and the chemist. *Vide " Lilium medicinæ " of Bernard Gordon—Watson (of New York) on ancient medicine.*

SECONDLY. That of the abdominal viscera for the performance of the functions thereof.

THIRDLY. That of the vessels which receive the various fluids of the cholera and fleuma (bile and phlegm).

FOURTHLY. That of the kidneys, supplying those fluids which pass to the bladder. From hence can be discerned all the signs of disease, the fluidity and colour of the urine indicating the evil and good signs.

### URINAL DIAGNOSIS.

§ 141. Should urine abound in water, or resemble red, black, or green wine, or oil, or blood, or the urine of beasts, and a skilful person consider the essential causes thereof, attentively studying the same, he will understand which of these humors chiefly predominate, whether the fleuma, the cholera, the sanguis, or the melancholia. It is necessary that the urine be collected in a glass vessel, and left to settle till the second hour, when, by the light of the sun, the physician should judge the indications thereof.

### SIGNS IN ORDER.—BLACK URINE.

i. If the urine be black, it will be necessary to renovate that patient's constitution by the most skilful means possible, frequently employing the bath and oil. Then the urine should be again examined, and if it should seem saffron-like and turbid, know that there is a painful disease in the person, produced by heat and dryness.

### SINOPLE.

ii. If the patient be attenuated and evidently declining in strength, his veins prominent, or red (transparent,) and the urine similar in colour to sinople, it proceeds from the sanguis. By bleeding the patient in the left arm, he will be restored with little trouble.

### THICK, OILY, OPAQUE AND SANGUINOLENT.

iii. If the urine should be thick, oily, deep red, not transparent in the rays of the sun, and sanguinolent, it indicates
languishment and weakness of body, from excess of fever.

### CURDLED.

iv. If the urine be curdled, it indicates a long continued
fever.

### RED AND CHANGEABLE.

v. If the urine be red, or brimstone-like, and seeming to
change its appearance frequently, it indicates a dangerous
fever.

### CLOUDY AND GREENISH.—A CLOUD ON THE SURFACE.

vi. If the urine be cloudy and greenish at the commencement of a fever, or in two days afterwards, when secreted it
seems thicker and thicker, the patient is sure to die.    If
these signs increase in number, though the urine does not
thicken, it indicates a tedious fever.

If there be a sky appearance on the surface of the urine,
it indicates a future fever.

### FOUL URINE.

vii. If the urine seem foul in fever, it indicates heat and
blindness, pain of head and shoulders, with deafness.    If
the patient is not relieved in seven days, he will die.

### OILY.

viii. If the urine seems like oil during the heat of a fever,
it indicates death, delirium or erysipelas.    If it is not
quickly removed, it indicates a softening of the brain.

### FIERY, AND PASSED WITH PAIN.

ix. If it assumes a fiery hue, and is passed with pain, this
indicates that the patient's food and drink are not properly

digested. It is accordingly expedient in such a case for the patient to restrict himself to spoon diet.

### BLACK OR RED, WITH SEDIMENT.

x. If it be black or red, and there be sediment in the bottom, with retention, pain in the kidneys, and pain in micturition, the patient is in danger. If the urine be passed frequently, and in small quantities, then it indicates a stone in the bladder.

### BLUISH WHITE, &c.

xi. If the urine be bluish white, during the heat of a fever, or reddish brown or red, accompanied with bleeding at the nose, it is attended with great danger.

### WHITE.

xii. In persons with a diseased liver, when thin urine becomes white, it indicates future agony, but if it disappears suddenly, it indicates a boil.

### BILIOUS.

xiii. If in the heat of a fever it has the colour of bile, being thick, with a whitish cloud and whitish granules floating thereon, it indicates a long continued languishing.

xiv. If more is passed than is proper, during the heat of a fever, and the colour is not good, though passed freely, it indicates danger at hand. If the urine is not natural, when passed, and it subsequently assumes a healthy colour, it indicates that the patient will pine away from future torment.

xv. If a man in the heat of a fever passes his urine sufficiently natural, but with white gravel therein, the fever not decreasing, it indicates danger.

xvi. If it abounds in water, the fever will increase, but he will be in no danger.

xvii. If the urine be dark, during the heat of a fever, the turbidness not subsiding, his illness will resolve itself into an ague in four, or perhaps three days.

xviii. If it be red, with much sediment, it will indicate a fever.

xix. If it has the colour of water, the fever will increase, but there will be no danger.

xx. Urine during the heat of a fever, if it be viscid and filthy, abounding with a gravelly sediment, with a cloudiness on the surface, indicates a tedious illness.

xxi. The urine of fever having sandy sediment, being sanguinolent in colour within, indicates disease of the kidneys.

xxii. If the urine should be frothy, like bubbles on water, let him not be surprised at the occurrence of any disease, as it indicates a fever at hand.

xxiii. If the urine be white in the morning, and afterwards red, it is well. It only signifies the proper flux of the body.

xxiv. If it be red first, and afterwards black, or if the urine has a mixture of those two colours, it indicates death.

xxv. If it be greasy on the surface, bubbles ascending therein, it is a bad sign.

xxvi. If it be greasy on the surface, and white sediment in the bottom of the vessel, it indicates pain in the viscera or joints.

xxvii. If the urine be blue, it indicates a disease of the viscera.

xxviii. An ill looking red urine, containing a gravelly sediment, and having a cloudiness on the surface, is a bad sign.

xxix. If it be very white, it is unfavourable. If it is dark in the morning, so much the worse.

xxx. If it be greasy, and preceded by great pain, it is indicative of death. If it be transparent, with a cloudiness thereon, the death of that patient will be nigh at hand. If it be light coloured in the morning, and lighter after dinner, it will be all the better. If it be red with a sediment, it indicates no danger. A dark hepatic urine indicates danger. A pale splenetic urine is dangerous. A red urine from dyspepsia is dangerous. A clear urine indicates a healthy condition. And thus it ends.

## BLEEDING.

§ 142. In bleeding, the blood should be permitted to flow till the colour changes, and the stream of blood from black should flow till it is red. If thick, let it flow till it becomes more fluid. If it is watery, let it flow till it becomes thicker.

## HEALTH.

§ 143. To secure constant health, drink daily, the first thing, a spoonful of the juice of the mallows.

## BIRDS AND FLIES.

§ 144. To drive away birds or flies, put the mugwort in the places where they frequent, and they will disperse.

## SPECK IN THE EYE.

§ 145. For a speck in the eye, put therein the juice of the ground ivy.

## INTOXICATION.

§ 146. In order to be delivered from intoxication, drink saffron digested in spring water.

## A TUMOR.

§ 147. For a tumor. Apply a cock or a hen thereto till the animal dies.

## FALLING SICKNESS.

§ 148. For falling sickness. Let a dog be killed, and, unknown to the patient, put some of the gall in his mouth. It will never attack him again.

### PROGNOSIS OF DEATH.

§ 149. In order to form a prognosis of the fate of a sick person, bruise the violet, apply to the eyebrows, and if he sleeps, he will live, but if not, he will die.

### CHASTITY.

§ 150. If you would preserve yourself from unchaste desires, eat rue in the morning.

### URINARY CALCULI.—TO DISSOLVE.

§ 151. To destroy urinary calculi. Take saxifrage, which grows in stony places, (it has obtained its name from its virtues in this respect,) temper with wine and pepper, drinking it warm. This will break the stone, and promote the passing of water. It will also promote menstruation, and cure diseases of the kidneys and uterus.

### AGAIN.

Another way (of dissolving the stone) is to take the saxifrage and the seed of the gromwell, digesting them in boiling water. Let the patient drink this for six days, and he will be cured without fail.

### AGAIN.—EXPERIMENT.

Another mode is to take the blood and skin of a hare, burning them to ashes. Then mix a quantity of this powder in warm water, and let the patient drink a spoonful of the mixture, fasting, and it will disintegrate the stone, causing it to be expelled. If you would wish to prove this, put a spoonful of the same powder in water, and deposit any calculus you please therein, and it will instantly slacken it.

### THREE THICK INCURABLE ORGANS.

§ 152. There are three thick incurable organs : the liver, kidney, and heart. The reason why they are so called is.

that when disease has affected either of them, no relief can be given, but a painful death.

### THREE THIN INCURABLE ORGANS.

§ 153. There are three thin incurable organs; the pia mater, small intestines, and bladder. They are incurable for the same cause as the others.

### THREE COMPLAINTS WHICH OCCASION CONFINEMENT.

§ 154. There are three complaints which occasion long confinement. Disease of the knee joint, of the substance of a rib, and of a lung. For when matter has formed in either, a surgeon does not know when he may be cured till he sees him well.

### HEMORRHOIDS.

§ 155. For hemorrhoids. Apply the calcareous droppings of peacocks (pounded) with fern roots, and it will cure it.

### HYDROPHOBIA.

§ 156. The bite of a mad dog. It is a good thing to eat the root of radish.

### BARRENNESS CURED.

§ 157. To render a woman fruitful, let her frequently eat lettuce, hot tallow, and pepper.

### GREATEST REMEDY.

§ 158. What is the greatest remedy (or effort of surgical skill ?) To remove a bone from the brain (to trephine) with safety.

### LEAST REMEDY.

§ 159. What is the simplest remedy ? To scratch one's hand until it is irritated, and then to spit upon it forthwith.

## PAIN.

§ 160. An antidote for pain: seek the dittany, which may be obtained from cunning men; it is the best in all complaints.

### A TUMOR.—REMEDY.

§ 161. For a tumor. Take the daisy and plantain (in powder,) mixing the same with drink, till it is thickened. Take also dust scraped from blue stone (sulphate of copper,) and administer to him in drink. It will cure him, if it is given him ere he sleeps.

### SWELLING AFTER INJURY.—REMEDY.

§ 162. For a swelling, the result of an injury. Take the juice of the yellow bed straw, the juice of the plantain, rye meal, honey and the white of eggs. Make into a plaster, and apply thereto.

### BOILS.

§ 163. For boils. Take the juice of the morella (mushroom,) plantain, barley meal, and the white of an egg.

### STRANGURY.

§ 164. For strangury. Take the dead red nettle, and parsley. Make a plaster thereof, and apply to the stomach below the navel.

### WARTS.

§ 165. To remove warts. Take the inner bark of the willow, make into a plaster with vinegar, and apply it.

### HEARTACHE.

§ 166. For the heartache. Take the bark of the keginderw, the bark of the stinking goose foot, the plantain, and the shepherd's purse, boiling them in ditch (stagnant) water.

till it is wasted to a third.    Take this water and make it
into a gruel, with wheaten flour.

Another way is to take caraway water and goat's milk in
equal parts, mixing plantain juice therewith, and boiling
river granite therein.   Let this be given the patient nine
days, unmixed with any other drink.

### DYSPEPSIA.

§ 167. For pain in the chest (dyspepsia.)   Take a large
quantity of black thorn berries, bruise briskly in a mortar,
mixing very new ale therewith.   Put this mixture in a new
earthen pot, over its edges in the earth, for nine days and
nights, giving it the patient to drink the first thing in the
morning, and the last thing at night.

### TO MAKE VINEGAR.

§ 168. To make vinegar.   Take clean barley, and put in
wine over night till the eve of next day.

### TO PROMOTE THE UNION OF BONE.

§ 169. To promote the union of bone.   Take comfrey,
and bruise with wine, pepper and honey, drinking it daily
for nine days, and they will unite compactly.

### EYE SALVE.

§ 170. To make an eye salve.   Take the juice  *   *   *
and the juice of fennel root, celandine, lesser celandine, sow's
lard, honey, a little vinegar, an eel's blood, and a cock's
gall, letting them stand in a brass vessel till an efflorescence
takes place.   This has restored sight to those who had quite
lost it.

### DIGNITY OF MEDICINE.

§ 171. Let all men know that it will be vain to seek anything except by effort.   There can be no effort without

health ; there can be no health without temperance in a
man's nature, and temperance cannot exist in a man's nature
without moderate heat in his extremities.  God has decreed
a supervision of the manner in which we should conserve
the health, and has revealed it to his own servants, the
philosophers and chosen prophets, who are full of the Holy
Spirit, and whom God ordained to this profession.

§ 172. The Latins, the men of Persia and the Greeks
(say,) what we choose we love, what we seek we think of.
Therefore let all men know that God has given the men of
Greece a special gift, to discern every art, and the nature of
all things, to a greater extent than other nations, with a
view to the preservation of human health.

§ 173. The philosophers and wise men foreknew that man
was formed of four elements, each being antagonistic to the
others, and each consequently requiring continual aliment,
which if it do not obtain, it will succumb.  If a man partakes of too much or too little food or drink, the body will
become weak, fall into disease, and be open to injurious con-
sequences.  If he partakes temperately of food and drink,
the body will acquire strength, and the health will also be
preserved.

### MODERATION.

§ 174. The philosophers have said. whosoever shall eat or
drink more or less than he should, or shall sleep more or
less, or shall labour more or less from idleness or from hard-
ship, (being obliged to over exert himself :) or who, used to
being bled, refrains from doing so, without doubt he will not
escape sickness.  Of these things we shall treat presently,
and of what is most suitable for our use.

### SAYINGS OF THE WISE AS TO FOOD.

§ 175. Wise men have declared, whosoever refrains from
eating or drinking immoderately, and will only partake tem-

perately of food and drink, as his constitution requires, shall enjoy health and long days, that is, a long life. Philosophers never said anything to the contrary. Desire, love, and the reception of worldly honour, these things fortify and assist life, so that they be gratified temperately. On which account, whosoever desireth life and permanence, let him seek that which is permanent and tends to prolong life.

### MODERATION A MEANS TO PROLONG LIFE.—HIPPOCRATES AND HIS DISCIPLES.

§ 176. Whosoever would prolong life, should restrain his appetite, and not eat over abundantly. I have heard that Ipocras[1] having attained to old age, whereby he had to suffer much from infirmity and the weight of years, was addressed by his disciples, thus:—" Thou great teacher of wisdom, didst thou eat and drink abundantly, wouldst thou have to endure all the weakness which thou dost?" Then Ipocras:—" My sons, (said he) I eat a proper portion seeing I live, I should not live if (with a view of prolonging mere human life,) I partook of food too frequently. Eating is not the one thing needful, when the prolonging of life is the object aimed at, for I have seen many die from too much eating."

### EAT SLOWLY AND SPARINGLY.—MEN OF ARABIA.—TWO RULES TO PRESERVE HEALTH.

§ 177. Whosoever, restraining their appetite, refrain from gluttony, and eat slowly, these shall live long ; which may be thus proved. The men of Arabia, who dwell in mountains and pathless woods, are the most long lived (of mortals,)

---

[1] Hippocrates was a native of the island of Cos, and was regarded as the father of medical science. He delivered Athens from a dreadful pestilence in the beginning of the Peiopenesian war, and was publicly rewarded with a golden crown, the privileges of a citizen of Athens, and the initiation at the grand festivals. He died in the 99th year of his age, B. C. 361, free from all disorders of the mind and body ; and after death he received with the name of *Great*, the same honours which were paid to Hercules.

as these circumstances prevent excessive eating and drinking. The health may be preserved in two ways. First,—
that is, by partaking of such food as is most suitable to the
time of life and the constitution, restricting himself to that
sort of diet which he was reared upon. Secondly,—by
evacuating duly, what is poured into the stomach from above.[1]

## A THEORY OF DIGESTION.

§ 178. Let all men know, that the human organism is
antagonistic to food and drink, (decomposing both in the
process of digestion,) and that every (animal or human)
being is (naturally) verging upon disease. Also, animal
organisms are corrupt from superabundant heat, which dries
the spirit (anima) by which the body is nourished. Animal
bodies also are corrupt from excessive heat of the sun, which
dries the (animal) spirits ; and this is particularly the case

---

[1] The following "Prescriptions about health and life" are attributed to
Cattwg the Wise.
1. He that would attain a long life, let him play until he is twenty, labour
until he is forty, and rest to the end of his days.
2. Let him arise with the lark, sing with the lark, and retire to rest with the
lark.
3. Let him eat when he has an appetite, drink when he is thirsty, and rest
when he is fatigued.
4. Let him avoid food that is too dainty, drink that is too strong, and work
that is too heavy and troublesome.
5. Let him avoid too much food, too much drink, and too much labour.
6. Let him avoid contention, love peace, and divest himself of too many cares.
7. Let him be merry, generous, and just.
8. Let him have but one wife, be strong in the faith, and have a clean
conscience.
9. Let him be meditative in the morning, industrious at noon, and social in
the evening.
10. Let his meditation be pleasant, his games innocent, and his air salubrious.
11. Let his clothes be not old, his furniture be clean and sweet, and let him
be content with his lot in life.
12. Let his dress be light, his food be light, and his heart be light.
13. Let his disposition be affectionate, his genius lively, and his friends numerous.
14. Let him keep the law of his country, the rule of his vocation, and the
commandments of his God.
15. Thereby, his body will be healthy, his mind easy, and his conscience pure.
16. His life will be long, his end will be bliss, and his God will love him.—
Myv. Arch. iii. p. 56.

M

with the bodies of the animals upon which we feed.   When
the body is hot, strong aliments are required, as then they
can be digested.

### FAT AND DRY CONSTITUTIONS.

§ 179.  When a (man's) body is fat and dry, luxurious
juicy food is proper for him, for they will easily assimilate.
In this way a man may preserve his health.   Let him confine himself to such food as is suitable to his constitution.
This has been proved.

### A HOT HABIT.

§ 180.  If a man's body be constitutionally hot, hot aliment is proper for him.

### A COLD HABIT.

§ 181.  If a man's body be constitutionally cold, cold aliments are proper for him.

### A HUMID OR DRY HABIT.

§ 182.  If the body be constitutionally humid or dry, cold
aliments are forbidden him.

### WHAT FOOD MOST SUITABLE FOR WEAK OR STRONG STOMACH.

§ 183.  Strong food is most suitable for a hot  stomach, as
such a stomach is comparable to fire consuming  loose flax.
Weak  food  is  most  proper  for  a cold  stomach, as such a
stomach is comparable to fire consuming straw.

### HEALTHY DIGESTION.

§ 184.  The signs of a healthy digestion are, that the body
be active, the understanding clear, and the desire for food
frequent.

### SYMPTOMS OF INDIGESTION.

§ 185.  The  signs  of  indigestion are, heaviness of body,
with irritability of feeling superadded, a languid performance

of duty, swelling of the face, frequent yawning, dimness of sight, frequent eructations, attended with a bitterness of taste, (in the mouth,) this bitterness-occasioning cardialgia, which extending to the body and limbs, occasions a dislike for food.

### HOW TO ACT AT GETTING FROM BED, AND SUBSEQUENTLY DURING THE DAY, WITH OTHER HYGENIC MATTERS.

§ 186. When rising from bed, walk a while, stretch your limbs, contracting your head and neck. This will strengthen your limbs, and the contracting of the head will cause the (animal) spirits to rush from the stomach to the head, and from the head, when you sleep, it will fall to the stomach again. In the summer, bathe in cold water, for this will keep warmth in the head, which will occasion a desire for food. Then array yourself in fair garments, for a man's mind delights in fair things, and his heart is rendered lighter. Then clean the teeth with the dry bark of the hazel, as they will become all the fairer in consequence.* Your speech will be also most distinct, and breath sweeter. The standing posture should be at times practised, as it will do you much good, relieving the dura matter (membrane of the brain,) clothing your neck with power, investing your countenance with greater beauty, giving strength to the arms, improving your sight, preserving you from paleness, and adding power to your memory. Conversation, walking in company, and eating and drinking according to your usual habit, should be done in moderation. Use moderate exercise in walking or riding, as this will invigorate the body, and remove cardialgic pains, so that a man will be more hearty, strong, and the stomach will be warmer as well as your nerves more elastic.

---

* Giraldus Cambrensis assures us that the Welsh, in the 12th century, paid great attention to their teeth, rubbing them with either the leaves or the bark of the hazel, and refraining from hot meats and drinks, so that they were of dazzling whiteness.

## WHAT TO EAT.

§ 187. When you eat, take that for which you have the greatest relish if you can, particularly leavened bread. If you eat simple food it will be more easy for the stomach to digest it. If (when unused thereto) you should nevertheless eat two kinds of food, plain and strong food, eat the strong first, for the inferior portion of the stomach is hotter than the superior, as the lime is nearer, from whence more heat will be derived.

## RULES FOR EATING AND DRINKING.

§ 188. When you eat, do not eat away all your appetite, but let some desire for food remain. Drink no water with your food, as it will cool your stomach, preventing its digesting the food, and quenching the warmth thereof. But when you drink water, drink it sparingly, choosing the coldest water you can get. When you have done eating, take a walk in some well sheltered level piece of ground. When you feel inclined to sleep, do not sleep too much. Rest on your right side, then turn on the left, and double yourself. If you should feel pain in your stomach (cardialgia) and heaviness, put on extra clothing, in order to withdraw the heat from the stomach, drinking warm water, as this by producing vomiting will remove the unhealthy matter from your stomach. Walking much before food will heat the stomach. Much walking after food will injure the stomach, because undigested (in consequence of the labour) the food will fall to the inferior part of the stomach, and there generate many diseases. Sleeping before food will make a man thin, but sleeping after food will make a man fat. The night is colder than the day, and consequently the stomach will digest sooner by night than by day, because the colder the weather, the better will the stomach digest, as the heat falls from the extremities, and concentrates itself about the stomach. If a man who is in the habit of eating twice a day, should do so once only, it will injure the stomach. If a man in the habit of eating once only daily, should do so twice, it will be hurtful to the stomach. If from eating at one period of the day, we change to another, it will do harm to the stomach. At all times, if necessity should arise, obliging one to make a change in ones habit, let it be done gradually. Also do not eat, till the stomach has become empty, and this you may know from the sense of hunger and the thinness of your saliva. If you eat without hunger, the animal heat will freeze. If you eat when hungry, your animal spirits will be as hot as fire, and whosoever does not then take food, his stomach will fill up with insalubrity, which will produce headache.

# Physicians of Myddvai.

---

### INTRODUCTION.

The following Work is a book of remedies, which have been proved to be the best and most suitable for the human body, through the research and diligent study of Rhiwallon the Physician, and his three sons, even Cadwgan, Griffith, and Einion, who were Physicians to Rhys Gryg, ab Griffith ab Rhys ab Tewdwr, their Lord, who gave them rank, lands, and privileges at Myddvai, for their maintenance in the practice of their art and science, and the healing and benefit of those who should seek their help.

Herein, therefore, by the help of God, is exhibited the art of healing the injuries and diseases to which the human body is most subject, and the method of their management.

In the name of the FATHER, of the SON, and of the HOLY GHOST. AMEN, and so may it ever be.

### FLATULENT DYSPEPSIA.

§ 1. Take parsley seed, bruise well, and boil in the juice of the same. Let it be drank warm, the pain being present.

### ACUTE GASTRODYNIA.

§ 2. Take buck bean and powder well. Also, burn a quantity of gorse or broom seed in an iron pot, and reduce to fine powder. Pour a gallon of strong old mead upon the ingredients, then cover it up well and boil, and let it stand covered till cold. You should then drink as much thereof as you may require, night and morning fasting; at other times you should drink nothing but water till you have recovered your health.

### ANOTHER.

§ 3. Drink a decoction of blessed thistle for nine mornings, and refrain therefrom for nine mornings following, then drink and refrain as before for nine mornings; and again in the same way for nine mornings more. Let your diet be wheaten bread, and the milk of kine.

### A COLYRIUM.

§ 4. Take a penny pot full* of the best white wine, and as much in quantity as a hen's egg of copper ore, heat the ore in the fire till it is of a red heat, and quench it in the wine, repeating this process nine times. This fluid being put in a well covered glass vessel, and kept so covered for nine days, will be fit for use when wanted; a drop or two being put in the eye night and morning. When wine cannot be got, strong old mead, or old cider (which is the wine of apples) may be used.

### TO BREAK AN IMPOSTUME OR ABSCESS.

§ 6. Take a small portion of the herb called the herb of grace,† a portion of leavened bread, and half a spoonful of glue, boil these ingredients in the sediment of old ale, mixing them well together until the mass thickens; when required for use let it be applied hot to the impostume.

### FOR THE TOOTHACHE.

§ 7. Take distilled water of red roses, a small portion of beeswax, and a little fresh butter, say an equal quantity of each; let the ingredients be mixed together in a dish upon embers, then let a linen cloth be dipped therein, and applied to the affected jaw as hot as it can be borne.

### OINTMENT FOR AN ULCER.

§ 8. Take four portions of rosin, two of wax, one of lard, and four of verdigris; let these ingredients be boiled

* Half a Pint.    † Rue.

together on a slow fire, and strained through a coarse cloth. It should be kept in a well covered leaden vessel.

### FOR ALL KINDS OF ACHES.

§ 9. Take linseed, boil in milk, and apply to the painful part.

### TO HEAL A WOUND.

§ 10. Take yellow wax, melt on a slow fire, and take bruised cummin seed, mix with the molten wax, then stir these ingredients with a stirrer until cold. Apply this as a plaster to the wound.

### ANOTHER.

§ 11. Take bruised linseed, the white of an egg, a small portion of sheep's cream, and a little honey, make them into a plaster and apply to the wound.

### FOR A BURN OR A SCALD.

§ 12. Roast a dozen eggs stone hard, then take out the yolk and put in a frying pan, fry them till they become an ointment, and strain; anoint the injured part with the same, then take a bladder, spread mucilage of lime twigs thereon, and apply to the injured part.

### FOR HŒMORRHOIDS.

§ 13. Take smoke dried goat's flesh, desiccate completely, and reduce to as fine a powder as you can; lay some thereof on live coals in a fire-proof utensil, and put the same in a commode and sit thereon.

### AN OINTMENT TO PROMOTE THE REMOVAL OF A SLOUGH FROM AN ULCER.

§ 14. Take a spoonful of good vinegar, a spoonful of honey, a little verdigris, and the same quantity of aloes,* boil together and keep ready at hand for use.

### A LOTION TO WASH AN INFLAMED PART.

§ 15. Take the greater plantain, honey suckle,† and white roses, distil together, and in the product put some camphor, and let it remain in this water constantly.

---

* Elyf *pro* Elyw or aloes. It cleanseth wounds and suddenly healeth them. Lond. Disp. 1679.

† Gwinwydd *pro* Gwyddwydd. It is a corruption used in many parts of Wales.

### FOR AN INFANTILE AGUE OR INTERMITTENT FEVER.

§ 16. Boil the leaves of the common cinquefoil in milk, using as much of the herb as will be expedient. Let this be the child's only drink till he is well. This is also generally the most successful remedy for those of mature years.

### ANOTHER.

§ 17. Let some crab apples be roasted, and take some of the pulp, and half as much honey; let this be the child's only sustenance for a day and a night.

### FOR A MALIGNANT INTERMITTENT PROCEEDING FROM THE HEART.

§ 18. Take some white wine whey and reject the curds, then take some horse dung warm as it comes from the beast, and mix well with the posset, then strain and boil a small portion of the blessed thistle therein, or if more convenient add thereto a spoonful of the distilled water of the same; let the patient drink as much as he can of this for nine mornings fasting.

### FOR AN OPACITY OF THE CORNEA.

§ 19. Take the juice of parsley, and half as much of honey, and drop into the eye with a feather, keep the eye closed afterwards as long as a hundred is counted, and let this treatment be perseveringly followed.

### ANOTHER.

§ 20. Take the juice of celandine, drop into the eye, and close as long as a hundred is counted; let this treatment be perseveringly continued.

### TO CURE A PAIN IN THE CHEST.

§ 21. Take wall pepper * in small fragments, the dregs of small beer, wheat bran, and mutton suet; pound well in a mortar, then boil together on a slow fire and apply to the chest.

### TO OVERCOME HABITUAL CONSTIPATION.

§ 22. Take a new layed egg and remove the white, fill up the egg with fresh unsalted butter, then warm and eat it; do

* Ciarllysg *pro* Clauarlys.

this frequently if you are naturally disposed to constipation.

## TO PRODUCE A DIURETIC EFFECT.

§ 23. Take some haws, put them in a vessel of red earthenware, mix therewith a good quantity of honey, then put in an oven with bread; of this take four spoonfuls three times a day.

## ANOTHER.

§ 24. Separate the stones of haws from the pulp, and dry well, then reduce to a fine powder and keep in a dry place; then, when you need it, take a spoonful of this powder and a spoonful of honey, and make a confection thereof; this should be taken at night by going to bed, and again in the morning fasting, food being refrained from for three hours subsequently. If needful, let this be repeated, and you will have a thousand chances of being cured.

## FOR WORMS IN CHILDREN.

§ 25. Take as much as will stand on three golden crowns of wheaten flower bolted through a fine silken sieve, put it in a glass vial, and pour thereon as much spring water as will suffice to bring it to the consistency of milk, and no more; then let it be given the child to drink, and dead worms will be seen in his evacuations. This is a very excellent recipe.

## ANOTHER.

§ 26. Take the child's hair, cut it as small as you can, and mix as much as will stand on a golden crown with the pulp of a roasted apple, or with honey, and this will kill the worms.

## FOR A MALIGNANT SCALD OR RINGWORM.

§ 27. Take some snails and prick them all over with a needle till a kind of water exudes from them, and with this water wash the scald or ringworm, then bind some honeysuckle leaves on the part; let this be done night and morning, and in a short time you will be cured.

2 R

### FOR A HŒMOPTYSIS, THE CONSEQUENCE OF THE RUPTURE OF A BLOOD VESSEL IN THE LUNGS.

28. Take the dung of mice and dry in the sun, or at a distance before the fire, then powder; let as much as will stand on a groat be put in half a wineglass of the juice of the plantain mixed with some burnt honey, and let the patient drink thereof night and morning, continuing this treatment till he is cured.

### TO CURE A FETID BREATH.

29. Take rosemary leaves and flowers if to be had, and boil in white wine with a little myrrh and pellitory of the wall,* and you shall witness a wonderful result if you gargle your mouth therewith frequently.

### FOR A VESICAL CALCULUS.

§ 30. Take the powder of golden rod, called in Latin *Virga aurea*, and mix a spoonful thereof with a newly laid egg gently roasted, and give it the patient for breakfast, he not being permitted to take any food for four hours afterwards, and he will pass urine in less than half an hour afterwards. Let him continue to do this for ten or twelve days and he will get rid of the stone without pain. This is also very useful in flatulent dyspepsia.

### FOR AN EPIPHORA

§ 31. Take red cabbage leaf, and spread some white of egg thereon, then cover your eyes therewith in going to bed.

### FOR THE BITE OF A MAD DOG.

§ 32. Take as much as can be contained in half a wallnut of the powder of the spear thistle, dried in the shade, mix with a wine glassful of the best white wine, and drink it three times daily for three days, and by the help of God you will be cured.

### FOR INFLAMED EYES.

§ 33. Take juice of ground ivy, and woman's milk, equal parts of each. Strain through fine linen, and put a drop in the painful eye, and in both eyes, if needful.

* Canel *pro* Canhauawl.

### ANOTHER.

§ 34. Take distilled fennel water, and a portion of new honey, then mix together. Put a drop or two in the eye. It is proven.

### ANOTHER.

§ 35. Take the leaves of the red fruited bramble,* and the leaves of the common plantain, boil in spring water till it is reduced to the half, and apply to the diseased eye.

### ACOLLYRIUM FOR AN ACUTE OPHTHALMIA.

§ 36. Take a handful of red sage, and boil in as much smith's water as will cover it† till it evaporates to a half, then filter well. Put a pennyworth of aloes, and as much white copperas‡ in the liquor when removed from the fire, then wash thine eyes therewith.

### FOR A PTERYGIUM OR WET IN THE EYE.

§ 37. Take the white of an egg warm from the nest, rejecting the yolk, add thereto the size of a small nut of aloes in powder, and a little burnt honey, incorporate well together and add as much water as will enable you to filter the mixture through a fine cloth. Put a drop or two in each eye (or rather in the one requiring it) three times a day.

### FOR AN ACUTE PAIN IN THE LEG.

§ 38. Take a quantity of leavened dough in a very advanced state of accidity, the same weight of mutton suet,§ and of black soap, incorporate them together and spread on linen cloth; then apply to the inflamed leg, changing twice a day, and by the help of God it will be cured after three or four dressings.

### TO STRENGTHEN THE SIGHT.

§ 39. Take eyebright and red fennel, a handful of each, and half a handful of rue, distil, and wash your eye daily therewith.

---

* Drysi pro Dyrysi, i.e. Rubus Suberectus.

† The water in which Smiths quench Iron.

‡ Sulphate of Lime.

§ Gwer mân pro maullwyn, i. e. the "small ones of the wood,"—a very primitive term for sheep.

### FOR A HEADACHE.

§ 40. Take a piece of raw beef, and lay it on the nape of the neck, taking it away each night in going to bed; do this as often as needful.. It is proven.

### FOR THE GOUT.

§ 41. This disease is mostly confined to the feet and hands. Take wood sage, pellitory of the wall, wheat bran, cow's dung, and salt, boil together in wine or cider vinegar, and apply as a plaster to the painful part.

### TO MAKE A PLASTER FOR ALL KINDS OF ACHES.

§ 42. Take a pound of crude wax, half a pound of rosin, one sixth of a pound of thus, and a pound and a half of ram's suet, boil together and strain into a clean basin, then place the basin on a cinder fire in a stove; saturate a piece of linen in this, and apply to the painful part.

### FOR A COUGH.

§ 43. Take mustard seed coarsely powdered, boil with some figs in strong ale, and drink.

### FOR A RINGWORM.

§ 44. Take the roots of red dock and salt them, then put the same in vinegar, and give them a boil, then wash the ringworm with the liquor.

### FOR HYSTERIA.

§ 45. Take rosin and pound it well, then put it in white wine, and the gum of the bay tree,* swallow it, and you will obtain benefit thereby.

### TO CURE ONE WHO TALKS IN HIS SLEEP.

§ 46. Take southernwood, and pound it well, and add thereto some wine or old mead, strain well and let the patient drink a portion thereof night and morning.

### FOR THE TOOTHACHE.

§ 48. Take shepherd's purse and pound into a mass, then apply to the tooth.

* Lliwydden *pro* Llawrwydden.

## ANOTHER.

§ 49. Take the root of the water flower de lys,* and masticate. If there be a cavity in the tooth put therein a fragment of the root, but avoid swallowing the saliva, as the juice of this root is poisonous, and if you swallow it you will become delirious for days, if it does not prove fatal.

## FOR A DANGEROUS COUGH.

§ 50. Take sage, rue, cummin, and pound them like pepper, then boil together in honey, and make into a confection. Take a spoonful thereof night and morning, and by the help of God you will obtain benefit.

## FOR SORENESS AND GANGRENE OF THE MOUTH.

§ 51. Take rosemary tops, sage, honeysuckle, and mallows, of each half a handful, and boil together well in as much spring water as will cover them, until it is reduced to a third, then take some pure honey boiled in spring water with as much as a pigeon's egg of alum, and boil in the filtered decoction of herbs till reduced to a third, then keep in a glass bottle well corked, and wash your mouth therewith.

## A DRAWING OINTMENT.

§ 52. Take mercurial ointment, May butter, rosin, suet, and new wax, then take round birthwort, great ox eye, betony, milfoil, hoary plantain, sage, smallage, marigold, and pound well; boil the butter and herbs together on a slow fire for two or three hours, and if the butter dries up add more as there may be occasion. When this boiling is finished strain off the butter well under a press, and add the wax and the mercurial ointment thereto as well as the rosin and the suet, and boil together on a fire for an hour, then let it cool in a clean vessel and keep.

## AN ANTIDOTE FOR POISONED FOOD OR DRINK.

§ 53. Take rue, bruise well and pour white wine thereon, (as much as will cover it) and if there be no wine, then ale, or mead; let the liquor and the herb be stirred well

* Vide Davies, under " Gellhesgen."

and strained. Let a draught of this be given to the patient in the morning fasting, and another in an hour, and he will be cured.

### FOR INFLAMMATION OF THE MAMMÆ.

§ 54. Take agrimony, betony, and vervain, and pound well, then mix them with strong old ale, strain well, and set some milk on the fire; when this boils add the liquor thereto and make a posset thereof, giving it to the woman to drink warm. Let her do this frequently and she will be cured.

### FOR A HOARSENESS.

§ 55. Take the spotted persicaria and boil, then pound in a mortar well; rub the throat with it, and the patient will be cured.

### FOR A STRANGURY.

§ 56. Seek some mouse chickweed, and wild sage, as much of the one as of the other; then make into a powder, and mix with drink, cider being best, or else old mead, if no cider can be got.

### TO EXTRACT A TOOTH WITHOUT PAIN.

§ 57. Take some newts, by some called lizards, and those nasty beetles which are found in ferns during summer time, calcine them in an iron pot and make a powder thereof. Wet the forefinger of the right hand, insert it in the powder, and apply it to the tooth frequently, refraining from spitting it off, when the tooth will fall away without pain. It is proven.

### FOR HŒMATURIA.

§ 58. Take agrimony, bruise well, and mix the mass with wine, ale, or mead to drink, and you will obtain a cure.

### FOR A DIARRHŒA.

§ 59. Take the roots of the red fennel, (*pyrethrum inodorum*) pound in a mortar well, and mix with goat's milk, drinking for nine mornings; it will be of benefit, and stay the purging. It is proven.

#### FOR AN OBSTINATE PAIN IN THE STOMACH.

§ 60. Drink the juice of the tansy in old ale, and you will be effectually cured.

#### FOR DYSPNŒA IN THE CHEST.

§ 61. Seek the roots of the elecampane, wash clean and scrape, then boil in white wine vinegar when scraped. Dry them, reduce into powder, and boil the powder in honey, and add powdered pepper thereto ; keep in a box and take a spoonful night and morning. This will cure the patient.

If there is dyspnœa and cough with expectoration in a person, seek three cinders and set before the sick person, then let him spit upon the cinders ; if the expectorated matter smells offensively he will die, if not he will recover.

#### FOR THE BITE OF A MAD DOG.

§ 62. Seek some plantain, and a handful of sheep's sorrel, then pound well in a mortar with the white of eggs, honey, and old lard, make into an ointment and apply to the bitten part, so that it may be cured.

#### TO PROMOTE THE FLOW OF MILK IN A WOMAN'S BREAST.

§ 63. Seek some red fennel, and administer to a woman in ale, and it will produce enough milk to nurse her child.

#### FOR DEAFNESS

§ 64. Seek red onion, and boil in oxymel, then add thereto a handful of oat malt, rue, and red fennel, and boil in the liquor; put this, in the warmth of milk, in the ear night and morning, plug the ear with black wool, so that it may not come out; it will improve the hearing wonderfully. It is proven.

#### TO PREPARE A BLESSED COLLYRIUM TO CLEAR THE EYE.

§ 65. Take red roses, wild celery, vervain, red fennel, maiden hair, house leek, celandine, and wild thyme, wash them clean and macerate in white wine for a day and a night, then distil from a brass pot. The first water you obtain will be like silver, this will be useful for any affection of the eye, and for a stye.

### FOR AN EPIPHORA.

§ 66. Take the flowers of betony, and eat, and it will clear the eye.

### ANOTHER.

§ 67. Anoint the eye with the juice of celandine and fresh honey, and you will obtain great benefit.

### ANOTHER.

§ 68. Take white wine, the juice of celandine, and the juice of red fennel; boil in the white wine until it is reduced to a third; anoint your eye with this and it will keep it clear and strong.

### FOR A STYE OR PAIN IN THE EYE.

§ 69. Obtain the yolk of an egg, and wheaten meal, add a little sulphate of copper, incorporate them together and lay upon a cloth, and apply to the eye in going to sleep. It will cure it by the following day; let this be done for three days.

### FOR PAIN IN THE EYE.

§ 70. Seek the gall of a hare, of a hen, of an eel, and of a stag, with fresh urine and honeysuckle leaves, then inflict a wound upon an ivy tree, and mix the gum that exudes from the wound therewith, boiling it swiftly, and straining it through a fine linen cloth; when cold insert a little thereof in the corners of the eyes, and it will be a wonder if he who makes use of it does not see the stars in mid-day, in consequence of the virtues of this remedy.

### TO STRENGTHEN THE EYE.

§ 71. Seek house leek, red rose leaves, and celandine, pound together and boil in white wine, or strong and clear old ale; boil briskly, and strain through a fine clean linen cloth, wash your eyes therewith night and morning, and you will be cured.

### FOR A COLD OR CATARRH, AND ALL KINDS OF PAIN IN THE SHOULDERS, ARMS, AND LEGS.

§ 74. Take wild thyme, and bruise small, boil in the lees of strong ale till it is thickened, and apply thereto as hot as the patient can bear it. Let this be persevered in for nine days, and he will be effectually cured.

### FOR A THORN IN THE FLESH.

§ 75. If a thorn enters into a man's body either in his feet or hands, take the root of the black chameleon thistle or the leaves, and the white of eggs, and refined rye meal, (or barley if there be no rye) apply thereto in the form of a poultice, and it will extract it.

### FOR TERTIAN AGUE.

§ 76. Take a large handful of betony, a handful of year old broom, and a handful of sage, wash clean and bruise in a mortar, mix with strong ale, strain and let it be drank nine times successively. This will restrain it,

### FOR SUPPRESSION OF URINE.

§ 77. Seek broom seed, and ground into fine powder, mix with drink and let it be drank. Do this till you are quite well.

### ANOTHER.

§ 78. Take broom seed, counting nine, and devoting the tenth to God; grind the seed into fine meal and take in drink, or as a confection in boiled honey. If a woman or maid should do this, neither pain or abscess will ever take place in her mammæ.

### FOR A SPRAIN.

§ 79. Seek the lees of strong old ale, the suet of a black wether, or a goat, and wheat groats, boil well and spread on a cloth as warm as can be borne, and apply to the injured part three times. This will cure it.

### FOR THE GOUT.

§ 80. Seek the avens, pimpernel, betony, the vervain, an equal portion of each, of ground ivy four portions; boil them in as much white wine as will cover them, and let a good draught thereof be drank night and morning; thus you will obtain a cure. Let this be drank the first thing every morning, and the last every night, for nine mornings, in order to relieve the stomach; then apply a piece of fresh beef half an inch thick to the foot or hand, and this will completely cure you.

### FOR DYSPNŒA AND HOARSENESS.

§ 81. Take a large quantity of the vervain, boil in water till reduced to a third, and strain; add the root of the mallow, cut small, and boil again. Let this be taken warm at night and cold in the morning, keeping it in an earthenware grenn.*

### FOR THE EVIL.

§ 82. Take the juice of rue, cummin, and powdered pepper, boil in honey and make a confection thereof. Let this be taken the first thing in the morning and the last at night.

### FOR A BLACK JAUNDICE.

§ 84. Seek the tail of salmon, dry slowly and reduce to a powder, let it be taken on ale, and the patient will be cured.

### FOR DEAFNESS.

§ 85. Take some elm rods, and lay them upon the embers, then receive the water that exudes from the rods in a clean vessel, and get the oil of a black eel, as much honey, and as much of the juice of betony, mix them together, drop into the ear and plug with the wool of a black lamb. This will effectually cure the patient.

### FOR PLETHORA.

§ 86. Seek bean meal, honey, and the yolk of eggs, form a cake thereof and bake on the hearth under a pan, with embers covering the pan; let the patient have some of this cake to eat frequently.

### TO AVOID ENEMIES.

§ 87. If one goes to battle let him seek the vervain, and keep it in his clothes (on his person,) and he will escape from his enemies.

### TO MAKE HEALING PLASTER.

§ 88. Seek half a pound of pitch, quarter of a pound of wax, half a pound of suet, and powder of gall stone, boil

---

* Grenn, a measure equivalent to the ½ of a ton. "The load of two men upon a bar in every grenn."—*Welsh Laws.*

these ingredients together, stirring them well so that they may be thoroughly incorporated; then it should be poured into a pot or into water, so that it may be formed into a roll. This plaster being spread on linen or white kid, is useful for all ulcers from which there is a profuse watery secretion.

### FOR SUPPRESSED MENSES.

§ 89. Seek rue, and pound well, and express the juice into wine or strong ale, strain and let it clear, then let the woman drink thereof, and she will recover.

### TO IMPROVE THE HEARING.

§ 90. Seek young ash shoots (of the size of rods,) cut, and lay on a tripod over the fire, then receive the drops which will exude from the ends, and take a spoonful of honey, the ends of house leeks, the heads and stalks of leeks, some mustard in flour, and a shell full of the oil of eels; let the whole be boiled together, carefully stirring them whilst boiling. Let it be injected warm with a syringe into the ear, the same being filled with the wool of a black lamb, and the patient will be cured.

### A PLASTER FOR ERYSIPELAS, AND THE REMOVAL OF PROUD FLESH.

§ 94: Take the juice of wood sage and honey mixed with salt and vinegar, mix the ingredients together well, then add a portion of rye meal and boil so that a cataplasm may be formed thereof. Make use of this cataplasm in conjunction with the drink recommended for the gout, and the patient will soon recover.

### FOR AN AGUE OR ARDENT INTERMITTENT.

§ 95. Take two pennyworths of treacle, a pennyworth of saffron, and a little hartshorn grated fine, put in a cupful of ale and mix well together drinking it for three mornings; then seek some sprigs of red raspberries, the leaves of sweet-briers, wood sorrel, and malt, make a drink, and take a hearty draught thereof three or four times a day; whoever does this will recover.

### AN APERIENT DRINK.

§ 96. Take a pennyworth of stibium * and grate as fine as flour, then mix with half a pint of sound ale, warm and let the patient drink it in the morning fasting, afterwards get a quart of posset, and in half an hour let him drink it at thrice; when it has acted, make a warm drink with spring water, put some good butter and honey therein, then let the patient drink it two or three times and he will recover.

### ANOTHER.

§ 97. Take the fruit of the buckthorn, express the juice and mix two spoonfuls thereof with a full draught of good ale wort, let the patient drink it, and if it does not act let him drink another draught without the buckthorn; when it has acted let him take for food some warm oatmeal gruel made with spring water, mixing therewith some honey, butter, and unsifted wheaten bread, let this be done three times in nine days and it will purge from the body all corrupt humors; after this course let him live for nine days farther on milk food and wheaten bread with the bran retained, alternately with the warm water and flour before mentioned.

### ANOTHER.

§ 98. Take a handful of leaves of damask roses, boil in the wort of good ale, and drink, attending to the diet as aforesaid for nine days.

### ANOTHER.

§ 99. Take of honey, and the juice of the fruit of the buckthorn, an equal quantity, boil together on a slow fire, and keep in a glass bottle well covered, take two or three spoonfuls thereof when required, and in half an hour afterwards a hearty draught of the wort of strong ale.

### A CONFECTION FOR A SORE MOUTH.

§ 100. Take a spoonful of the juice of sage, a spoonful of the juice of elder, two spoonfuls of the juice of cloudberry, the pulp of a hot apple, and three spoonfuls of honey, boil

* Reguius of Antimony.

on a slow fire stirring continually till it becomes a thick confection. Keep it in an earthen pot, covering it well, so that it may be kept for use. When a case of sore mouth occurs, take as much as a pigeon's egg and let it be retained in the mouth till it is dissolved, and it will be of service.

### ANOTHER.

§ 101. Take elder leaves, honey suckle leaves, sage, rosemary, and briers, boil well in as much water as will cover them, then sweeten with honey and wash your mouth therewith, retaining the liquor in your mouth as long as you can; then eject it three times, and afterwards drink a hearty draught thereof to cool your stomach.

### ANOTHER.

§ 102. Take four spoonfuls of honey, the juice of four oranges, three spoonfuls of the juice of sage, three of the juice of blackberries, and three of the juice of cloudberries, boil on a slow fire till it becomes a thick confection; keep in a covered pot, and put as much as a pigeon's egg in thy mouth, retaining it till it dissolves.

### FOR A COLD HUMORAL CATARRH.

§ 103. Take half a pint of the juice of cleavers, and a spoonful of honey therein night and morning.

### ANOTHER.

§ 104. Take half a pint of blackberry juice, containing a spoonful of new honey, night and morning.

### FOR AN INFLAMMATORY CATARRH.

§ 105. Take the juice of cleavers, the juice of water cress, the juice of sorrel, and the juice of elder, equal parts of each; drink half a pint of this night and morning for nine days, and live the next nine days upon milk diet and wheaten bread, ground through and through; let no other food or drink be taken, and it will be well to take a cathartic two or three times before this medicine, in order to clear the system of corrupt humors.

#### FOR HUMORAL FLATULENCE, WEAKENING THE BODY. AND MIND.

§ 106. Take the juice of apples, raspberries, plums, or blackberries, strained; set upon a slow fire, adding thereto a spoonful of honey for every draught, and giving it a slight boiling; then drink a hearty draught thereof for nine days, and take for food bread made of highly roasted acorns, no no other food being taken during the time, and you will recover.

The best juice of fruit, should they be in season, is the juice of sloes, and of blackberries. When no acorns can be procured, dry the roots of nettles before the fire at a distance, and grind to powder; make it into bread, and subsist thereon.

#### ANOTHER

§ 107. Take a spoonful of mustard seed three times a day, wash down the throat with good old mead, and subsist upon a milk diet with well baked wheaten bread; let your meals be slight and frequent.

#### AN OINTMENT FOR THE ANKLES AND JOINTS.

§ 108. Take the rhodri, or (as others term them) radishes, and the suet of sheep or goats, pound them well together till they become an ointment, then put the ointment in a pan, adding thereto a little honey and salt, boil them well on a slow fire, and strain well; with this anoint the painful joint, and it will be cured by the help of God.

#### TO EXTRACT IRON OR FRAGMENTS OF WOOD FROM A WOUND, AND TO OPEN IT.

§ 109. Take the roots of nettles, goose grease, and honey, pound them into a plaster and apply to the wound. It will mysteriously open the wound and extract what may be in it.

#### FOR INFLAMMATORY WOUNDS, WHEREBY THE PATIENT IS PREVENTED FROM SLEEPING.

§ 110. Take holly bark, mallow, the middle bark of the elder, equal quantities of each, and add thereto lard and wine in the same proportions; boil well until it becomes thick, then take a cloth and spread the ointment thereon, and spread some warm on a tent also; insert this in the wound, and cover it over with the anointed cloth; apply some powdery unguent on the wound with the tent, and by the help of God it will be healed.

### A GOOD HEALING SALVE FOR WOUNDS.

§ 111. Take oil of olives, or, if none can be got, some lard and wine, in equal quantities, boil together well, stirring it continually whilst boiling; when it has thickened keep in an earthen vessel or bladder, covering it well. When required anoint the wound therewith.

### AN OINTMENT FOR AN EXTERNAL INFLAMMATION.

§ 112. Take the cream of kine, and white wine or strong apple cider, or else hard old mead; boil well together (equal quantities of each) till it becomes thick, stirring it continually; when cold, keep in a bladder or box, and when needful anoint the part therewith.

### FOR BRONCHITIS WITH DYSPNŒA.

§ 113. Take the roots of parsley, red fennel, river star tip, and pound well; take three quarts of strong black wort and boil what is proper of the herbs therein till the three quarts are reduced to one, then take six pennyworth of powdered anise, as much as will sweeten it well of clarified honey, and boil in the above liquor, and set aside to keep in a warm place; this is termed an expectorant medicine, and will certainly destroy the cough.

### TO PREPARE CLARIFIED HONEY.

§ 114. Take one proportion of honey, four of spring water, and put in a clean brass pot to boil; when the wax and other impurities rise to the surface, remove it with a bassel * until it ceases to produce scum, then boil on a moderate fire till the water is completely evaporated, and the honey left clarified in the pot; put it afterwards in an

---

* From Baselard an ornamental dagger much worn in the time of Henry V. A spatula is the term now in use.

earthen pot, and cover it up well. It is the best sort of honey for medicine or dietetic purposes.

### AN ANODYNE OINTMENT.

§ 115. Take the pulp of crabs and boil in wine until the wine is evaporated completely, mix rosin, clear honey, and old lard therewith, then boil well and strain; anoint the painful part with this ointment frequently, and by the help of God the pain will be removed.

### FOR A BURN OR SCALD.

§ 117. Take the roots of the lily, wash them clean and boil briskly in water, then mix them well with the white of eggs, ointment of petreolum, or the ointment of lime twigs, (or if the last cannot be got) good kine's cream, or fresh unsalted butter; apply this to the burn, and the more the better of it.

### FOR A SWELLING, HEAT, OR SPRAIN,
A RIGOR, SUCCEEDING A JOURNEY, OR FOR ERYSIPELAS ON THE LOWER EXTREM-
ITIES ; HOWEVER GREAT MAY BE THE PAIN, REDNESS OR CORRUPT CONDITION OF
THE DISEASED PART, EVEN THOUGH MANY OTHER MEDICAMENTS MAY HAVE FAILED,
THIS WILL HEAL IT.

§ 118. Take white alum and reduce to powder, then mix it with spring water giving it three boilings, and should any scum appear, remove it carefully until none remains, then keep it most carefully. A pennyworth of this solution in a quart of water will be enough to make a lotion, which should be applied frequently to the diseased part with a linen cloth, and it will reduce the swelling, the heat, the redness, and the pain. Indeed if you continue to wash it in this way, any disease even phagadenic ulcers, or gangrenous erys-elas will be cured by this water, thus perseveringly applied by a fire. When the whole is used make another supply, and observe that a pennyworth of the alum will be enough in a quart of water; do this and you will be cured. It is proven.

### FOR A SUNBURN OR THE LIKE EFFECT FROM ANY OTHER HEAT.

§ 119. Take marsh pennywort and cream, half and half, and boil on a slow fire till it becomes a thick ointment; keep it in a box covered.

### FOR ITCH OR PSORIASIS.

§ 120. Take the root of elecampane washed clean, boil in pure water; when the roots are softened, pound, then add thereto thick kine's cream. Mix it for an ointment and anoint your whole body with it as you go to bed, once in three days, (that is three times in nine days,) and drink a hearty draught of the water in which the roots were boiled, three times a day for nine days, and you will be cured of the eruption, and will be strong in body, for the water is useful to heal and strengthen the stomach and lungs.

### AN OINTMENT FOR PNEUMONIA.

§ 121. Take suet and honey, boil together, and when they have boiled enough take nine pieces of fine flannel and dip in the ointment; let each cool, and when cold apply the nine to your chest, from one armpit to another, and from the shoulder to the navel; let it remain there for nine days, then remove one away daily till the whole are removed. When this is going on, take wheaten bread ground through and through, with some pure honey spread thereon every morning, and some of the same bread with cow's milk at noon, then baked apples and goat's milk at night, taking between the meals a spoonful of pure honey. This by the help of God will cure you.

### ANOTHER MEDICINE FOR PNEUMONIA.

§ 122 Take the white horehound, and pound well, then add some pure water thereto, letting it stand for three hours, then strain well through a fine cloth, add a good deal of honey to the strained liquor, and put on a slow fire to warm; take half a draught thereof every three hours, and let your diet be the best wheaten bread and milk; when thirsty, take an apple, and cover it with good old cider, eat the apple, in an hour drink the cider, and let this be your only diet.

### ANOTHER.

§ 123. Take half a man's meal of kine's milk, and add thereto two spoonfuls of pure honey. Take for food some

2 T

good wheaten bread with this drink three times a day.
Between the meals take a spoonful of the juice of horehound, and a spoonful of honey mixed.

When neither these herbs nor any other can be got fresh,
in order to get their juice, then get the herbs dry, and boil in
what will cover them of water in an iron pot, till it evaporates to the half, then express well through a fine cloth, after
this add half the quantity of honey, boiling the second time
till it is evaporated to a third, keeping it in a glass bottle
well corked.

### ANOTHER.

§ 124. Take for your only food a slice of the best wheaten
bread with honey, and for your only drink the breast milk
of a healthy young woman, for nine days without intermission; then instead of the breast milk, take goat's milk
for another nine days, and subsist upon that for a longer
period if needful.

### FOR STRANGURY AND THE STONE.

§ 125. Take the milfoil, and saxifrage, pound with
warm water, and let the patient have this liquor for nine
days as drink, nor let him take any other drink, and by
God's aid he will recover.

### ANOTHER.

§ 126. Take the blood and skin of a hare and make a
powder thereof, mix with the cider of red rinded apples,
mead, or beer, and drink it with either, but prefer cider or
mead. Let the patient drink this only, and it will disintegrate the stone, causing it to be expelled. If you should
wish to prove this, take a spoonful of this powder in water,
and put in a hole made in an acid stone, and by next day it
will certainly have dissolved it.

### FOR STRANGURY AND RETENTION OF URINE.

§ 127. Take smallage, a herb very much like the garden
parsley, having a roast meat sort of taste, rue and betony,
with a quart of white wine; pound the herbs well, and boil
in the wine till it is reduced to the half, then strain well

through a fine cloth, and give it to the patient at three draughts, and he will certainly be cured.

## FOR A PAIN IN THE CARDIAC REGION.

§ 128. Take the centaury, pound well, boil in old ale and express well, afterwards boil to the half, take that with twice as much honey, and boil moderately; take a cupful thereof fasting for nine days, and it will remove the pain and oppression from the region of the heart without fail.

## ANOTHER WAY OF PREPARING THE SAME MEDICINE.

§ 129. Take the centaury, boil well in old ale, then remove the herbs from the ale, and pound well in a mortar, boil again well, and express through a fine cloth, take this juice mixed with twice the quantity of honey, boil moderately and habituate yourself to take it fasting for nine days, and through the help of God it will heal the oppression and pain about the heart.

## A VALUABLE OINTMENT FOR ALL KINDS OF ACHES.

§ 130. Take old lard, a he-goat's and a sheep's suet, yellow wax, wormwood and primrose, bruise in a mortar, boil in butter, then put in the suet, lard, and wax, boil well and express strongly through cloth, keep carefully and it will ease all sorts of aches.

## AN OINTMENT FOR ALL NERVOUS DISORDERS.

§ 131. Take earthworms and the bulb of an onion, make a hole, and put the earthworms in, then light a fire underneath to roast them, after that apply to the affected part, leaving it there for three nights without removing.

## AN OINTMENT FOR GENERAL USE.

§ 132. Take a gander's fat, the fat of a male cat, a red boars's fat, three drams of blue wax,* water cress, wormwood, the red strawberry plant and primrose, boil them in pure spring water, and when boiled stuff a gander with them, and roast them at a distance from the fire, the grease issuing from it should be carefully kept in a pot. It is a

* Cupriated wax.

valuable ointment for all kinds of aches in a man's body, and
is like one that was formerly made by Hippocrates. It is
proved.

### FOR AN OPACITY IN A MAN'S EYE.

§ 133. Take a rook's gall and mix well with the white of
an egg, put in your eye, and take a little fine linen and lay
thereon; do this night and morning, you will surely be
cured.

### FOR AN INJURY IN THE ELBOW, KNEE, OR LEGS.

§ 134. Take lard, or pig's fat once melted, spread on a
cloth or flannel, and apply to the swellings. If to the elbow
or knee, mix some juice of rue therewith, and it will cure an
injury of the joint. It is proved.

### FOR A SWELLING, AND HEAT, OR INFLAMMATION
#### OF AN ERYSIPELATOUS NATURE, OR ANY OTHER KIND.

§ 135. Take elm bark and bruise well, rejecting the
epidermis, boil down to the thickness of honey, remove the
bark, and add barley meal and unsalted butter, boil into a
cataplasm, lay on a flannel and apply to the disease. If it is
supposed that there is a fragment of bone therein, use a
large quantity of bark in the poultice, and it will bring it
into union with the adjoining bone, if it is used with
perseverance.

### FOR PAIN AND NOISE IN THE EAR.

§ 136. Take a loaf of wheaten bread (ground through) hot
from the oven, divide in two, and apply to both ears as hot
as it can be borne, bind, and thus produce prespiration, and
by the help of God you will be cured.

### FOR CARDIALGIA IN A MOIST STOMACH.

§ 137. Take grains of paradise, and powdered cloves, eat
for a week, and by God's aid you will be cured.

### A PLASTER TO REDUCE A SWELLING.

§ 141. Take the tutsan, cinquefoil, vervain, mallows, lard,
and butter; boil the herbs well in water, then remove and
pound the herbs well, setting them on the fire in the water a
second time, with butter and lard, mix and boil till it forms
a cataplasm, and apply to the swelling, and it will reduce it
without fail.

### FOR THE JAUNDICE.

§ 145. Take the leaves which grow on the branches of the hawthorn and the mistletoe, boiling them in white wine or good old ale, till reduced to the half, then take it off the fire and strain. Drink this three times a day and you will be cured.

### A DRINK FOR RIGOR OF STOMACH AND BODY.

§ 147. Take a handful of rosemary, a handful of hyssop, a handful of sage, a handful of feverfew, a handful of red fennel, pound well and boil in a gallon of good strong wort made from barley malt, keeping it in an earthen vessel, covering it carefully, and setting aside for three days; then take three draughts thereof, fasting every morning, and another at night warmed blood heat. Take also a pennyworth of grains of paradise, a pennyworth of saffron, and a pennyworth of canella bark powdered fine in a mortar, and cast a portion on the surface of the drink, doing this in the drink as long as it lasts. It has been proved valuable for all pains in a man's body.

### FOR PNEUMONIA.

§ 148. Take a proportion of the sea beet (called in Latin beta) rejecting the branches and tops, and take three gallons of pure water, boiling therein; then take the beet out, letting the decoction boil, after a while remove from the fire, and let it cool to the temperature of wort, then pour it upon some fresh lees (of ale) permitting it to ferment as long as it will do so, then give it the patient for nine meals as his only drink; then take the beet and mix with butter and powdered melilot, giving it the patient to eat for nine meals, and by the help of God he will recover. It is also an excellent medicine for tertian ague.

### FOR AN AGUE.

§ 149. Take a handful of the water flower de lys, three quarts of good strong ale, pound the herbs, and boil in the ale till it is reduced to three quarts, then strain; then take a pennyworth of the powder of the grains of paradise, and boil a second time slightly. Take it at four times a day before the ague fit, and you will recover.

## FOR THE INTERNAL PAIN CALLED STONE.

§ 150. Take the herb called butterwort, which grows in meadows and on mountains, its leaves embracing the earth, and having a blue barren flower, gather your cowl full of these herbs, and pound them well in a large wooden milk pail. Then take twice as much water cress, and pound those briskly, afterwards take a red cock, kill, feather, eviscerate, and clean well; then put in a brass pot, in at least two gallons of pure water, and boil in the water with the herbs, till the bones become loose, when they should be taken out, and the bones removed; return the flesh again to the pot as well as the herbs, boil briskly the second time till you find the mixture thickening, and the ebulation ceasing in consequence of its thickness ; now take it off the fire, and strain the whole through a strong cloth. Take the strained matter and set on the fire, then take a half-pennyworth of powdered pepper, and cast into this liquor, afterwards remove it from the fire to cool, stirring the meanwhile ; administer some of this to the patient with his food and drink each meal, till the morbid product is found passing away from him in a dissolved condition. I have proved this to be effectual in the case of those of all ages. It is called " *The blue confection for the Stone.*"

### WHEN A MAN IS SWOLLEN FROM THE POISON OF A SPIDER.

§ 151. Take nine cloves of garlic, and peel carefully, a spoonful of treacle, a quart of strong new ale, mix these together and give them to the patient to drink freely, at the same time cover him with abundance of clothes so that he may perspire well. If he can retain this position for an hour he will escape, even though the integument had become mottled. This medicament is also useful for a person bitten by an adder.

### FOR SWELLING AND PAIN IN THE SHOULDERS, OR THE JAWS, AND UNDER THE EARS.

§ 152. Take the celandine, the roots of red fennel, the heads of leeks, red wine and butter, pound them together and apply them cold as a plaster to the part, and you will truly recover by the help of God.

### FOR SCABS AND ERUPTIONS ON A MAN'S FLESH.

§ 153. Take the celandine, the root of the elecampane, and wood sorrel, boil them in as much water as you please, till it is evaporated to the half, wash the diseased part with this fluid and it will be healed.

### FOR PAIN IN THE BACK.

§ 154. Bleed from the back of the foot near the great toe, and fillet the limb, having bathed it in warm water, and the patient will surely get well.

### FOR A PAINFUL ERYSIPELAS IN THE LEGS AND MEMBERS.

§ 155. Take the herb called the buckthorn plantain, and boil in three gallons of water, till it is reduced to a quart, bottle, then add a gallon of ale, and boil till it is reduced into a bottle again, finally straining it. Keep it in a clean vessel and let the painful part be anointed therewith frequently.

### FOR STRANGURY AND THE ATTENDANT PAIN.

§ 156. Take saxifrage and parsley, pound them well together, and boil with honey in old ale, finally straining. Drink of this night and morning, and you will be cured in the name of God.

### FOR ULCERATION OF THE EARS.

§ 157. Take the seed of the ash, otherwise called ashen keys, and boil briskly in the water of the sick man, Foment the ear therewith and put some therein on black wool. By God's help it will cure it.

### FOR THE JAUNDICE.

§ 158. Take the largest apple you can have, and scoop the eye out, removing the core of the apple with a bone or wooden scoop, fill it up with the juice of the white ox eye, (by some called the great daisy) and saffron, then re-insert the eye in its place, and bake the apple under the embers, when sufficiently baked remove from under the embers, and pound thoroughly. Let the patient eat it, and he will certainly recover.

### FOR A CHRONIC GASTROCELE.

§ 159. Take the bark of the black thorn, scrape off the epidermis, and boil the under bark in water as long as beef is boiled; afterwards boil an egg hard, and take the yolk and fine wheat flour, mixing well together; then take the third part of the liquor wherein the bark was boiled, and the mixture of meal and yolk, make bread of them and bake on the hearth stone; this should be eaten night and morning. The patient should carefully abstain from any other drink than the liquor of black thorn or red wine, and he will recover.—PHILIP THE PHYSICIAN.

### FOR FAINTINGS OF THE HEART.

§ 160. Take the juice of fennel, and honey, measure for measure, boil well, eating as much in quantity as a hen's egg night and morning, and you will recover.

### FOR HARDNESS OF THE ABDOMEN.

§ 161. Take two spoonfuls of the juice of holly, drinking it three times a day for nine days, and by God's help you will recover.

### FOR A MOIST STOMACH.

§ 162. Take the roots of leeks, and make into powder by desicating them at a distance from the fire, and powdering in a mortar; take a spoonful of this powder in a good draught of red wine, and drink it the last thing at night, two hours after your supper for three days, when by God's help you will recover.

### FOR A PNEUMONIA.

§ 163. Take the three following herbs, even mugwort, tansy, and red fennel, a handful of each, pound well and make them into a potion with good sound old ale, boil them on a slow fire, straining carefully, and drinking it cold for three meals, and by God's aid it will remove the pain under the pectoral muscle and shoulder, curing the patient.

Another way of preparing it is to pound the herbs well, pouring thereon three cupfuls of ale or old mead. Having left them to stand to cool for half an hour, strain well through a clean cloth, giving it in three portions to the patient once every three hours, and by God's help he will recover.

### AN OINTMENT FOR ALL SORTS OF DOLOURS.

§ 164. Take broom flowers, or (when not to be had) the branches and leaves, primroses, the roots of water hemlock, the leaves of eryngo, mugwort, and red dock, pound them well in a mortar, and make an ointment by means of butter ; anoint the diseased part frequently and it will be cured.

### FOR SOLUTION OF THE LIVER.*

§ 165. Take a little wild tansy, pound well with wine, express, and then drink it three times a day for three days, and by God's help you will recover. When no wine can be got, take strong sound ale or mead instead.

Borage will remove the red hue [of the evacuations,] if it is pounded with wine and drunk. It will strengthen a man's memory and intellect, being truly a warm astringent tonic.

### TO RESTRAIN THIRST IN A HEALTHY OR SICK MAN.

§ 166. Take centaury, and pound with warm water, then strain, when cold let it be drunk, and it will remove cardialgic pains, and cure the patient.

### FOR PAIN IN THE FEET, AND SWELLING IN THE LEGS.

§ 167. Take the roots of the dwarf elder, and remove the bark, boiling it well, then pound them in a mortar with old lard, and apply as a plaster to the diseased part.

### FOR AN OPACITY OF THE CORNEA.

§ 168. Take the leaves of the red garden strawberry, and pound with a hen's fat and unsalted butter, anoint your eye when you go to sleep with this ointment, so that it may enter into your eye, and you will recover.

### ANOTHER.

§ 169. Take a hen's fat, unsalted butter, and powdered aloes, boil them together and let them cool, then anoint your eyes when you go to sleep.

---

* One of the imaginary diseases of the old humoral pathology, probably bilious diarrhœa or dysentery.

### FOR STRANGURY.

§ 170. Take the juice of the leek, honey, powdered pepper, and vinegar, pound well till they are incorporated, and administer to the patient in three doses, and it will cure him.

### FOR DYSPEPSIA, STRANGURY, AND PAIN IN THE PERINŒUM.

§ 171. Take two handfuls of tansy, pounding them in a mortar, then boil them in spring water for the time required for beef, when they will become a thick mass. Cast some barley meal upon the surface, mix well and lay upon a cloth or flannel. Apply this cataplasm to the painful part frequently, repeating it until nine times; afterwards take two quarts of perry, a quart of the blessed water* of rulandus, (or the emetic water,) add some to the wine as warm as the patient can take it, and let him drink it night and morning. Do not permit him to take the warm drink first and then the emetic water afterwards. Let him follow this plan as long as the liquor lasts. Whilst taking these things procure some ram's flesh, boil well in spring water, then remove from the fire, take out the meat and let the water cool. Remove the surface fat, make it into a ball and melt, boil this tallow with some of the blessed water on a slow fire till it becomes an ointment, the vessel containing it being covered well meanwhile.† Let the affected part be rubbed backward and forward with this ointment. Take some oven baked or gridle baked bread, and ram's flesh for food, and do not take any other kind of food for a long while, for in persevering in this plan you will recover, as has indeed been fully proved.

### TO HEAL A BURN, EVEN WHEN INVOLVING THE JOINTS OR VEINS.

§ 172, Take the shield fern, (by some called the great fern,) extract the juice of the roots, (the out side being first scraped) and mix the same with some white of eggs. Spread

---

* Aqua Benedicta Rulandi was a wine of antimony, and identical in property and strength with that now in use.

† This again has its modern representative in the antimonial ointment of the Lond. Ph.

in the injury with a feather night and morning, and the patient will recover.

### TO REMOVE A DEAD BONE IN MAN OR BEAST.

§ 173. Take the cucumber, (called in Latin *cucumer*) the bugle, and pepper, in wine, drink this nine times fasting, and you will certainly recover.

### FOR INFLAMMATION OF THE MAMMÆ.

§ 174. Take groundsel, tutsan, and old lard, pound them well in a mortar and apply to the inflamed organ, as an emollient first, then next day take the plantain, and a gloveful of betony, boil them with water to the half, lay them on a flannel or cloth, and apply to the part, when the patient is going to rest, giving her a cup of wine, and she will obtain natural sleep that night.  i. h. u. y.

### TO DESTROY PARASITES ON THE HUMAN BODY.

§ 175. Take rue, pound well, wrap up in a cloth, and rub the flesh smartly therewith, this will destroy them.  It is also excellent for those hectic prespirations which so weaken a man.

### FOR ANY KIND OF WOUNDED INTEGUMENT.

§ 176. Take the feverfew, bruisewort, ribwort plantain, common plantain, and sage, an equal portion of each, bruise them briskly in a mortar, and boil in unsalted butter till the butter disappears, then strain well and keep in a box. Anoint any bruised skin with this.

### THE FOLLOWING IS A POTENT OINTMENT FOR EXTRACTING EVIL HUMORS FROM WOUNDS.

§ 177. Take feverfew, mugwort, the devil's bit, plantain, and mallows, pound them well and add some unsalted butter, fresh yellow wax, rosin, and suet, boil well, and the virtue of the herbs will be communicated to the butter, suet, wax, and rosin, strain through a cloth, and keep in a box. It will extract the venom from all sorts of wounds, and heal them.

There are three wounds of membrane which the surgeon should not meddle with, even the membranes of the brain, a wound of the intestines, and the urinary bladder, for they should be left to God, nevertheless they will be frequently healed as is often the case in men wounded in battle.

Neither food nor drink should be allowed such patients, save sweet milk, and woman's milk.

### FOR WORMS IN THE STOMACH.

·§ 178. Make a powder of turnips, by slicing them and roasting them before the fire. They should be ground and given to the patient to eat cold, for nine mornings fasting, or at nine separate times, and he will be cured.

### FOR THE BITE OF AN ADDER.

§ 179. Take the juice of plantain, of ground ivy, and olive oil, equal quantity of each. Give the patient a good draught thereof, and anoint the wound with the same. It will destroy the poison and cure the patient.

### ANOTHER FOR AN ADDER'S BITE.

§ 180. Take the brain of a red cock, and the juice of the fern, called hart's tongue, pound them well and mix well with white wine or milk. Let the patient drink a full draught of this, washing the wound therewith, and he will be healed.

### FOR A FRECKLED FACE.

§ 181. Anoint it with a bull or a hare's blood.

### FOR SWELLING IN A MAN'S JOINTS OR LIMBS.

§ 182. Take centaury and pound well, strain it well in combination with water through a clean linen cloth. Let the patient drink it.

### FOR EXCESSIVE THIRST.

§ 183. Take centaury, and a little bastard pellitory, pound them well, and express into a strong wort of barley malt, or let the herbs stand in the wort, in an earthen vessel till next morning; this given to the patient to drink in the morning will remove his thirst.

### FOR AN INTERNAL SWELLING.

§ 184. Take plums, boil in goat's milk, and when cold let the patient drink it in the morning, and as late as he can in the evening.

### FOR THE RINGWORM.

§ 186. Take some brimstone, and grind fine, also ox tallow and dock root, boil the root and tallow together, and when cold add the powdered brimstone and mix with the tallow as much thereof as will make a hard ointment. This will destroy the ringworm.

### FOR A HEADACHE.

§ 187. Whoever is frequently afflicted with a headache let him make a lotion of the vervain, betony, chamomile, and red fennel; let him wash his head three times a week therewith, and he will be cured.

### FOR DEAFNESS.

§ 188. Take ram's urine, the oil of eels, the house leek, the juice of traveller's joy, and a boiled egg, let him mix and drop into the ear little by little, and it will cure him.

### AN OINTMENT FOR AN OLD SPRAIN.

§ 189. Take a handful of ivy leaves, and pound well with the dung of goats, and fresh butter, mixing them together well. Let this be applied as a plaster to the sprained part, and it will be healed.

### FOR A HEADACHE.

§ 190. Take ground ivy, pound well with red wine, and apply as a plaster to the forehead of the patient.

He that will not take food when hungry, his stomach will be filled with wind and disease, which will produce headache. Taking as food dry bread with salt mutton will cure it.

### FOR ALL KINDS OF PAIN.

§ 191. Take a quantity of broom flowers, water flower de lys, primrose, a handful of the roots of red nettle, water hemlock, the leaves of eryngo, and the leaves of plantain when in seed, with a quart of seeds,* mix and pound well with unsalted butter, and boil briskly, strain through linen, and keep in a covered box. This is a precious ointment for any kind of pain.

* Probably "the four greater hot seeds—Anise, Carui, Cummin, and Fennel."

### TO DESTROY WORMS IN A MAN'S STOMACH, WHEN NAUSEA IS PRODUCED.

§ 192. Take the herbs called honeywort, pound it well with some white wine, warm some thereof and administer to the patient fasting for three mornings, and it will cure him.

### FOR PAIN IN THE BACK OR HIP.

§ 193. Take the mouse-ear chickweed, and pound well, boil it with butter, and strain, then anoint the back with it before the fire, and the patient will get well.

### FOR CHRONIC HEPATITIS.

§ 194. Take the root of the melilot, anise-seed, betony, and elecampane, pound them well with strong wort or white wine, strain carefully and drink night and morning, till the pain is removed, when by God's help you will obtain a cure.

### TO CURE DIMNESS OF SIGHT.

§ 195. Take the juice of red fennel, celandine, a little vinegar or verjuice, an eel's blood, and a cock's gall, mix these ingredients together, and set aside in a clean vessel till fermentation takes place; take some of the clear liquor and put in a blind man's eyes. Science tells us that by this means, sight lost may certainly be recovered.

### FOR THE PAIN AND SWELLING OF ERYSIPELAS.

§ 196. Take fern root, and pound well, then mix with a little warm water, rubbing it with your hands; then express through linen, and make a plaster thereof with barley meal and the white of eggs, spread with your thumb on a cloth, and apply to the disease.

### FOR ALL COMPLAINTS OF THE EYES, PARTICULARLY OPACITIES.

§ 197. Take the wild or garden tansy, and boil well in white wine till the virtue of the herbs is extracted; then remove from the fire, strain clean, and permit it to cool and clear. Afterwards take of the clearest portion, and put some camphor therein, and leave it till it is dissolved.

Introduce some of this collyrium to the eye, and whatever disease afflicts the eye, it will cure it. Aristobolis states that this is proven.

## FOR GASTRIC PAINS.

§ 198. Take a little tansy, and reduce to fine powder. Take with white wine and it will remove the pain.

## ANOTHER.

§ 199. Take some tansy, and southernwood, then boil together well with salt, eat them frequently when fasting, and you will recover.

## FOR AN ŒDEMATOUS WOUND OF THE SCALP, IN CONSE-QUENCE OF A FALL.

§ 200. Take an ounce of bay salt, three ounces of crude honey, one of cummin, and two of turpentine, mix these ingredients well on the fire, then spread on a linen cloth for a plaster, and apply to the head warm; it will remove the œdema and contusion. Let neither oil, tallow, nor any other grease whatever be added to any plaster required for the head.

## FOR A MALIGNANT DISEASE OF THE MAMMÆ.

§ 201. Take hemlock leaves, bruising them well and boiling with fresh butter in a pan on the fire. Apply it to the breast as warm as possible on a white cloth, and it will cure it; or the leaves may be pounded well with some fresh butter, or olive oil, being spread as before on a white linen, and applied as hot as it it can be borne to the breast.

## FOR CANKER OF THE MOUTH.

§ 202. Take a cupful of wine or claret, and a sprig of rosemary, boiling them together; put in a piece as big as a nut of frankincense, a spoonful of honey, and two of water, mixing them well together. Wash the mouth frequently, and it will be cured.

## TO PRODUCE GOLDEN HAIR.

§ 203. Take the bark of rhubarb, and infuse in white wine, wash your head therewith, dry with a fine clean cloth, then by the fire, or in the sun if it be warm. Do this once and again, and the oftner you do it the more beautiful your hair will become, and that without injury to the hair.

### TO REMOVE WARTS FROM THE HANDS.

§ 204. Take the juice of sheep's sorrel, and bay salt, wash your hands and let them dry spontaneously. Do this again and you will see the warts and freckles disappear. It is also an useful remedy for eruptions and ringworms.

### TO KNOW WHETHER A PATIENT WILL LIVE OR DIE.

§ 205. Take breast milk where a boy is nursed, and some of the urine of the sick person, drop the milk from the end of your finger to the urine, if it remains on the surface of the urine, the sick person will live, if not, he will certainly die.

### ANOTHER.

§ 206. Take the flower of the daisy, and pound well with wine, giving it the patient to drink ; if he vomits it, he will die of that disease, if not, he will live, and this has been proven true.

### FOR A BURN.

§ 207. Take fern roots, and pound well with butter, apply it as a plaster to the injury, and it will remove the ardent pain.

### FOR A VIOLENT HEADACHE.

§ 208. Take the leaves of foxglove, and pound with milk and mutton suet, till it becomes a plaster, apply to the head as warm as it can be borne.

### HOW TO PREPARE ANOTHER REMEDY.

§ 209. Take oaten groats, the leaves of the foxglove, suet, and sweet milk, pound together till the ingredients become incorporated into a plaster, set upon the fire till it is warmed, and apply to the head as warm as it can be borne.

### FOR THE SMALLPOX.

§ 210. Take quicksilver, oil of turpentine, white lead, blue stone, and lard, melt these ingredients into an ointment, mixing them well in order to kill the quicksilver, one portion being taken in hand (to kill the mercury) when the other is finished. Long pepper and treacle in sage wine should be administered in order to drive out the eruption.

### A HEALING OINTMENT FOR BRUISES.

§ 213. Take feverfew, ribwort plantain, garden sage, and bugle, equal parts of each, pound them well and boil in unsalted May butter, then express through a fine linen, and keep in a box. Anoint the disease therewith and it will cure it. If there be dead flesh therein, take some aloes, or sulphate of copper, or red precipitate of mercury in powder, and mix with some of the ointment, then it will destroy the dead flesh, and promote the healing of the sore.

### FOR WARTS ON A MAN'S HANDS OR FEET.

§ 214 Take puffballs, and pound with salt butter or fresh, make a plaster, and apply to the part where the the warts are situated, and it will unroot them.

### FOR A WART.

§ 215. Take an eel and cut its head off, anoint the parts, where the warts are situated, with the blood, and bury the head deep in the earth; as the head rottens, so will the warts disappear.

### FOR A THORN OR ARROW-HEAD, WHICH HAS ENTERED A MAN'S BODY AND CANNOT BE EXTRACTED.

§ 216. Seek the roots or leaves of the spear thistle, and the white of an egg, mix together and apply to the wound. It will extract the foreign substance.

### FOR THE BITE OF A MAD DOG.

§ 218. Seek some cowslips, pound them, mix with milk, and administer to the patient as his only drink for nine days, being first strained through a fine cloth; others boil the cowslips with the sweet milk, straining them under a press, and administering as a drink to the patient, for nine days. The patient should drink as much as he can thereof, abstaining from all other aliment for the time.

### TO PREVENT DREAMS.

§ 220. Take the vervain, and hang about a man's neck, or give him the juice in going to bed, and it will prevent his dreaming.

### TO DESTROY A WORM IN THE TOOTH.

§ 221. Take the roots of the cat's ear, bruise, and apply to the patient's tooth for three nights, and it will kill the worm.

### TO CURE ALL KINDS OF ERUPTIONS.

§ 222. Take some onions and pound in water or vinegar, wash the affected part therewith, and it will remove all sorts of eruptions.

### FOR NOISE IN THE HEAD, PREVENTING HEARING.

§ 223. Take a clove of garlic, prick in three or four places in the middle, dip in honey and insert in the ear, covering it with some black wool. Let the patient sleep on the other side every night, leaving the clove in the ear for seven or eight nights unchanged. It will prevent the running of the nose, and restore the hearing.

### A SAFE PLASTER FOR ALL SWELLINGS.

§ 224. Take some cream, (or in the absence of cream, fresh milk,) set on the fire, adding thereto some crumbs of white bread, wax, and a little honey: when it has boiled nearly enough, add a portion of mutton suet, and oil of olives. If the heat in the swelling is considerable, add some white of eggs, mix well and apply to the swelling.

### A PLASTER TO REMOVE PAINS, ACHES, AND INFLAMMATION.

§ 225. Procure (if you can) the milk of a one coloured cow, oatmeal, a little mutton suet, and a handful of parsley, pound together and boil well, then apply warm to the disease, and it will speedily ease it.

### TO DISPERSE A SWELLING.

§ 226. Take the juice of plantain, the white of eggs, clarified honey, and barley meal, mix them together and apply as a plaster to the swelling. Proven.

### ANOTHER.

§ 227. Seek the juice of water pimpernel, the white of eggs, honey, and wheat or barley meal; make a plaster, then apply to the disease, and it will heal it.

### TO REMOVE PAIN AND SWELLING.

§ 228. Take rye meal, white of eggs, and the juice of plantain; then apply as a plaster to the disease, anointing it first with honey, and by God's help it will cure it. If required, this should be done two or three times.

### TO REMOVE A SWELLING.

§ 229. Take the leaves of foxglove, mutton suet, oatmeal, and milk, apply as a plaster to the swelling, and it will cure it.

### TO PROMOTE THE FORMATION AND POINTING OF AN ABSCESS.

§ 230. Take the leaves of foxglove, pound with wine, suet, and barley meal, applying it thereto as a plaster warm.

### ANOTHER.

§ 231. Take curds in ale, together with sheep's milk.

### TO DESTROY FLEAS.

§ 232. Take a hedgehog, roast it, receiving the oil in a vessel, anoint a stick with some of this oil, and lay it where there are fleas, and as many as are to be found in that room will be attracted thereto.

### FOR ALL MANNER OF ACHES IN THE THIGHS, FEET, ARMS, OR ANY OF THE JOINTS.

§ 233. Take a small quantity of broom flowers, lily flowers, eryngo leaves, and red dock leaves; pound them well and make an ointment of them with butter, then anoint the diseased part therewith, and it will be cured.

### FOR THE VERTIGO, CALLED MIGRAN, OR HEMICRANIAL HEADACHE.

§ 234. Take a live hare, behead it, skin, and boil or roast, then open the head, taking some rosemary flowers, and powder the same, put them in the head, mixing with the brain, and baking or roasting it. Let the brain be then eaten, the patient sleeping afterwards, and it will be found really useful.

### FOR THE FALLING SICKNESS, CALLED FFLAMGWST, AND IN LATIN EPILEPSIA.

§ 235. Take the blood of a newly brought forth lamb, who has never suckled, mix with two spoonfuls of good ale, and drink it fasting for three mornings. This is proven and wonderful.

### TO ALLEVIATE HOOPING COUGHS WHEN PRODUCING CEREBRAL DISTURBANCE.

§ 236. Seek a pennyworth of cummin seed, two penny-worths of the seed of the English galingale, called glingal,* and the same of cannella; powder these ingredients well together, then take on warm drink, and it will be of benefit.

### FOR THE MALIGNANT CARBUNCLE OR PLAGUE.

§ 237. Seek a good handful of red sage, a handful of rue, the same of garlic, pound well in strong ale, or wine, or good mead, finally straining through a fine cloth, and by God's help you will recover.

### FOR A PROLAPSUS ANI.

§ 238. Take the herb called cleavers, whose seed adhere to the hose of those who get among them, and are found in round grains of the size of pepper on the terminal branches of the plant; pound them well and boil in butter till an ointment is formed, which should be expressed and the anus anointed therewith.

### FOR THE MIGRAN OR VERTIGO.

§ 239. Get frankincense, yellow wax, and honey, compound them well together, then apply in the form of a plaster to the forehead, and it will be truly useful.

### FOR A CHILD WHO HAS BECOME PARALYSED IN HIS LIMBS.

§ 240. Perhaps that he has lost the power of his limbs from weakness in his spine, if so, take oil of turpentine, and oil of olives, and mix together, anointing the child's back therewith night and morning. This will strengthen him.

### FOR PAINS IN THE THIGHS, FEET, ARMS, AND ALL JOINTS.

§ 241. Take oil of turpentine, butter, sheep and goat's suet, boil in a pan well, straining through a cloth. Anoint the painful part with it well.

* Cyperus longus.

FOR A STICH ORIGINATING UNDER THE ARM OR BREAST, AND EXTENDING THROUGH THE SHOULDER.

§ 242. Make an ointment with thick cream, broad leaved dock, and nettles; apply this as a plaster so as to bring it to the surface. It is indeed a good application.

FOR THE BITE OF A MAD DOG.

§ 243. Take primrose, pound small, express the juice under a press, and mix with milk, giving it the patient to drink nine times.

FOR RHEUMATISM, OR STIFFNESS IN THE SHOULDER AND LIMBS.

§ 244. Make an ointment with butter, rue, frankinsence, and three pennyworth of the blessed water,* anoint three times a week for a summer's month, or if it be winter, remain in a warm room, and beware of cold.

FOR AN INSANE PERSON.

§ 245. Take betony, boil in a quart of strong ale, and use for drink, and you will certainly recover.

FOR A MAN WHO IS WEAK IN HIS INTELLECT OR MAD.

§ 246. Take a quart of red wine vinegar, and half as much of the juice of celandine,† mixing them together; then take a cupful of a potion prepared from spring water and betony, (bruised together and strained) the first thing in the morning, and the last at night. Let the same herbs be boiled for him in order to strengthen his head, an emulsion being prepared from linseed, in which the herbs shōuld be boiled. The patient should be confined in a dark room. This is an effective treatment.

FOR THAT INFIRMITY OF THE HEAD WHICH IS TERMED BRAIN FEVER, OR FRANTIC DELIRIUM, OCCASIONING DERANGEMENT OF MIND, AND CALLED IN LATIN PHRENESIS. IN THIS COMPLAINT THE PATIENT IS HARDLY CONSCIOUS WHAT HE UTTERS; IT IS OCCASIONED BY WATER UNDER THE FONTENELLE, PRESSING ON THE BRAIN AND MEMBRANES, AND HINDERING SLEEP AT NIGHT.

§ 247. Get linseed, pound in a brass mortar, make an emulsion therefrom with pure water, boiling it as you do porridge. Powder as much as can be contained in

* Aqua Benedicta Rulandi.     † Celandine is an active drastic Cathartic.

the hollow of your hand of anise-seed and ginger, let the same be mixed with. the emulsion and given to the patient to drink, four times in the day and night for nine days. The diet should be nourishing, the drink of a tonic nature, and the patient should be put to sleep in a dark room.

### FOR INFLAMMATION, ATTENDED WITH SWELLING AND PAIN IN THE MEMBERS, FEET, AND HANDS.

§ 248. Take asparagus, pound well and make into an ointment with butter, then anoint the diseased part therewith. It is truly useful.

### FOR ALOPACEA.

§ 249. Take water cress, bruise well and express the juice, wash your head therewith and scrub it well. The same juice may also be taken internally, and you will be cured.

### FOR HYSTERIA.

§ 250. First take an emetic, then the following dry herbs, cloves, mastic, grains of Paradise, and wood of aloes, a pennyworth of each, pound together well, let a portion be taken dry every morning, and in an emulsion at other times.

### TO REMOVE AN EXFOLIATION OF BONE FROM THE SKULL.

§ 251. Take betony, vervain, and rue, pound well with honey, wheaten flour, and the white of eggs, making it into a plaster, and applying to the injured part.

### A PLASTER TO REDUCE A SWELLING.

§ 252. Take barley flour, and the white of an egg, mix, and apply as a plaster to the injury.

### FOR A HŒMATUREA.

§ 253. Take a handful of each of the following herbs, even parsley, plantain, and shepherd's purse; pound thoroughly, and strain with goat's whey, drink a cupful fasting every morning. Continue this and you will recover.

### FOR AN EPITHELIAL CANCER.

§ 254. Take ground ivy, and foxglove, pound well, boil in stale urine and tallow or suet, strain, and anoint the injury therewith.

### TO OBTAIN SLEEP.

§ 255. Take eryngo, and mugwort, called orpin, mix with milk, and form into pills, administering unto the patient, and he will sleep presently.

### FOR AN INFLAMMATION THE RESULT OF MECHANICAL IRRITATION, BOTH HEALING IT, AND SOOTHING THE ITCHING.

§ 257. Get parsley, and pound small, boiling well in butter, cast a pennyworth of black soap to the boiling ointment, mixing it well; strain, and anoint the diseased part night and morning. It is proved. In order to promote the healing of the skin, so that it may be white as the whole skin, get oatmeal gruel made with water, and apply an oatmeal poultice as a broad cake to the part, first washing it with the gruel. This will presently heal it.

### FOR THE SCROFULA, CALLED BY SOME THE EVIL.

§ 258. Take oil of olives, four pennyworth, white lead, two pennyworth, frankincense, a pennyworth, blue stone, and wax, a pennyworth, oil of turpentine, the same, mercury, three pennyworth, colophane,* a pennyworth, and lard; mix these ingredients together, and apply repeatedly to the affected part, removing the former previous to each fresh application.

### FOR A SWELLING IN A MAN'S THROAT THAT PREVENTS HIM FROM SPEAKING.

§ 259. Take hog's lard, and stale urine, boil together, and dip a piece of flannel therein, wrapping it round the throat, use for three days; but if it be an abcess, put some clarified butter on flannel, and it will mollify it, and also prevent it from suppurating.

### A PLASTER TO REDUCE A SWELLING, RESULTING FROM AN ACCIDENT.

§ 260. Take mallows, chamomile, maiden hair, chickweed, and ground ivy, boil them well in the stalest urine you can get. Apply to the affected part as a plaster, and it will reduce the swelling.

* Black Rosin

### TO STRENGTHEN THE TEETH AND MAKE THEM WHITE.

§ 261. Take elecampane, and scrub your teeth therewith briskly, it will make them firm, white, and healthy.

### FOR A LIVID INFLAMMATION OF THE FLESH.

§ 262. Get eryngo, the leaves of the red alder, parsley, broom flowers, and the stinking iris, pound them well together and make into an ointment by means of butter and black soap. Anoint the painful part therewith, and it will heal it.

### TO RESTRAIN A HŒMORRHAGE.

§ 263. Get beans, or rather bean meal and suet, boil them together and apply as a plaster to the injury. It is really useful.

### FOR A NAUSEA.

§ 265. Get a pint of the juice of fennel, and boil it with a pint of clarified honey, taking a spoonful every morning fasting as well as the last thing at night, for nine days.

### FOR A MAN WHO TALKS IN HIS SLEEP.

§ 266. Take a pint of the juice of betony, and a pint of ale wort mixed together. Drink, and by God's help it will do you good.

### FOR ABSORPTION OF THE GUMS.

§ 267. Take two pennyworth of the blessed water,* of the distillation of white wine,† and of white wine vinegar, of each two pennyworth, mix them together, and wash your mouth with the same as long as it lasts.

### FOR HŒMATUREA.

§ 271. Take milfoil, and a third part of the juice of red fennel, temper it with red wine, and let the patient drink it warm, and he will be cured.

### FOR THE DYSENTERY AND ITS ATTENDANT PAIN.

§ 272. Take sloes when fully ripe, and dry them either in a strong sun heat, or before the fire, (but at a distance,) that they may become so dry, that they may be powdered.

---

* Aqua Benedicta.    † Brandy.

Let it be kept in a glass bottle, well corked.   When there is a person ill of this complaint, mix a spoonful of this powder with a pint of good, strong, and sound old ale, strong old cider, or good old mead, warming it well and giving it to the patient to drink for three mornings fasting.   It will remove the pain and cure the disease.

Also for this disease get some strong new linen cloth, and put in it as much in quantity as a goose's egg of the finest wheaten meal you can get.   Tie up the meal in this new cloth, and boil in a gallon of spring water till reduced to a quart; then let it cool, and boil a little with milk as a gruel. Let the man have this for his daily food.   It is proven.

### TO REMOVE THE PAIN ATTENDANT UPON DYSENTERY.

§ 273.  Take wheaten bread and old cheese, slice it thin and boil in milk, mixing a good quantity of pepper therewith.   Make use of this, for it is good.

### FOR PARALYSIS OR HEMIPLAGIA, THE BLOOD BECOMING SLUGGISH AND VISCID IN THE VEINS.

§ 274.  Take a handful of the leaves of foxglove, and a handful of the leaves of red nettles, pound them well, then boil in a quart of good honey, strain carefully and keep in a vessel.   Boil therewith three pennyworth of the blessed water,* or distilled wine,† or cider; then take two gallons of stale urine, boiling it well, and skimming it carefully as it boils.   Take a quantity night and morning, and anoint your joints well therewith by the fire, rub them afterwards with the preserved ointment, rest your shoulder on an elevated place, and exercise yourself in walking frequently. It is good.

### FOR A SWELLING UNDER THE NAVEL, SOMETIMES LONG, SOMETIMES ROUND, LIKE A BALL BETWEEN THE FLESH AND SKIN.

§ 275.  Take a quart of red vinegar, pound a handful of leeks, roots and leaves, boiling a pennyworth of stale bread therewith well.   Apply this as a plaster fresh every night, and it will remove it.

* Of Rulandus.     † Brandy.

2 Y

### FOR A THORN.

§ 277. Take betony, (by some called bitton) old lard, and agrimony, pound them together and apply thereto. This will extract it.

### FOR A POISONOUS THORN.

§ 278. Take boar's lard, black soap, and the yolk of eggs, mix them together and apply as a plaster to the part, and it will extract it.

### FOR PAIN IN CONSEQUENCE OF A THORN.

§ 279. Take broom tops and a boy's urine, boil them briskly, and apply as a fomentation to the part, and it will ease it. The fat of a wild cat is also good. Take also oil of olives, and a pennyworth of camphor, pounding them well together and applying as an ointment to the part.

### FOR A WHITLOW ON THE FINGER.

§ 280. Take rue, cummin, the fat of bacon, and wheat flour, boil in white wine and oil of turpentine, mix together carefully and apply to the part ; when ripe let it be opened and dressed, it will then heal like any other wound or contusion.

### FOR AN IMPOSTUME.*

§ 281. Take mugwort, and bruise briskly, mix with the yolk of eggs, apply to the part and it will cure it. There will be a spreading inflammation of the skin,—a livid hue,—a burning pain at the bone,—and the tendons will slough away in an impostume of the finger. Thus is the disease known.

### ANOTHER.

§ 282. Take a snail out of its shell, and bruising it small, pound into a plaster and apply to the finger, this will ripen and break it, then it should be dressed like any other wound.

### ANOTHER.

§ 283. Take water pimpernel and pound well, mix carefully with oil of roses, and apply as a plaster to the part.

* Or Whitlow.

### ANOTHER.

§ 284. Take rue, and wild valerian, pound them well and boil with rosin and yellow wax, apply as a plaster to the part. It is useful for all kinds of swellings in a finger or any other joint.

### ANOTHER.

§ 285. Take rue, water pimpernel, southernwood, wild valerian, a snail, and lard, pound them into a plaster and apply to the part, changing every night. Others boil the bruised herbs in lard, adding the snail (bruised and boiled carefully) thereto, compounding the whole into a plaster, so using it.

### ANOTHER.

§ 286. Take a little sulphate of copper dried and powdered, mix it well with the yolk of eggs, and apply to the part and it will heal it quickly, easing the pain and reducing the swelling.

### TO IMPROVE THE SIGHT.

§ 287. Boil fennel in water, and wash your eyes with the same water morning and evening, and it will improve it for you.

### FOR A WEB IN THE EYE.

§ 288. Take a cow's, a hare's, and an old cock's gall with a small quantity of the blue matter formed of rue and celandine. You should have equal parts of each, (the cow's gall only being in excess,) and they should be tempered together with wine. Being applied to the eye it removes the web.

### AGAINST INTOXICATION.

§ 289. Take a handful of betony and pound well, expressing in water and straining carefully; drink some of this before you have taken any food or drink, and you will not get drunk that day.

### A GOOD EMETIC FOR THE HEAD AND STOMACH.

§ 290. Take three spoonfuls of the juice of betony for three mornings successively, put in your nostrils with the tip of a wing, and it will be a good emetic for the head and stomach.

### FOR INTERMITTENTS AND FEVERS.

§ 291. Take dandelion and fumitory, and add to some drink, of which take a good quantity morning and noon, and you will be certainly cured.

### TO DESTROY A CANCER.

§ 292. Take a piece of unburnt limestone, black pepper, orpiment,* called in Latin *auripigmentum*, strong vinegar, rue, honey, barley meal, equal parts of each, boil in a pan or pot till they can be reduced to a powder, then they should be powdered and boiled a second time. This powder is good to destroy a cancer or scrofula.

### ANOTHER FOR THE SAME.

§ 293. Take the root of the dragons,† cut them small, dry and make into a powder, take nine pennyweights of this powder, boil in wine well and give it to the patient to drink, warm, for three days fasting, and it will cure him; and I warrant him he will never have it again.

### FOR DEAFNESS.

§ 294. Take a small branch of ash, a foot in length, putting the middle part in the fire, and keeping the water proceeding from the two ends; then take the juice of rhubarb, wine, and the fat of a newly caught eel, take an equal part of these substances, mixing all together, and put in the ears as you go to sleep. It is also useful in these cases to drop some stale urine into the ears, covering it over with black wool.

### THUS IS A MAN PRESERVED FROM HYDROPHOBIA.

§ 295. Let him not eat cheese, nor butter, nor eggs, nor sea fish, nor beef, nor rye bread, nor new bread, and let him drink nothing but sweet milk, water, or buttermilk, with a draught of wine or mead once in twenty four hours. Let him also refrain from venery, and by help of God he will be preserved.

---

* Yellow sulphurate of Arsenic.          † Arum dracunculus.

#### FOR AN INCISED WOUND OR INJURY OF A TENDON, VEIN, ABDOMINAL WALLS, OR BONE, WHEN INFLAMING AND SUPPURATING.

§ 296. Take goat's milk and linseed, boiling them together, then take the milk of a one coloured cow and bean meal, mix together, boiling it for a long space of time, then removing it and applying as a plaster to the part, leave it there till the next day or longer, and it will reduce the swelling and pain, extract the venom from the flesh, promote the union of the tendons, remove dead flesh, disperse contusions, and procure sleep for the patient. If needful some healing salve should also be used.

#### TO RE-OPEN A WOUND OR ABSCESS WHICH HAS CLOSED OVER, AND TO HEAL IT.

§ 297. Again, to the same ointment * add a portion of wax, rosin, black soap, a small quantity of honey suckle leaves, and plantain, pound together, boil on the fire, strain through a cloth and keep in a pot. Apply this in the manner of a salve, and the wound will be healed.

#### TO PROMOTE THE SECRETION OF URINE, THE GROWTH OF FLESH, SKIN, AND BONES.

§ 298. Take a handful of red roses, spring water, the juice of celandine, honey, juice of hemlock, fennel, tutsan, burdock, a spoonful of a suckling child's urine, and red wine, mix these ingredients together, warm them a little, then remove from the fire, strain and keep. Let this be applied to a sloughing wound, and it will cleanse and heal it.

#### FOR AN ILL CONDITIONED ULCER.

§ 299. Take good cheese, pound it carefully, mixing therewith some clear honey, anoint it frequently with this, and cover it with cabbage leaves. This will cleanse it in three days, for it is excellent.

#### FOR A WHITLOW.

§ 300. Take honey, yolk of eggs, and wheaten flour, mix together and apply as a plaster to the diseased part as may be needful. It is indeed a good application.

* i. e. the healing salve.

### FOR A DISEASE OF THE LEG, CHARACTERISED BY GATHERING AND SUPPURATING, RED GRANULATIONS, SPREADING TOWARDS THE TOES, BEING OF A LIVID REDNESS.

§ 301. Procure three pennyworth of roses, two pennyworth of olive oil, a pennyworth of oil of turpentine, a spoonful of honey, a little wax, three pennyworth of red lead, a little mutton or stag's suet, a small quantity of sulphate of copper in powder, and a spoonful or two of the blessed distillation,* or the distillation of red wine,† mix and temper them in a pot on the fire till the whole are thoroughly warmed. Anoint the disease therewith and it will benefit it.

### FOR AN OFFENSIVE SORE.

§ 302. Take barberry, called in Latin *boxus*, boiled in ale or wine, wash the sore therewith and it will benefit it ; or take the leaves and pound well with wine or mead, straining it under a press, keeping in an earthen vessel on the fire till it is warmed thoroughly, washing the sore therewith.

### TO PREPARE AN OINTMENT FOR SCROFULA.

§ 303. Take yellow wax, rosin, suet, elecampane, and celandine, pound them well together and boil, then strain through a clean cloth, and anoint the part so as to heal it.

### FOR THE SCROFULA.

§ 304. Take the vervain and pound well, filling some vessel with it to the brim, add thereto as much water as will fill it, and let it stand over night, then strain ; let this be taken as the sole drink. You may add white wine to the pounded herbs instead of water, and drink of it as much as you wish once in the twenty four hours. Take this herb also and pound small, with oil of olives, boiling together and straining under a press ; after this add thereto some yellow wax, honey, and stag's suet, boil till it becomes an ointment, keep in a vessel and anoint the diseased part therewith. If you also take the roots of this herb, wash it clean, dry it well, reduce it to powder, and mix it with wheaten flour in the proportion of a third, in order to make bread,

---

* Aqua Benedicta Rulandi.     † Brandy.

then subsist upon this bread and goat's milk as your only food, you will recover sooner. This is well proven.

#### A PLASTER TO REDUCE THE SWELLING, AND TO EXTRACT WORMS* FROM SCROFULOUS ULCERATIONS.

§ 305. Take the milk of a one coloured cow, and oatmeal, boil well to the consistency of a child's pap, spreading it thick on a cloth, adding honey on the surface, this will extract the worms and reduce the swelling, disenvenom the flesh, remove the hardness, and heal the sore. This is proven.

#### FOR HEAT AND INFLAMMATION IN THE LIVER, HYSTERIA, PAIN IN THE LOINS, AND PAIN IN A MAN'S SHOULDERS.

§ 306. Take centaury, and livergreen, pounding them well, and filling a vessel therewith, adding an equal quantity of water and wine; let it stand covered for about six hours, then strain under a press, and drink as much as you can fasting night and morning. Take for food a broth made of mutton, and the following herbs, viz:—borage, lettuce, fennel, parsley, and a little honey; let it be your only food. Make also a lay with wood, fern, or nettle ashes, and boil in it two or three pennyworth of lard, let it cool till next day, then remove the surface and preserve in a vessel. Anoint your shoulders and other painful parts, then by God's help you will recover.

#### FOR A BURN.

§ 307. Mix your own urine with cow dung, let it clear, pour this portion to a vessel, and wash the part therewith.

#### FOR SWINE POX.

§ 308. It is an eruptive skin disease forming white vesicles, from which clear water is poured forth. Take broom seed and lard, boiling and straining them; mix two pennyworth of black soap well with it, and anoint your whole body therewith. It is truly good.

---

* These " worms " were generally imaginary, being only portions of disintegrated structures.

### FOR A WOMAN AT THE CHANGE OF LIFE.

§ 309. Make a gruel with oatmeal and spring water, add thereto a pinch of cummin, and a pinch of the stone called cryth,* or in Latin *creta*, or when this is not procurable, a lime stone powdered as fine as possible and sifted through a fine cloth or silk. Mix this with the gruel, and let her take a cupful thereof each end of the day for a week, and it will be useful to her.

### TO EXTRACT A TOOTH WITHOUT PAIN.

§ 310. Seek some ants with their eggs and powder, have this powder blown into the tooth through a quill, and be careful that it does not touch another tooth.

### FOR TREMBLING OF THE HANDS.

§ 311, Put pounded mugwort in water over night, and wash your hands therein. It will benefit you if you wash your back and nape of the neck with this water,—it will strengthen you miraculously.

### FOR HYSTERIA.

§ 312. Get feverfew, wormwood, and the inner bark of ash, boil well in perennial spring water, strain, and drink, fasting for three mornings. This will procure you a recovery, so that you will not be afflicted ever again.

### FOR BLEEDING OF THE NOSE.

§ 313. Take a handful of nettles, and put in a cloth to your nostrils, plugging your nostrils with some of the same. It is good.

### ANOTHER.

§ 314. Take a small sheet of iron and put in the fire till it is hot, but not red hot, drop the blood thereon, and when there is a sufficient quantity, scrape it off, and blow into the nostrils with a quill, and this will restrain the bleeding from the nose, from a wound, or a cut, wherever it be on a man's body.

### FOR A PATIENT WHO IS BURNT.

§ 315. Take a handful of mallows, of snails shells, of pennywort and linseed, pound them in a brass mortar,

* Chalk.

and mix them together, so that they be intimately incorporated; apply this to the swelling or sore, and retain it there continually, never leaving it uncovered. If you like you may syringe it with soft water so as to wash it. In consequence of the plaster, a watery discharge will come from the nose. It is a good application.

### TO KNOW WHETHER THE PATIENT WILL LIVE OR DIE.

§ 316. Anoint the patient's heel with some hog's fat, and give the remainder to a dog to eat. If the dog will eat it, the patient will live, if not he will die.

### TO CAUSE THE HAIR TO GROW.

§ 318. Take the barberry, and fill an iron pot therewith, fill it up with as much water as it will contain, then boil on a slow fire to the half. With this water, wash your head morning and evening. Take care that the wash does not touch any part where hair should not grow.

### ANOTHER.

§ 319. Take two spoonfuls of olive oil, two spoonfuls of new honey, and an onion as large as a pigeon's egg, pound them together in a stone mortar till it becomes an ointment, and anoint your head therewith night and morning. Wear a leathern cap till the hair is grown. It is best to pound the onion well before it is added to the ointment.

### TO REMOVE THE HAIR SO THAT IT DOES NOT GROW AGAIN.

§ 320. Take ants with their eggs, and reduce to powder, mix the seed of henbane in powder therewith, and apply to the place required, rubbing it on well till the part is warm, twice a day. This will destroy the hair at the roots so that it will not grow in that place again. You may mix it with water so as to form a paste, and anoint the place therewith night and morning.

### TO DESTROY PEDICULI.

§ 321. Take the gum resin, called olibanum, and lard. Boil them together and anoint the head, or any other part requiring it. This will destroy them.

2 z

### FOR FRECKLES OF THE FACE.

§ 322. Anoint your face with a hare or bull's blood at night, before you sleep, and wash it in the morning with some butter-milk.

### TO EXTRACT A TOOTH.

§ 323. Take ivy gum and leaves, burn them into a powder in a new earthen pot, mix this powder with the juice of the herb petty spurge, and insert the paste in the tooth so as to fill the cavity. It will cause it to fall from your jaw, but have a care that it does not touch another tooth.

### FOR STRANGURY.

§ 324. Pound mallow leaves and garlick together with white wine, drink it and in any case you will make water.

HERE IS A METHOD OF PREPARING A STOMACHIC BEER WHICH IS USEFUL FOR PARALYSIS, SHAKING PALSY, LATENT AGUE, FULLY DEVELOPED INTERMITTENTS, COLDNESS ABOUT THE HEART, RHEUMATISM, CARDIALGIA, STRANGURY, HERNIA HUMORALIS, AND COLD IN THE NERVES AND VEINS.

§25. Take a handful of rosemary, of sage, of agrimony, of bedstraw, of hyssop, both the leaves and branches, of the roots of mallows, of elecampane. of radish, of saxifrage, a handful of each, pound them well in a mortar together, and boil in three gallons of strong ale wort till it is reduced into one gallon, remove it from the fire to cool, and strain through a clean linen cloth; take a quart of pure honey and add to this wort, boiling until it is reduced to a quart, meanwhile skimming it carefully; remove it to cool, and take six gallons of strong new ale, dregs and yeast included, and put in a clean brewing tub, cover it and let it stand for three days and nights; then put in a strong cask, and take a pennyworth of cloves, of ginger, of grains of paradise, a little fennel seed, a pennyworth of caraway, a small quantity of the seed of English galingale, and as much as the whole of canelle bark; powder them fine as the finest wheaten meal, and put them in a small linen bag, hang this in the cask, (a small stone being included in the bag to weigh it down) and leave it there. Drink some of this liquor the first thing in the morning, and the last in the evening. It is as safe for a man to drink it as spring water.

The following are the special virtues of these various herbs,—the rosemary is a stimulant, the sage will remove the fever, bedstraw is for the paralysis, hyssop for the chest, agrimony for the bowels, saxifrage for the bladder, radish for the stomach, elecampane for the joints, cloves and ginger for the nerves, pink for the kidneys, grains of paradise for the brain, galingale and canelle for the lungs and veins. It is proper that every person should take of this drink for the cure of the diseases above mentioned. If he should be the subject of any other disease, let him add the herbs proper for the same, and partake of this drink frequently. You will in consequence have a healthy body, a more youthful look, greater elasticity of limbs, a stronger sight, a more determined will, more freedom in walking, and a sweeter breath. This is the best beer of all, and the most healthy drink in the world.

### A GENTLE APERIENT.

§ 326. Take a hen's egg, removing the embryo, and mix with some sound ale, both egg and ale together; drink it fasting in the morning, fast subsequently for three hours and you will be benefited.

### FOR NAUSEA OF STOMACH IN CONSEQUENCE OR COLDNESS IN THE SAME, THE FOOD BEING REJECTED, AND THE BOWELS CONFINED.

. § 327. Take two cupfuls of white wine, or an emetic every other day, take treacle, a quart of red wine, a pennyworth of mustard, three pennyworth of aloes, boil these ingredients together and keep in a vessel; take two spoonfuls warm in the morning fasting. Take a pennyworth of pepper, two pennyworth of fennel, boil them in clarified honey. The leaves of the fennel are superior to the seed.

### FOR A DRY OR OBSTRUCTING COUGH, SO SEVERE THAT THE FOREHEAD BECOMES COVERED WITH PERSPIRATION, YET WITHOUT ANY EXPECTORATION.

§ 328. Get these ingredients—a pennyworth of pepper, a pennyworth of fennel seed, two pennyworth of anise-seed, a pennyworth of cummin seed, two pennyworth of liquorish root, a pennyworth of canella bark, a pennyworth of grains of paradise, powder these fine, and boil in a quart of honey on the fire till it becomes a clear bay colour ; remove and keep in a clean vessel. Take a spoonful fasting in the morning, and another the last thing in going to bed, avoiding meat diet, and eating nothing but food made of corn.

### FOR SPASM IN THE LEG OR OTHER MEMBER.

§ 329. Take a pennyworth of black soap, three pennyworth of quicksilver, two pennyworth of oil of olives, frankincense, the vital water called the blessed distillation* four pennyworth, and boar's lard, compound these ingredients effectively till they become as white as a neck cloth, let the painful part be rubbed briskly with this ointment morn and eve. It is proven.

### FOR A COUGH.

§ 330. Take a quart of milk, and a pennyworth of garlick, then pound together, boiling in milk and straining; drink as you can thereof, and use garlick also with your food. Let lean and fresh meat be your diet.

### FOR ARTICULAR RHEUMATISM, AND PAIN IN THE HIPS OR THE SHOULDER BLADE WHEN WALKING.

§ 331. Take two pennyworth of black soap, three pennyworth of quicksilver, three pennyworth of water of life,† a pound of red boar's lard if one can be procured : when the lard is molten cast in the soap, and strong water; mix greatly, and when cold cast in the quicksilver, rub the ingredients together till they are as white as lawn. Rub the painful part with this ointment by the fire night and morning as long as required.

### FOR THE PLICA POLONICA.

§ 332. Shave the head once a week for a year, and wash every night with a strong decoction of sage, then every morning with cold sea water, or salt and water once a week,

---

* Aqua Benedicta.

† Aqua vita. It was prepared at this time by distilling ale, small wine, and the lees of strong wine, in which anise-seed had been mascerated. The same name has been also given to brandy and spirit of wine.

anoint your head with a hen or an eel's fat; when you have so anointed it apply the following cataplasm as warm as possible to your head. Take the whitest fermented wheaten bread, boil in sheep's milk, add thereto a spoonful or two of honey, a large spoonful of oil of chesnuts, and the yolk of an egg, incorporate these ingredients well together, and apply as a plaster to your head, let it remain there twenty-four hours, and when you have removed it wash your head well with a decoction of fennel and soap, scrubbing it carefully. Let your diet be an abundance of milk, and a sparing quantity of meat, or roasted or boiled apples, with milk, as often as you can procure them.

### FOR PULMONARY COUGH.

§ 335. Get the roots of mallows, figs, and elecampane, in powder, make it into a confection with honey, by incorporating together in a mortar. Take a large spoonful, at least morning and night, two hours before and after food, and accustom yourself to a diet of goats' milk, and apples.

### TO EXPEL THE POISON OF ERUPTIVE DISEASES FROM THE BLOOD. IT IS IN CONSEQUENCE OF THE ERUPTIVE POISON THAT SCROFULA, TUBERCLES OF THE LUNGS, ALL ERUPTIONS OF THE SKIN, AND ALL PHLEGM OF THE HEAD AND STOMACH, WITH MANY OTHER DISEASES OF THE HEAD AND EYES, COME.

§ 336. Take cleavers,* (which are recognised by their round seed which adhere to the clothes when ripe) and pound them well; fill up an earthen vessel therewith, and pour thereon as much boiling spring water as the vessel will admit, let it stand an hour and strain through a clean linen cloth; let this be your only drink for nine days. When cleavers cannot be obtained, water-cress may be used. For food take milk, and as many roasted or boiled apples as you can, with the milk, and a slice of wheaten bread and honey. Do not take any meat save fresh mutton, or soup made of the same, cleavers, water-cress, and white field trefoil being boiled therein; boiled nettles, or water-cress and vinegar should be taken with the meat instead of bread. It is proven.

---

* It is remarkable that Cleavers has again come into much credit as an anti scorbutic. The whole section is worthy of attention.

### FOR DERANGEMENT OF MIND.

§ 337. Take linseed, pounding them thoroughly, and making a thin gruel therewith (as you would oatmeal porridge,) with a cupful of pure water, pound and mix betony with this gruel, finally removing the herbs, then boil the gruel till it has become as thick as porridge,—upon some of this porridge cast powdered betony, aloes wood, fennel, and anise-seed; let the patient drink three or four spoonfuls daily, and he should be put to sleep in a dark room. It is proven.

### FOR COUGH AND DYSPNŒA.

§ 338. Take the root of elecampane, two pennyworth of black pepper, and the same of the roots of mallows. Let them be powdered and made into a confection with clarified honey. Take as much as a pigeon's egg the first thing in the morning, and the last at night. It is proven.

### TO DISPERSE SWELLINGS FROM HANDS OR FEET.

§ 340. Take red nettles, hemlock, and sage, with which make fomentation for the patient, surround the affected part therewith, and wash it with your own water daily. It is proven.

### TO RELIEVE CONSTIPATION.

§ 341. Take the roots of the gladwyn, the inner bark of elder and the juice of the house leek; pound them well in a mortar, and mix them with old ale, then strain through a clean cloth and give to the patient to drink when fasting. This will speedily relieve him of his constipation, and he should not take any other drink till his bowels are moved.

### FOR A HŒMATURIA.

§ 342. Take fennel seed and the seed of parsley, or the leaves when the seed cannot be had; pound them well and mix with goat's whey, strain carefully, and let the patient drink a quart thereof for fifteen days, night and morning; let him avoid salt and acid diet, and use light and hot fresh meat with wheaten bread well fermented; also a broth made with parsley and oatmeal, boiled in water. Let this be used and he will recover.

#### FOR UNCONSOLIDATED CANCER.

§ 344. Take dog's dung become white, and glass, powder
the glass as fine as you can, mixing the two together with
some oil of olives; (rancid oil is the best;) heat them together
on the fire, then apply to the disease, and the patient will
be cured.

#### FOR A CARBUNCLE OR CHRONIC ULCER.

§ 345. Take a portion of virgin wax, the same quantity
of frankincense, and pitch, with half as much of walnut
wood, pound these four ingredients, adding some verdigris,
grind them fine and put in a pan, melt and stir them well
so that they may not adhere to the pan; when they have
completely melted and become incorporated, remove from
the fire, strain carefully and apply to the disease. It is
truly useful.

#### FOR THE FRENCH CARBUNCLE OR PLAGUE.

§ 346. In dangerous times when contagious distempers
prevail, thus may the contagion be avoided; get three small
branches of rue, as much of the walnut, and a fig or two;
eat them together and you will be preserved. It is proven.

#### ANOTHER TO CURE THE DISEASE.

§ 347. Take the fœces of a young child between ten and
twelve years of age, and reduce into fine powder, then put
two spoonfuls at most thereof in a cupful of white wine.
Let it be administered to the patient six hours at farthest
after he has sickened; the sooner the better it is done.
Many have proved this.

#### FOR THE CRUSTED TETTER,* CALLED KING'S WORM.

§ 348. Get ivy leaves, pound and boil in mutton and the
lees of stale urine, boil them well and strain, then mix two
pennyworth of black soap therewith, and anoint the part
with it.

#### FOR HEMATEMASIS.

§ 349. Take betony and sage, scrape and powder, then
cast a pinch of this powder into an hen's egg, roast it and

* Impetigo.

eat before it is hard, do this daily for a week or more, and use some acorn powder with your soup, and drink (warm) daily till you recover. Let your diet be light, fresh, and warm, with wheaten bread well leavened, as it is beneficial This is also useful for seminal weakness.

### FOR SPASMS.

§ 351. Take sixteen figs, sixty nine bees, and remove the heads, legs, and wings away, reduce the bees to a powder, and add to the figs, with as much honey as may be needful, pound the whole together, and make into pills of the size of haws ; let the patient have one at the commencement of the spasm, another smaller in the end,—mean while he should be kept walking about. This treatment should be perseveringly followed till the patient recovers.

### A COLLYRIUM.

§ 353. Take a quart of spring water, situated in a shady place, and add thereto as much in quantity as a nut or two of sulphate of lime, boil for twenty four hours in a well covered earthen pot, for an hour it should boil briskly, and for an hour it should cool on the ground, when it should be strained through a fine clean linen cloth. It should be kept in a bottle, and it will be none the worse for seven years. A drop at a time should be inserted in the patient's eye.

### AN OINTMENT TO CLEAR THE EYE.

§ 354. Get the daisy, eye bright, strawberry leaves, red fennel, betony, milfoil, field scabious, knapweed, roots of the burr-reed, leaves of the honeysuckle, ground ivy, and vervain ; take equal parts of each, and pound well with butter. Let them stand for a week, and on the ninth day boil them well, finally straining through a clean linen cloth ; keep it in a well covered glass vessel, and insert as much as a grain of wheat thereof in the eye. It should be used for two days and nights in order to remove an opacity, web, or membrane from the eye. This ointment should be put in the eye the third night, and it will become clear and bright. It is proved.

### TO PREVENT SPEAKING DURING SLEEP.

§ 355. Take the seed or leaves of rue, and pound with vinegar till it becomes a mass, then mix it well in old ale, strain through a clean linen, and let the patient drink it.

### TO PREVENT DREAMING.

§ 356. Take the vervain, and hang about a man's neck, or let him drink some of the juice in going to bed; certainly he will not dream if he does so.

### TO RELIEVE THE PHLEGM IN BRONCHITIS.

§ 357. Take unsalted butter and honey in equal parts; mix together carefully, and anoint your chest therewith. It is a good remedy.

### ANOTHER FOR THE SAME THING.

§ 358. Take wild celery, and boil in good wine vinegar, wash your chest with the hot vinegar, and apply the boiled herbs to your chest for three or four hours.

### FOR A PUNCTURED WOUND IN A JOINT FROM A THORN OR NEEDLE, THE SAME BEING HEALED OVER.

§ 359. Take the finest wheaten flour and temper with white wine, then boil the same till it becomes thick, bind this about the injured part as hot as it can be borne, and it will open the puncture, extracting the corruption and poison. In the absence of wine use good ale.

### A MEDICAMENT FOR ULCERS IN A LEG, ARM, OR OTHER PART.

§ 360. Take water cress, wash clean and boil in pure water till they become tender, then pound them well in a mortar, put then in a clean frying-pan on the fire, mixed with a stag or buck's tallow, or with mutton suet and a quantity of the lees of wine, and the bran of wheat; fry the whole together for a poultice, and apply warm to the painful part. Do this three or four times as may be needed.

### THINGS THAT ARE USEFUL FOR THE BRAIN.

§ 361. Smelling musk and camomile, drinking wine moderately, eating the leaves of sage frequently, keeping the head

3 A

warm, washing the hands frequently, walking moderately, sleeping moderately, listening frequently to a little music and singing, smelling red roses, washing the eyebrows with rose water, drinking water in going to sleep, reading a little before going to sleep, and light diet.

### THINGS THAT ARE HURTFUL TO THE BRAIN.

§ 362. For all brains the following things are hurtful; gluttony, drunkenness, late eating, much sleeping after food, tainted air, anger, depressed spirits, much standing bare headed, eating much or hastily, too much warmth, excessive watching, too much cold, curds, all kinds of nuts, frequent bathing, onions, garlick, yawning, smelling a white rose, excess of venery, two much music, singing and reading, strong drink before sleeping, restless sleep, too frequent fasting, frequent wet feet.

### FOR A BURN OR SCALD.

§ 363. Take the white of an egg, lay on a pewter plate and mix with a little frankincense, rubbing them together into a uniform consistency; then take some fine linen and dip in some oil of olives, the oil of pinetops,* or some other oil most easily obtained. Apply the same linen to the part, spread the ointment of white of eggs and frankincense over it.

### AN OINTMENT FOR CONFUSED NOISE IN THE HEAD, HINDERING HEARING.

§ 364. Take a head of garlic, then peel and perforate it five or six times about the middle, and dip in new honey; insert it in your ear, covering it over with black wool, and rest each night on the other side. Let this remain seven or eight days, and it will remove the noise from the head, and restore the hearing.

### FOR A BURN.

§ 367. Take linseed oil, and apply to the part with a feather, it will extract the fire, and heal the injury in as beautiful a way as any other remedy.

* Turpentine.

### FOR THE STONE OR STRANGURY.

§ 368. Take a quart of white wine and make a posset thereof, remove the curds, and add four pennyweights of the scrapings of white soap to the whey; boil and drink thereof as warm as you can.    It is really useful.

### FOR RETENTION OF URINE.

§ 369. Take a flint, heat it white in the fire, and warm your drink of strong ale therewith.

### A DIURETIC.

§ 370. Take the fourth part of a handful of parsley, and as much of red fennel, bruise them well and put in a cupful of old ale, drink the ale and it will benefit you.    It is proven.

### TO RESTRAIN BLEEDING FROM RECENT WOUNDS.

§ 371. Take the leaves of leeks, pound with honey and wheaten flour, incorporate these together carefully away from the fire, and apply cold to the wound.

### A GOOD COLLYRIUM.

§ 372. Take rotten apples, and strain with some spring water; wash your eyelids therewith, and it will cleanse and brighten your eyes.

### ANOTHER.

§ 373. Take sulphate of zinc and dissolve in spring water, and when you go to bed wash your eyelids therewith, droping some to your eyes.

### FOR DISEASE IN THE SHOULDERBLADE, THE LIVER, AND THE BREAST.

§ 374. Habituate yourself to eat nine pepper daily, and it will do you good.

### FOR ALL KINDS OF HEAT AND INFLAMMATION IN THE FACE, EVEN IF IT WERE ERYSIPELAS.

§ 375. Take a quart of smithy water, a handful of the leaves of sage, a handful of the leaves of the elm, or of the inner bark thereof, and a pennyworth of frankincense; boil these together to the half, and keep in an earthen vessel; anoint the face therewith.

### FOR PAIN IN THE LIMBS, BACK, OR SHOULDERS.

§ 376. Take the blessed distillation,* or brandy, and sheep's foot oil, put in a vessel and warm together well, anoint the painful part therewith, covering the patient with an abundance of clothes afterwards.

### AN APPROVED REMEDY FOR A PAIN.

§ 377. Pound wild celery, and put in some blessed distillation, or brandy, strain and add some molten boar's lard thereto ; mix it well and anoint the painful part therewith.

### FOR PAIN OR SWELLING IN THE THIGHS.

§ 378. Take a quart of sage wine, and a handful of thyme, boil together, and when half boiled add some fresh butter, then boil down from a quart to a pint, when you go to bed wash your feet well therewith ; then dip a linen cloth therein, and apply three or four fold to the painful members as hot as you can bear it for six or seven nights, it will do much good without doubt. If you have any brandy or blessed distillation, add a spoonful thereto when sufficiently boiled, mixing it well.

### TO RESTAIN HŒMORRHAGE FROM A WOUND OR THE NOSE.

§ 379. Take an old linen cloth, and wet it thoroughly in red wine vinegar, or if you have not that, then in any vinegar, burn the linen and apply the powder to the wound ; it will restrain the bleeding quickly. If the bleeding should be from the nose, blow up some of the powder through a quill.

### A PLASTER FOR A SORE, WOUND, OR SWELLING, NOT YET MATURE.

§ 380. Take some meal and boil in fresh milk till it is as thick as stirabout ; put in a pan with a portion of suet, and boil well ; mix it thoroughly for a plaster, and apply as hot as you can to the part.

### FOR THE BITE OF A DOG.

§ 381. Take the dittany, garlick, and the white of an egg, make it into a plaster, apply to the wound, and it will cure it.

Aqua Benedicta Rulandi.

### TO MATURE CARBUNCLES.

§ 382. Take a pint of fresh milk, set on the fire and add thereto a portion of bruised mutton suet, and a handful of oatmeal, break and beat it carefully whilst boiling; let it boil till it becomes thickened, so that you may spread it on a clean linen, then apply it to the diseased part. When it breaks, dress it with some turpentine on white leather, piercing it with many holes.

### FOR DEAFNESS OF THE EARS.

§ 383. Take some juice of leek and goat's gall, mixing them well together, drop some of this into the ear, and cover it with wool.

### FOR BLINDNESS.

§ 384. Take some celandine seed mixed with the morning dew, and pound well in a mortar, strain the juice and mix it with an equal part of clear honey, boil it briskly to a third, keep in a glass vessel, and drop to your eye when needful.

### FOR THE ITCH.

§ 385. Take dock root and butter, pound the roots and strain through linen, purify the butter, boil the juice and butter, and keep in a pan, when needed melt it, and anoint the skin three times, i.e., every other day, and you will be cured.

### FOR A SLOUGHING ULCER.

§ 386. Take black wool, soap, and the powder of baked beef, pound them together and apply to the sloughing part. It will cure it.

### FOR PAIN IN A JOINT.

§ 387. Take the crumbs of wheaten bread, fresh from the oven, crab apples, betony, and dandelion, pound them together well in a mortar in equal parts, boil them in good red wine till they become a plaster, apply to the painful part as hot as it can be borne, and it will break out in the form of boils.

### THINGS HURTFUL TO THE HEART.

§ 388. Onions, peas, cummin, garlick, sorrow, anger, too much care, too much travelling, drinking cold water after a journey, and bad news. If a man wisheth health and long life, let him carefully maintain a merry heart, let him neither eat, drink, nor do what will harm it, for as the wise man says, —" A merry heart and all is well."

### FOR PAIN IN A JOINT.

§ 389. Take water chickweed, the leaves and blossoms of primrose, and a flintstone, pound them well together and boil with May butter; anoint the painful part with it warm. Let it be kept in an earthen pot.

### FOR A BOIL.

§ 390. Take mallows, boil in spring water and make into a plaster, then apply to the disease.

### ANOTHER.

§ 391. Boil pennywort in sheep's cream, and apply thereto.

### FOR CHILBLAINS.

§ 392. Take dry dead leaves gathered from the surface of a bog, and pound well. Take the white of an egg and pound with the herbs, adding some May butter thereto; incorporate the whole together and apply as a plaster. It will cure it.

### FOR THE TOOTHACHE.

§ 393. Take the roots of the water flower de lys and bruise smartly, strain through linen, and inject through a quill to the nostril farthest from the painful tooth.

### FOR A BURN.

§ 394. Take fern and pound well with sheep's milk, let it be applied to the burn with a feather, it should be stirred carefully before it is used.

### TO RESTRAIN HŒMORRHAGE FROM A WOUND.

§ 395. Take rue leaves, pound well and apply to the wound.

### ANOTHER.

§ 396. Scrape off the rind from a branch of broom, make it into a ball, insert in the wound, and bind firmly.

### FOR CUTANEOUS ERUPTIONS.

§ 397. Take the leaves of the lily and ground ivy, pound them well together, then take mutton suet and fry the whole conbined, express through a cloth and anoint the part therewith.

### ANOTHER.

§ 398. Take oat straw and burn, cover the scald therewith and rub it. It will dry and cure it.

### TO PREVENT DREAMING.

§ 399. Take the leaves of betony, and hang about your neck, or else drink the juice in going to bed.

### FOR A CANCER IN THE MOUTH, ON THE BROW, OR ANY OTHER PART.

§ 400. Take eight or nine leaves of sage, and pound well with some salt and vinegar, apply it as a plaster to the part.

### A MEDICAMENT FOR BLINDNESS.

§ 401. Take twelve grains of fair wheat, and lay upon some cold clean polished iron, then press another iron (red hot) upon the wheat; a substance like honey will exude from the wheat, which apply to the painful eye with a feather.

### TO RESTRAIN HŒMORRHAGE WHEN ONE OF THE PRINCIPAL VEINS IS DIVIDED.

§ 402. Take a piece of salt beef, both fat and lean together, as much in size as will fill the wound, lay it on the embers till it is warmed through, and insert it warm in the wound; it will stay the bleeding.

### FOR A PAIN IN THE LIMB, WHETHER ATTENDED WITH SWELLING OR NOT.

§ 403. Take water pimpernel and mix with honey, the yolk of an egg, and best wheaten meal; let this be applied as a plaster to the painful part; if the part be disposed to suppurate it will hasten that termination, if not it will remove the pain, and heal the disease.

### FOR THE KING'S EVIL.

§ 404. Take the root of the lily and bake under the embers till it is dry, reduce it then to a powder, and mix with goose grease or lard, dress the sore therewith and it will heal it.

### TO REMOVE EXFOLIATIONS FROM THE SKULL OR ANY OTHER BONE.

§ 405. Take betony, vervain, and rue, mix them with wheaten meal and the white of eggs, pounding the whole together till they become completely incorporated. Let it be applied as a plaster to the part.

### FOR ALL SORTS OF CUTANEOUS ERUPTIONS, INCLUDING RINGWORM.*

§ 406. Take onions, pounding them small and boiling in water or vinegar, let the affected part be washed with this, and it will heal a scald head or any other eruption on any other part of the body.

### FOR THE ITCH.

§ 407. Take dock roots, bruising them thoroughly in new butter, and then frying the whole mixing and compounding the mass whilst so doing. Anoint the patient therewith and he will be cured.

### ANOTHER.

§ 408. Take the roots of elecampane and clean them well, then boil them in spring water, and when boiled sufficiently, incorporate them with good thick cream, or unsalted butter, so that they may be made into an ointment ; let your flesh be anointed with this three times in nine days, viz., once in three days. Drink also a good draught of the water in which the roots were boiled night and morning, for this is an antidote to the specific virus whose existence in the blood and fluids occasions eruptions on the skin, carbuncles, and such like.

### FOR CARBUNCLE.

§ 409. Take black wool and incorporate it with some black soap, and bind this upon the disease or carbuncle.

### FOR CANCER OF THE MOUTH.

§ 410. Take the juice of plantain, vinegar, and the distilled water of red roses, mix and wash the mouth therewith frequently.

* Favus.

#### FOR AN ERUPTIVE VIRUS IN THE BLOOD AND FLUIDS.

§ 411. Take water chickweed, pound well and express the juice under a press ; drink a cupful three times a day on an empty stomach. It is truly good.

#### ANOTHER.

§ 412. Take chickweed, the leaves or the inner bark of elm, water cress, and scurvy grass, pound them well and express the juice under a press, let it be your only drink for nine days, and as a diet confine yourself to good wheaten bread prepared with yeast and goat's milk; it is proven. This medicine and the former one will destroy the eruptive poison in the blood and humors, also that of the inveterate eruption called in Latin *Scabies*,* and every kind of eruptive poison in the blood. Pneumonia and numerous other diseases, more than an ignorant person would believe, are occasioned by this kind of blood poison.

#### FOR A BURN OR SCALD.

§ 413. Take black soap or white, and bind to the injured part.

#### FOR AN ERUPTION OF THE FACE.

§ 414. Take best wheaten meal, mix with vinegar and honey, and apply to your face.

#### FOR CARBUNCLES AND BOILS.

§ 415. Take wheaten meal refined, lard, May butter, and sage, pound together and make a plaster thereof, which apply to the carbuncle till it maturates and draws out the matter.

#### FOR PAIN OR SWELLING IN THE MAMMÆ.

§ 416. Take the bark of the thornless holly, pound well and mix with good old ale, strain and administer it to the patient as a drink ; it is proven that by the use of this the gathering of the breast will be prevented.

---

* Scabies or itch—Scabies does not depend upon a *virus*, but upon the presence of an insect,—the *Acarus Follicularum*.

## ANOTHER.

§ 417. Take milfoil, and an egg (with its shell,) pound together carefully, and apply as a plaster to the breast ; it will certainly cure it.

## FOR PAIN IN THE LEGS.

§ 418. Take the herb called coltsfoot, (they are like burdock in appearance,) boil them well in the milk of a cow of one colour with oaten groats and May butter, and apply warm the painful part.

## FOR TIGHTNESS OF THE CHEST.

§ 419. Take hyssop and centaury in equal portions, pound them well and strain carefully, mix white of eggs with the strained juice, and drink for three days fasting.

## ANOTHER.

§ 420. Take rue, and boil well in vinegar, and administer to the patient.

## FOR HYSTERIA.

§ 421. Take mugwort, red fennel, and red mint, boil well in old ale, and strain carefully through a cloth ; drink it warm and you will recover.

## FOR A TERTIAN AGUE.

§ 422. Whoever drinks the juice of betony and plantain, mixed together, will recover.

## FOR PAIN OR SWELLING OF THE LEGS, FEET, OR ARMS.

§ 423. Take oatmeal, cow's milk, the juice of house leek, and mutton suet, boil together till it becomes a thick mass, apply as a plaster to the painful part, and it will remove the pain and swelling.

## FOR AN EPIPHORA OF THE EYE.

§ 424. Take some black snails, and boil in pure water, mix the oil which floats on the surface, and anoint the eye with the same.

## ANOTHER.

§ 425. Take lead and melt in an iron pot, remove, and pour vinegar thereon, cover it up carefully so that the vapour may not escape ; when cold and settled, let the clean liquor be decanted and kept in a glass bottle ; deposit in the bottle a fragment of *elyf** as big as a large nut. When required, mix it with equal parts of decoction of mallows, and wash your eye therewith, or mix the vinegar with white of eggs in equal parts, beating them together well. Let your eye be washed with the same.

### FOR HEADACHE.

§ 426. Take an apronful of sheep's sorrel, and boil in the milk of a one coloured cow till it is nearly dry, apply as a plaster to the head, the patient keeping his bed, being covered with clothes, so as to cause him to perspire.

### FOR A COLD IN THE LIMBS.

§ 427. Take the seed of nettles and boil in honey, anoint your feet and arms or other parts requiring it with the same, and it will remove the cold.

### FOR A PARALYSIS AFFECTING A MAN'S SPEECH.

§ 428. Take sage leaves, marjoram leaves, (roots when the leaves cannot be got) and pound the whole together in equal parts, strain, mix with good ale, and administer to the patient. It is well proven.

### FOR AN ULCER WHICH HAS HEALED OUTWARDLY, BUT IS INWARDLY PAINFUL.

§ 429. Take barley meal, the white of eggs, and honey, mix them together and make a plaster, apply to the painful part and it will benefit and heal it.

### FOR ONE WHO HAS DRANK POISON.

§ 430. Take fresh rue, wash and bruise well, then mix with white wine, strain and let the patient drink a good draught thereof.

### FOR SWELLING OF THE WOMB, OR HARDNESS OF STOMACH.

§ 431. Take linseed and boil in goat's milk, applying it as a plaster thereto.

---

* I am not satisfied as to what is intended by *Elyf*, it is usally rendered aloes, but what use aloes could be of here I do not see.  Tr.

### FOR PAIN OF THE WOMB.

§ 432. Take horse mint or tansy, bruise well, and strain carefully, boil with old ale and drink as warm as you can.

### FOR WORMS.

§ 433. Take the juice of tansy and milk, strain and boil well till reduced to a third, drinking it warm.

### FOR A SCALD HEAD.

§ 434. Take pitch and wax, boiling them together, shave the scald head carefully, applying the plaster to the same as warm as it can be borne, leaving it on for nine days.

### FOR PAIN AND OPACITY OF THE EYE.

§ 435. Take the yolk of an egg, fine wheaten meal, and a little sulphate of copper, mix briskly, applying it to the eye and it will remove the opacity.

### FOR AN OPACITY OF THE EYE.

§ 436. Put the juice of ground ivy in the eye, and it will cure it.

### FOR A RINGWORM.

§ 437. Take the white of an egg baked, and apply as a plaster on a linen cloth.

### FOR PAIN IN THE BACK.

§ 438. Take young broom, boil in spring water, and wash your back with the same.

### FOR DYSPNŒA.

§ 440. Take the strained juice of hyssop, and of centaury in equal parts, mixing them with as much again of the white of eggs; let this be your only drink for three days.

### FOR PAIN OF THE CHEST.

§ 441. Take parsley and sage, pound together and apply to your chest.

### FOR PAIN UND R THE SHOULDER.

§ 442. Take the juice of sage, and warm wine, one proportion of the juice, and two of the wine, drink it and it will benefit the pain under the shoulder, pain of the womb, and of the stomach.   It is also useful for headache, paralysis or muscular weakness; it is proven.

### FOR THE BLACK JAUNDICE.

§ 443.  Take thyme, rue, pennyroyal, hyssop, parsley roots, fennel, the leaves of birthwort, (called in Latin *chamærops)* and two spoonfuls of the anise-seed, boil the whole in a quart of water containing three spoonfuls of honey; strain through a clean cloth, and drink blood-warm.

### TO CURE A CANCER.

§ 444.  Take a cupful of red wine, three or four spoonfuls of honey, and as much as a large hazel nut of frankincense, mix and boil till reduced to a third, then strain and put in a bottle to keep, let the affected part be washed therewith frequently and it will cure it.

### FOR A HEADACHE.

§ 446.  Take a spoonful of the juice of betony, a spoonful of wine and honey, mix with it nine pepper corns, and drink morning and evening for nine days.

### TO HEAL A WOUND OR SWELLING, AND TO EASE PAIN.

§ 447.  Take a portion of oatmeal, the milk of a *myswynog*,* the juice of house leek and mutton suet, bruise together till they become a thick mass, apply warm as a plaster to the painful part, this will ease the pain and remove the swelling.

### FOR HÆMOPTASIS.

§ 448.  Take wild celery, mint, rue, and betony; boil in fresh milk, drinking it warm and it will cure you.

### FOR THE STRANGURY.

§ 449.  Take red nettles and parsley, pound well together, and apply as a plaster to the stomach.

### TO STRENGTHEN THE UTERUS.

§ 450.  Take acorns, roast hard and reduce to a powder, put a spoonful thereof in a drink of good ale, and drink warm

---

* A cow which has been a year without calving.

every morning for a week or nine days, lying in bed for an hour or two.

### A GOOD EYE WATER.

§ 451. Take rotten apples, strain with spring water and wash your eye therewith. This will clean and clear your eye wonderfully.

### FOR THE TOOTHACHE.

§ 452. Take holly leaves and boil in spring water till they are tough, then remove the pot from the fire, and put a kerchief about your head, holding your mouth over the pot in order to inhale the vapour. It will cure you.

### A PROVED REMEDY FOR THE TOOTHACHE.

§ 453. Take the roots of pellitory of Spain, wash clean and bruise well, and form of them three small balls with your hand, each about as big as a plum ; retain the first between your cheek and the painful tooth as long as you walk a mile with moderate steps, and as the saliva collects spit it away. When you think that the ball has been there as long as that, put in another and walk backwards and forwards for the same space of time ; after that put in the third, then lie in bed, and warm yourself well, and when you have slept you will be free from the pain. This I have often proved and have found to be a present remedy for the toothache.

### TO FIND WHETHER THE SKULL IS FRACTURED.

§ 454. If the integument is entire, shave the hair where the bruise is, and apply a thick new linen cloth doubled, spreading the white of an egg thereon, and binding it on the part for a night ; in the morning, let it be removed and see whether the linen be wet, for if the linen be moist and wet, there, certainly the skull is fractured.

### FOR FLATULENCE OF STOMACH.

§ 455. Take wild carrot's seed and make into pills of the size of peas by means of honey, take four every morning and evening for three days.

### FOR SORE LIPS.

§ 456. Take the root of the knapweed and pound well, adding some cold milk cream thereto, and mixing carefully, straining through a clean cloth. Anoint your lips with this salve.

### TO PROVOKE AN APPETITE.

§ 457. Boil centaury in clear spring water, and let the sick person drink nine spoonfuls thereof fasting for three days, and it will help him.

### FOR EVERY KIND OF VENOMOUS BITE.

§ 458. Take plantain leaves and drink their juice, take also the yew, and celandine in equal parts, and pound well together, tempering them with stale urine, then apply to the wound and it will ease the pain, reduce the swelling, and extract the venom.

### FOR THE BITE OF A MAD DOG.

§ 459. Take a handful of betony, a handful of wild sage, a handful of bitter night shade, and a cupful of standing water, pound the herbs well mixed with the water, and strain, mix a pennyworth of treacle therewith, and let the patient drink it two or three mornings. It is proven.

### FOR AN INFLAMED EYE.

§ 460. Seek cream, and as much again of the white of eggs, then dip a linen cloth of the size of the eye therein, and apply thereto.

### TO HINDER INEBRIETY.

§ 461. Take a handful of betony, bruise well, mix with spring water, and strain carefully; let it be drank fasting, and you will not get drunk that day.

### A GOOD EMETIC FOR THE HEAD AND STOMACH.

§ 462. Take three spoonfuls of the juice of betony for three successive mornings, and inject it through a quill into the nostril.

### FOR PAIN IN THE LIMBS.

§ 463. Take a handful of the herb called colt's foot, and as much of the leaves of burdock, pound and mix with the milk of a one coloured cow, oaten groats and butter being added, the whole being boiled well, and applied as a plaster to the painful parts as hot as you can bear it ; it will ease it.

### FOR THE SAME THING.

§ 464. Procure the same herbs, and wrap them (unbruised) about your feet night and day ; they will extract the poisonous water from your feet. At other times brown paper should be used in the same way instead of a hose ; it is proven.

### FOR THE CHILBLAINS OR PUSTULAR ULCERATIONS ON THE FEET AND HEELS.

§ 465. Take hot wax when combs are strained, and immerse your feet therein as hot as you can suffer it, stand therein a long while and you will be cured. It will absorb the purulent matter.

### TO REDUCE SWELLINGS OF THE WOMB.

§ 466. Take mercurial ointment, and May butter, or the lard of pigs slaughtered in that month, also wax and rosin, melting therewith orpine bruised, in equal proportions, only minding that the butter or lard should exceed the wax and rosin in quantity ; let them be boiled well and strained. With this ointment anoint the side in which the pain is situated, by rubbing it up and down as hard as you can. It is proven.

### FOR CONSTIPATION

§ 467. Take the roots of gladwyn, pound them as you would garlic with good old ale, letting it stand aside a space of time, straining, and warming as a potion for the patient ; it will certainly act as a laxative, for it is proven.

### FOR A BOIL ON THE BACK, WHEN THE SKIN IS ABRADED.

§ 468. Take a quart and a half of the best ale you can obtain, and boil it to a spoonful ; it is a good ointment for all sores of the back, being spread on new linen, and applied thereto ; the use of this will extract the impurity. Then dress it with a healing ointment. If there is a swelling in the leg, get the leaves of foxglove, bruise and apply thereto, covering the leaves with potter's clay. It is good.

### ANOTHER TO REDUCE THE SWELLING, AND EXTRACT THE POISON.

§ 469. Dress the ulcerated part with clarified honey, and it will benefit it.

### FOR MENORRHAGIA.

§ 470. Take the inner bark of the black thorn, rejecting the outer, and pound it well in the milk of a one coloured cow; this mixture being administered to the woman, will certainly be of use to her.

### ANOTHER.

§ 471. Take archangel, and pound well with strong red wine, straining it carefully; let this be given the woman to drink night and morning freely. The use thereof will be of great benefit to her. The archangel should be kept dry for winter, being taken as a powder then; a spoonful in in the wine warmed, as warm as it can be drank. The root pounded with the wine and strained is also useful, or the powder may be taken with the wine; the herb should be grown in a garden apart from other plants.

### FOR A THORN.

§ 472. Take common soap, apply to the part and it will draw it well. Leave on till it is extracted.

### FOR A SICK ANIMAL.

§ 473. Take black soap and boil in ale, let it be given the animal and it will purge him.

### FOR INFLAMMATION OF THE BREAST.

§ 474. Take plantain leaves and lard, pound them together and apply to the part.

### FOR A SWELLING OF THE STOMACH.

§ 475. Take goat's whey, and pound the herbs called ramsons, mixing together and straining. Let it be your only drink for three days.

3 c

### FOR RETENTION OF URINE.

§ 476. Take red nettles and parsley, pound them into a plaster together, and apply to the perineum.

### A GOOD HABIT FOR THE PRESERVATION OF HEALTH.

§ 477. Whatever sex you be, wash your face, hands, &c., with cold water every morning, scrubbing them well afterwards; wash your back and nape of the neck once a week also, scrubbing them well afterwards with a coarse cloth.

### TO DESTROY A WORM LODGED IN A MAN'S FLESH.

§ 478. Take the lard of a red pig, May butter, sage, and acorns, pound them well together till they become an ointment, and apply the same to the part.

### ANOTHER.

§ 479. Take the juice of sage, and a little of the distillation of wine,* anoint the part where the worm is lodged, and it will kill it.

### FOR BLEEDING OF THE NOSE.

§ 480. Take an egg shell and receive the blood in the same, then set on the fire to bake till it becomes a powder; blow this powder into the nostrils, and it will stop the bleeding. It is proven.

### FOR INFLAMMATION OF THE MAMMÆ.

§ 481. Take the bark of the thornless holly, and pound well, mixing it with good old ale, and straining; let this be administered to the patient and no doubt she will be cured. It is an approved remedy, and will prevent the formation of an abscess in the breast.

### ANOTHER.

§ 482. Take yarrow, and an egg, shell and all, pounding them together, and applying to the breast. It will not fail to cure it.

### FOR AN ACUTE PAIN IN ANY PART OF THE BODY.

§ 483. Take the lees of wine in the cask, half a gallon, the same quantity of the lees of good old ale, a *ffiol* full†

---

* Spirit of Wine or Brandy.

† See about this measure at the end of the Volume. Lit. a cupful.

of wheat bran, and the roots of the cinquefoil; boil well, pound the herbs carefully, then boil the whole together till the mass becomes tough; the more it is boiled, the better the plaster will be. Let this be applied to the painful part, and with God's help you will certainly be cured. It is proven.

### FOR GASTRODYNIA.

§ 484. Take camomile, bruise well, and boil in a pint of wine till it is reduced to the half; let it be given to the patient, and he will certainly recover.

### ANOTHER.

§ 485. Take wild carrots, and infuse in as much as will cover it of water, using it for drink. It is proven.

### TO HEAL A BRUISE, AND TO DRAW WATER FROM THE INJURED PART, OR FROM THE BRUISED BONES, AND DISPERSE THE SWELLING RESULTING FROM THE SUPERABUNDANCE OF HUMOR, TAINTED BLOOD, OR CORRUPTED FLESH.

§ 486. Take half a pound of mutton suet, and half a pennyworth of black soap, melt together, and add six eggs well beaten, yolk and white together, the whole being well mixed. Remove the mass from the fire to cool, mix it well and spread on a cloth carefully. Let this be applied to the injury daily or every other day till it is cured.

### TO DRAW HUMOR OR TAINTED BLOOD FROM A BRUISE OF THE SCALP.

§ 487. Wash your mouth clean, and anoint your head with oil of olives, letting some of it drop into the ears. Let this plan be followed for eight days, and you will be cured.

### FOR HAZE OF THE EYE CALLED THE ONGLE.*

§ 488. Take pepper and reduce to powder, mix with the marrow of the wing bones of an old goose, and bind up in a linen cloth, burning it upon a bake stone, till it can be reduced into fine powder. Let this be blown into the eye till it is cured.

* Onyx.

### ANOTHER.

§ 489. Take the flowers of the hawthorn, and the willow, making a distillation of them, use this night and morning, for it is useful for inflamed, painful, and watery eyes.

### ANOTHER.

§ 490. Inject the juice of the celandine into your eye through a quill twice a day.

### FOR THE ITCH.

§ 491. Take the leaves of the betony, pound and strain the juice, rub the skin well with the same night and morning for nine days. It will cure it.

### FOR A CONTUSION OF THE HEAD, OR A FALL, FRACTURING THE SKULL, AND LACERATING THE BRAIN.

§ 492. Take betony and pound briskly in a mortar, then boil well in the lees of red wine, let this be applied as a plaster to the head. This will cool the head, and bind the bones together.

### FOR A PAIN OF THE NATURE OF CARDIALGIA OR STRANGURY.

§ 493. Take clean oats, and fry in unsalted butter till they are browned; apply to the painful part upon a cloth, and it will be most certainly cured.

### FOR ERYSIPELAS.

§ 494. Take the dung of geese feeding on grass, hartwort, daisy, betony, and unsalted May butter, pound together, boil on the fire and strain; let it be kept in a clean vessel, and the patient anointed therewith. It will cure him.

### TO STRENGTHEN THE LUNGS, THROAT, AND CHEST.

§ 495. Get red fennel, and the top of hyssop bruised, also mallows, which boil in perennial spring water. Let the patient drink the same and he will certainly recover.

### FOR THE BITE OF A MAD DOG.

§ 496. Boil wild sage in as much as will cover it of ale or water; let it be used as ordinary drink for nine days.

### FOR ALL KINDS OF HURTFUL ACHES IN WHATEVER WAY THEY COME.

§ 497. Get parsley, plantain, daisy, garlic, and grains of Paradise, pound well in a mortar, strain and take the juice in ale. If the patient can obtain beef, he should not eat it when he recovers.

### FOR HOARSENESS.

§ 498. Take mugwort, red nettles, and plantain, boil them well in goat's whey; let a cupful thereof be drank every morning, and it will cure you.

### FOR HOOPING COUGH AND BRONCHITIS.

§ 499. Take ground ivy in milk and water, and administer to the patient every morning fasting, and in the evening. It will cure him.

### FOR A COUGH.

§ 500. Take a handful of white sage, pounding it well in a mortar, mixing with good old ale, and straining carefully under a press; make a posset of this ale, using the clear part, and you will be cured.

### ANOTHER FOR THE COUGH.

§ 501. Take powder of orpiment, and hard boiled eggs, twice a day for thirteen days, and you will recover.

### ANOTHER.

§ 502. Take the fat of a duck and of a hen, with the marrow of a fresh bone, make them into an ointment, and anoint your chest therewith, but not your stomach, then you will be cured.

### FOR AN ERUPTION OF THE HEAD IN CONSEQUENCE OF SUMMER HEAT.

§ 503. First get the lees of good strong ale, rosin, and rye meal, make three plasters thereof, and apply to your head for a week each, then wash it with stale urine, scrape it well, remove all the loose hair, bleed if the countenance is flushed, between each application, then get white of eggs and rye meal, and make three plasters, three times, washing the head clean after each application. This being done get elecampane root, dock root, fumitory, and the herb Robert, pound together, boil them with ox tallow, and strain carefully ; when cold get sulphate of copper, and a portion of sulphur, reduce the same to fine powder and mix with the strained ointment; incorporate the whole well with a spatula, stirring it from the centre till it becomes like thick honey, anoint the head well with this, then get butter and the above mentioned herbs of the earth, (not the powder of minerals), make an ointment thereof, and anoint therewith. It will cure it.

HÉRE IS A MEDICAMENT FOR A MAN WHO HAS AN ERUPTION OF THE HEAD, WHICH HAS PROVED INTRACTABLE.

§ 504. Get pitch and fresh wax, melt together, and apply as a plaster, as warm as can be borne, leaving it unchanged for nine days.

ANOTHER.

§ 505. Take sulphur and mercury, incorporate together with roasted garlic and fresh lard, mixing them well; with this anoint your head.

ANOTHER.

§ 506. Take two handfuls of crown imperial, (called *petilius* in Latin) before it is in flower, boil in a pot of strong whey till it is reduced to the half ; then wash your head therewith warm, scrubbing the scabs away. Again make a plaster of crown imperial, and apply to your head warm, leaving it there a night and a day, when it should be removed, a plaster being afterwards prepared with rye meal and spring water, applied on a linen cloth over the diseased part, leaving it on three days and nights; then it should be removed and the head washed with stale urine, the head being scraped to the flesh. Then take a red onion and make into a plaster, boiling and tempering with the juice of mountain mint and the lard of an old boar. This practice will cure it.

ANOTHER.

§ 507. Take pitch and wax, equal parts, melt them together and pour into a box, letting it stand in water till

cold, scrub the head, and wash as directed above, then take
a linen, apply to the head, and then apply another upon
that ; then take a portion from the box, reduce to powder
and spread upon the linen, after this apply another linen,
and then a bandage about the forehead and all, so that the
powder be not lost, letting it remain there seven or eight
days; each time you change it, the head should be washed
as before said. When you perceive that this process is no
longer needed, take the fat which is obtained from the feet
of 𝔯𝔯𝔢𝔲𝔯𝔢𝔰 when boiled, blow it from the surface of the
water wherein they are boiled into another vessel, preserving
it in a box, and anointing the head therewith till it is well.
It is proven.

### TO PROMOTE THE GROWTH OF HAIR.

§ 508. Shave the head clean with a razor, and take honey
with the juice of onions in equal parts, anointing and scrubbing the head well with the same every morning and night;
the head should be washed with the distilled water of honey.
It is proven.

### ANOTHER.

§ 509. Shave the head carefully, anoint with honey, and
sprinkle the powder of mollipuffs upon it.*

### TO CURE BILIOUSNESS, OTHERWISE CALLED HYPOCHONDRIA-
### SIS, OR DISEASE OF THE BILE.

§ 510. Take male fern, (the best is that which grows upon
the oak,) boiling it in strong ale wort, and drinking a hearty
draught thereof every other day, for eight days, subsisting
meanwhile upon a corresponding diet, consisting of fresh
meat, avoiding vegetables, and preferring well baked wheaten
bread, your drink being good wine, or ale, and milk mixed
in equal quantity, partaken of temperately. Take also
caraway seed in powder, fennel seed, wild carrot seed, anise
seed, canella, and such dry herbs mixed with your drink,
walk hard daily, and amuse yourself with song and harp,

* Lycoperdon Bovista.

another being the performer, not yourself. By following this plan you will (by God's help) recover.

### TO RELIEVE NAUSEA OF THE STOMACH.

§ 511. Take an infusion of the blood red pink, called in Latin *cariophilum major*,* mixed with honey, the powder of anise seed, and the powder of fennel, being sprinkled thereon, a good draught should be taken night and morning, and the flowers should be kept dry so that they may be at hand at all times.

### A PLASTER TO REDUCE A SWELLING THE RESULT OF A
#### WOUND, BLOW OR OTHER INJURY TO A MAN'S BODY, OR ON A MEMBER WHERE THE SWELLING CONCEALS THE INJURY.

§ 512. Take a handful of the leaves of smallage, (called in Latin *oleoselinon*) fine wheaten meal, and the white of four eggs, pound them well in a mortar, beating the white of eggs till it becomes thin, then adding the meal thereto, let the whole be mixed for a plaster, and applied to the part, and it will reduce the swelling completely, till the nature of the injury can be plainly discovered.

### FOR THE DROPSY, IN LATIN CALLED HYDROPS.

§ 513. Take fresh dough, and make thereof a large pie so that a goose or two capons at least may lie therein, and fill the same with the following salutary herbs, even two handfuls of sage, two handfuls of dwarf elder, one handful of betony, a handful of water cress, a handful of hart's tongue, a handful of parsley or smallage roots bruised, half a handful of hyssop, and half a handful of columbine, (called in Latin *aqilegia*); let all these herbs save the parsley be put in the cavity of the pie, then get an ounce of the powdered rootlets of leeks, an ounce of powdered anise seed, two ounces of powdered marsh mallows, put the whole in the above cavity, covering them well with dough; this pie being put in a hot oven for the time required for bread, and baked well, should be taken out, divided in four parts, put in an earthen pot of sufficient capacity whilst still hot, and two gallons of

---

* Dianthus Caryophylus or Clove Pink.

strong old ale, racked carefully from the lees poured thereon ; cover the vessel carefully, and leave it to macerate for a night, and from henceforth drink a fair quantity of the same three times a day, morning, noon, and night. This potion will prove a more effective diuretic to thee than anything else, a little broom ash being mixed therewith. Let it be drank as directed, and it will preserve thee from the dropsy, for it is proven.

THE WAY TO PREPARE BROOM ASH, WHICH IS EXCEEDINGLY USEFUL FOR DROPSY AND STRANGURY, BEING MIXED WITH DRINK OF LIKE NATURE, OR MADE INTO A CONFECTION WITH HONEY, OR INTO BOLUSES ; NO LESS THAN FOUR OF THE BOLUSES, OR AN EQUAL QUANTITY OF CONFECTION BEING TAKEN NIGHT AND MORNING.

§ 514. Take a large sheet of iron, or a bake-stone, heat it to a red heat, and put fresh broom (in full seed is best) thereon, turning them about well, that they may so burn, as to afford you a sixpenny cupful of ashes. The vessel in which it is kept should be covered carefully, so that no air can get into it or from it ; when it is required, let a spoonful thereof be taken mixed with a good draught of strong old ale, good old mead, or good white wine.

FOR ACUTE ERYSIPELAS ATTENDED WITH SWELLING, HEAT, AND BURNING IN A JOINT OR OTHER MEMBER.

§ 515. Take barley meal, and well made butter, moderately salted as if for eating, mix them together gradually in equal portions, and keep in a clean well covered vessel as long as you wish. Let some of this be spread on a cloth or linen and applied to the affected part ; should it ferment it ought to be worked with a wooden spatula, or if it becomes hard, tempered with white of eggs ; from the use of it you will recover through God's help. It is proven.

FOR A MALIGNANT ERUPTION.

§ 516. Take glass, powder and mix with black soap, then apply frequently to the part, and it will certainly heal it.

FOR ANY STIFF OR SWOLLEN ERYSIPELAS OF AN ACUTE NATURE BEGINNING IN A MAN'S LIMBS OR BACK.

§ 517. Take hemlock, mudwort, marsh mallows, red fennel, and the flowers of the water lily if you can obtain them,

3 D

or if not the common mallow, bruise them between your hands, and boil in the urine of the sick person for a long time, then put some unsalted butter therein, and boil briskly, remove from the fire and wash the affected part therewith whilst hot ; apply the herbs also as a plaster thereto on a cloth, leaving them a night; then warm again and apply thereto a second time, and continue this application till it is cured. The patient's own water is better than that of another man least he should be diseased, and the use thereof will certainly cure him.

## FOR THE ITCH ON A MAN, BEING A WATER THAT WILL CURE IT ON WHATEVER PART OF THE BODY IT BE.

§ 518. Take a bottle full of pure water, and put in a clean vessel on the fire, then take some aloes and an ounce of sulphate of copper, adding it to the water, boiling it well and removing it from the fire to clear; afterwards put it in an earthen pot and cover it well. When wanted, warm some thereof, and wash the part with a cloth. It will cure you and dry the eruption, so that it will fade away.

## FOR PARALYSIS.

§ 519. Take a few bay leaves, wild sage, wild strawberries, brookweed, the leaves of honeysuckle, and rosemary, pound them. in a mortar separately, mix with lard, divide into small balls, put in an earthen pot for ten days, then in a pan, bruising them well, warm them over the fire mixed with May butter or animal oil, and strain whilst hot through a cloth. It should be kept in a glass vessel and warmed by the fire when about to be used, which should be night and morning; by God's help it will cure the patient. It is proven.

## FOR THE GOUT, CHARACTERIZED BY SWELLING AND AGONISING PAIN IN THE JOINTS, FEET, HANDS, AS WELL AS THE STOMACH, THIGHS, AND THE HEAD, INDUCED BY THE DESICCATION ON THE HUMOURS INTO A CALCAREOUS EARTH. THIS COMPLAINT IS CALLED Arthritis* IN LATIN.

§ 520. Take the juice of tansy and clarified honey, equal parts of each ; if the complaint be hot, fry the ingredients

---

* " Gout (remarks Good) is one of the maladies which seems to have been common to England in its earliest ages of barbarism. It is frequently noticed

in a pan, keep carefully (but if cold, then let the remedy be also cold) and spread on a fine flannel, and let it be applied to the painful part. It is a good and proven remedy, as I can witness, for a woman lay bed ridden for four years of this disease, and she was restored in a month by the use of this remedy.

### ANOTHER REMEDY.

§ 521. Take a portion of rue, of coarse salt, of the white and yolk of an egg, and a little black soap; let the rue and salt be bruised together in a mortar, the egg and black soap being added thereto, mixing the whole well together. Apply it as a plaster to the affected part, and it will be cured.

### ANOTHER FOR THE SAME DISEASE.

§ 522. Get one or two onions, and roast thoroughly before the fire, then get some blessed distillation,* and put it over the fire in a retort, then bruise the onions small, and boil in the blessed distillation for a while, straining them into a dish through a clean cloth; with this let the painful part be anointed night and morning till it is well. Many Physicians state that this is a proven remedy, though such a cheap one.

### FOR THE SAME DISEASE.

§ 523. Take linseed, the lees of wine, and quick lime, equal parts of each, let them have a prolonged boiling, and apply as a plaster to the painful part. If the part be hot, let pennywort be bruised fine, and apply thereto; it will reduce the swelling and the heat. It is proven.

### FOR THE SAME DISEASE.

§ 524. Take a handful of sage, a handful of liverwort, and a handful of honeysuckle, boil in a gallon of standing

by the Anglo Saxon historians, and the name assigned it is fot adl, (foot ail.) In the Cottonian MSS. at the British Museum, lib. Vitel c. 3, we have the following prescription, which was once regarded as a specific. 'Take the herb datulus ortulosa, which we call greata cranleac (a species of iris or flag flower,) take the heads of it, and dry them very much, and take thereof a pennyweight and a half, and the pear tree, and the Roman bark, and cummin, and a fourth part of laurel berries; and of the other herbs half a pennyweight of each, and six pepper corns, and grind all to dust, and put two egg shells full of wine; this is a true leach craft. Give it to the man to drink till he be well.' "

* Aqua Benedicta Rulanda.

water till it becomes a quart, wash the painful part therewith, and when you have done washing it, apply the herbs thereto, and by God's help it will be cured.

### ANOTHER FOR THE SAME DISEASE.

§ 525. Take the yolks of three eggs hard baked, and reduce to a powder in a pan on the fire, strain them carefully ; this is an useful ointment for the gout, and for divers others diseases.

### ANOTHER FOR THE SAME DISEASE.

§ 526. Take the juice of pennywort, a little frankincense, the juice of plantain, (if in season) and two spoonfuls of the powder of madder, boil them well together in a gallon of spring water, (but do not let it be over boiled) and anoint the affected member therewith as hot as it can be borne ; let a linen cloth be also dipped in the decoction and applied thereto ; it will cure it.

### A NOBLE PLASTER FOR GOUT IN THE HEAD.

§ 527. Take two handfuls of barley bruised in a mortar, a handful of betony, bruised separately, viii of wine,* and half as much of wort, mix these with the barley and betony till it becomes a thick plaster, spread it on linen, and apply to the painful head as hot as can be borne, from the temporal bones to the middle of the forehead ; it will cure it.

### ANOTHER FOR THE SAME PAIN IN THE HEAD.

§ 528. Take rose water, vervain water, a woman's milk, and the white of an egg, mix together and apply to the head. If there is pain in the eye, drop some therein and it will cure it.

### FOR THE GOUT.

§ 529. Take half a measure of white wine, and of stag's tallow, or when that is not procurable, mutton suet with moderately coarse ground wheat; boil these ingredients till they become thick, take a quantity of garlic, peel carefully, pound well, and add to the former ; beware however that it

---

* See Weights and Measures at the end of the Volume.

be not hot, or the garlic will lose its effect. Mix the whole together, and apply as a plaster between the affected part and the healthy, so that it may attract it till it is cured.

## FOR EVERY KIND OF ACHE.

§ 530. Take tender brambles, sprigs of broom and rue, pound well, being first washed, and temper with oil of olives so as to prepare an ointment, wherewith the affected part should be anointed.

## FOR A COLD 'OR HOT DROPSY.

§ 531. Take anise-seed, and the seed of loveage, called in Latin *Levisticum Vulgaris*,* powder and mix the same with your food and drink. Spikenard of Spain may also be carefully added to that and any other kind of drink.

## A FOMENTATION FOR EITHER A COLD OR HOT DROPSY.

§ 532. Take some sprigs of white bryony, roots of red fennel and herb bennet, boil together in a pot till the herbs settle in the bottom, then pour it into a convenient vessel so that the patient may wash and foment himself therewith. Make also a soup with water cresses, and pork or mutton boiled together, giving it colour with saffron; this is useful through Jesus for all kinds of dropsies, whether hot or cold.

## FOR BLEEDING PILES.

§ 533. Get some blessed distillation of the best sort,† and dip a piece of fine soft linen therein, and push it up the rectum as far as you can, if the piles be internal; if external, let them be washed with the distillation for three or four days, at bed time.

## FOR THE SAME.

§ 534. Take viper's bugloss, and the leaves of the barberry tree, and pound together, forming them into small balls. Put a pan containing burning charcoal under a commode, casting the balls thereon, and let the patient sit well covered over the same.

* Ligusticum levisticum.
† Spirit of wine.

### ANOTHER.

§ 535. Let the patient sit in a chair over a hot foment-taton, composed of mallows, marsh pennywort, and cow's milk.

### FOR THE COLIC.

§ 536. Boil mugwort, spear-mint, dill seed, and fennel seed, in equal parts of milk and water, then drink a good draught thereof as hot as you can, and another draught when quite cold, using no other drink than water, and living by rule, rejecting butter, fat meat, and good ale. Dine upon mutton, and sup and breakfast upon the milk of kine or goats, with well baked wheaten bread. A good potion for this disease is finely powdered unburnt lime, a small spoonful thereof being taken at a time in milk and water.

### THE FOLLOWING IS A GOOD METHOD OF TREATMENT FOR A PERSON SUBJECT TO FREQEUNT ATTACKS OF COLIC.

§ 537. Two hours before breakfast every morning take a good slice of wheaten bread, made with the best barm, and toast brown and crisp before the fire, but be careful not to burn it ; eat this by itself, and do not drink anything after it. If you eat meat reject the fat, and prefer mutton to any other, well baked oven barm bread being used with it. You should only drink water or milk and water with your meals, habituating yourself to oaten cakes and gruels, with milk or honey, wine or cider, all garden vegetables being avoided. House fennel seed, caraway seed, and dill seed, ground also with your bread wheat, avoiding butter, pork, (particularly if old,) rich cheese, goose' flesh and duck.

### FOR AN ABCESS OR IMPOSTUME.

§ 538. Take cow's milk, linseed, and a few garlic, pound-ed ; boil them together, make into a plaster, and apply to the part.

### A WATER FOR ALL SORTS OF GOUT.

§ 539. Procure the seed of eringo, fill an earthen pot thereof, covering it very carefully, and bury it fully half a

yard in the earth, where it should be left from the first
Lady-day in harvest time, till the last Lady-day in spring;
it should then be opened, and you will find some clear water
in the pot; keep this carefully in a glass vial, for it is most
useful for all sorts of gout.

### TO CLEAR THE EYE.

§ 540. Obtain some fresh sprats, lay in the sun, or at
such a distance from a fire as will subject them to a like
heat till an oil exudes therefrom; mix this oil with honey,
and anoint your eye therewith.

### FOR A WATERY EYE.

§ 541. Take the leaves of red cabbage, and hen's fat, compound together thoroughly, and cover the eye therewith at
night, securing the same with a bandage.

### FOR PAIN IN THE EYE.

§ 542. Procure some of the juice of centaury, and of
celandine, boil them together, and apply the same to the eye.

### TO REMOVE EXFOLIATIONS OF BONE FROM THE SKULL.

§ 543. Drink the juice of betony three times a day fasting, the dose being three spoonfuls each time, and they will
come away.

### FOR A CANCER.

§ 544. Take knap-weed and goat's feet, calcine in furnace,
reduce to a powder, and apply to the cancer.

### FOR A GOUT, ATTENDED BY AN OFFENSIVE SUPPURATION.

§ 545. Procure the juice of bugle, and of ribwort plantain,
the white of an egg, mouse ear chickweed, and fine rye meal,
which make into a plaster, let this be applied upon the part
daily, being secured by a linen cloth, and it will cure it.

### FOR A BOIL

§ 546. Get some plantain, make a plaster and apply to
the part. It will cure it.

### FOR AN ABCESS OR IMPOSTUME OF THE HEAD, WITH DEAFNESS.

§ 547. Take wood sage well pounded and oil of almonds, boil and mix well in a silver spoon on the embers, then take some clean linen, give it a twist, dip in the ointment and insert in the painful ear, binding it till the matter is discharged. It is proven.

### TO EXTRACT A TOOTH BY MEANS OF A POWDER.

§ 548. Take the roots of nightshade with black berries,* and pound them well in goat's milk, then add the black berries separately pounded thereto, incorporate the whole into a pulp, and macerate in vinegar for xiii days; renew the vinegar three days, then powder the residue and add vinegar thereto for three times more, when this has cleared, decant the vinegar, and dry the sediment in the sun or near the fire in the like heat. Let the powder be put in the tooth if there be a cavity therein, and it will extract it without pain, and without delay.

### FOR HEADACHE AND WHOOPING COUGH.

§ 549. Take a red onion, pound small with a little bile, adding some honey thereto. Let this be boiled, and when boiled, let the patient † be put on his back, and pour some to his nostrils; then let him get up and sneeze, when he will be cured and eased.

### TO MAKE A CERECLOTH.

§ 550. Take two ounces of cod oil, two ounces of pitch, two ounces and a quarter of mastic, and an ounce of frankincense; mix them well together, and set on the fire, taking a quantity of plantain juice, and mixing therewith. Put the cloth in this molten fluid, so that it may absorb as much as possible thereof. Then set it aside to cool, warming it by the fire, when required, for a bruise or other injury on a man's body.

* Solanum nigrum.

..† "Y dynn ai dorr, &c."

## A METHOD OF MAKING A PLASTER ACCORDING TO ART, THOUGH TO CRUDE FOR INFLAMED ULCERS.

§ 551. Take smallage, senna, the roots of the lily, of the nightshade, (called morel,) and of the plantain ; let these be pounded very small, honey, clarified white of eggs, and fine meal being added thereto. Let them be carefully compounded, and mashed together, (not on the fire mind,) till they become thick like porridge ; spread on a cloth, and apply to the wound. It will remove the anguish, and restore the wound to its natural condition. This is the most excellent of plasters for all sorts of injuries.

## TO PREPARE A GOOD RESOLVENT APPLICATION TO REMOVE BLOOD OR BRUISE FROM AN INJURY.

§ 552. Take old bacon, melt in a pan, and let it stand till the salt settles in the bottom ; then take virgin wax in equal quantity, and frankincense in powder, melting and mixing them well with lard. When it has somewhat cooled, take a moderate quantity of mastic and frankincense, setting it on the fire again, and mixing well. When cold, add as much again of flour of sulphur to the frankincense, and mastic, mixing them well and diligently, till the whole resembles honey. Let it be kept in a box till required.

## TO PREVENT TEETH BECOMING YELLOW AND ILL SMELLING.

§ 553. Take the leaves of sage, powder with as much again of salt, and make it into balls. Bake them till they are burnt, and powder. Let your teeth be rubbed frequently therewith. It will render the teeth clean, white, and sweet.

## FOR CANCER.

§ 554. Take quick lime, pepper, horse mint, strong bile, honey, and barley meal, equal parts of each. Boil them well in an earthen vessel, powder, and apply to the cancer ; it will destroy it.

## ANOTHER.

§ 555. Take quick lime powdered, red precipitate of mercury, equal to a fourth part of the lime in quantity, and mix with as much honey as will make it into a mass. Put it in an earthen crucible, in a furnace, heated as for bread. When cold, keep it carefully covered in a glass vial, and apply as much as may be required upon the cancer. It will completely destroy it. Then apply a detergent plaster to the ulcer; when quite clean, dress it with healing salve or lint, and it will cure the patient.

### FOR DROPSY BETWEEN THE FLESH AND SKIN.*

§ 556. Take the parings of white sheep skins, boil until they become a glutinous mass, and apply thereto on linen.

### TO BREAK OR RE-OPEN ANY GATHERING.

§ 557. Take a portion of black soap, another of honey, and a third of fine wheaten meal, incorporate them together, and apply to the part. If you wish it to break quickly, add much soap.

### FOR MALIGNANT ST. ANTHONY'S FIRE, OF WHICH, IF A MAN SICKEN, HE WILL MOST PROBABLY DIE.†

§ 558. Take the warm dung of a pigeon,‡ and rye meal, a pound of each, pound together, and add thereto half a pound of vinegar, mix well, and apply cold to the diseased part, covering it with cabbage leaves, and binding the same carefully with a linen cloth. Let it not be removed for three days, and what is covered with the plaster, will be at any rate cured.

### FOR THE GOUT.

§ 559. Take wood sorrel, rue, agrimony, tansy, pimpernel, celandine, avens, ivy leaves, and ground liver wort, in equal parts; pound together well, strain, and drink the strained liquor. It is good.

### TO PREPARE AN OINTMENT FOR THE GOUT.

§ 560. Take the lard of a young pig, a horse's fat, a boar's lard, and the herb called feverfew, or in Latin *febrifuga*, pounded well. Mix them well together, and set on the fire till they boil, and when boiled till the virtue of the

---

* Ascites.     † Erysipelas Phlegmonoides.     ‡ Just killed.

herbs is extracted, strain, keeping the ointment in a glass well covered, and anoint the painful part by the heat of a fire.

### ANOTHER.

§ 561. Take wall cress, southernwood, sage, and as much as an egg of sugar; half fill a glass vessel with the same, and then fill up quite with salt.' The herbs should be pounded well in old ale, the vessel being left in the sun for a week, or near the fire in a like heat, and you will obtain an ointment therefrom, which should be kept carefully. Anoint the painful part therewith, then get wheat bran, white wine, and boar's lard; boil them together, and make into a plaster, applying the same as warm as it can be suffered to the swelling. This application will disperse it.

### ANOTHER.

§ 562. Take black snails, and bake them before the fire in an earthen vessel. Keep the oil in a clean vessel, and anoint the painful part therewith. It is beneficial for hot and cold gout.

### ANOTHER.

§ 563. Take pitch, virgin wax, frankincense, mutton suet, and boar's lard. Fry well together, strain, and keep in a pot; with this anoint the painful part.

### AN USEFUL OINTMENT FOR ERUPTIONS AND WOUNDS.

§ 464. Take the fat of bacon, melt and let the salt settle in the bottom; then take the fat, and add pitch, and frankincense, making an ointment thereof. Let it be applied as may be required.

### AN OINTMENT FOR A HEADACHE.

§ 565. Take the juice of dwarf elder, honey, wax, salt and frankincense, boil them together. With this anoint your head and brows.

### FOR THE GOUT IN THE STOMACH.

§ 566. Take a handful of tansy, pound the same, pour a quart of bottled wine thereon, and let it stand well covered for a night in an oaken vessel; then put it in an unglazed earthen vessel, boil gently, and strain. Let three draughts be taken thereof, one each night for three nights, the patient being covered well in bed afterwards, so that he may perspire, and this will cure him. It is well to sleep in flannel sheets or blankets.

### ANOTHER.

§ 567. Take an armful of tansy, of mallows, of wormwood, half as much of garden sage and rosemary; boil the same well in a pot, put a pound of salt in the water, and pour out the decoction into a vessel large enough to bathe in. Get in, and sit therein so that it may cover your ancles, then cover yourself with blankets, so that you may be kept in a full perspiration for two or three hours, adding more hot liquid as may be required, so as to keep up the heat. Drink three table spoonfuls of good old mead, mixed with powdered fennel seed, every half hour; then at the end of the time specified, let the bath cool, and when it is no warmer than new milk, get out, go to bed and cover yourself well with blankets, taking a spoonful every hour of the decoction of blessed thistle, for six hours, carefully avoiding cold for some days.

### PAIN IN THE JOINTS FROM COLD, WEARINESS, OR SPRAIN.

.§ 568. Take sea weed, boil in sea water, and anoint the painful part with the same, as hot as you can bear it; then apply the boiled sea weed thereto, well pounded in the manner of a plaster, as warm as it can be borne easily. This is a good remedy for every painful swelling, resulting from a fall or blow.

### FOR THE WHOOPING COUGH.

§ 569. Take pig's lard, powdered garlick, and a little honey, boil well, and anoint the feet of the patient therewith; then cover the feet with a flannel, and the bed in which the patient must lie with an abundance of blankets. The blankets should be removed when he has perspired freely, and the patient will certainly recover.

## FOR THE CANCER.

§ 570. Apply the juice of red onions to the ulcer, and make a plaster with the leaves of cow parsnip, stalks, flowers, and seed included, compounding the same with honey, vinegar, and a little frankincense.

## FOR INFLAMMATION OF THE LUNGS.*

§ 571. Take elder flowers, or in their absence, eringo flowers, or the leaves, or the green inner bark, and wood sorrel; boil in the whey of goat or kine's milk, and let it be your only drink for nine weeks. So that you may not be in want of the flowers, let them be gathered in their season, and dried in the sun. Keep them and boil them in the whey as required. When wood sorrel cannot be got, boil bruised apples with the flowers in the whey. This is useful for all sorts of fevers in the blood and humors.

## FOR A COLD.

§ 572. Take a pound of garlick, and pound well, adding thereto a quart of good bottled wine, or in the absence thereof good strong old mead; let it macerate well covered, strain under a press, and drink lukewarm. If the cold affects a joint, warm the remains of the garlick and apply to the part as warm as it can be borne. It is proven.

## FOR A WEB OF THE EYE.

§ 573. Take the juice of celandine, and a little honey, mix well and apply to the eye with a feather night and morning. It is proven.

## FOR THE BLACK FEVER.†

§ 574. Take anise-seed, fennel seed, and rue well powdered, to which add good white or bottled wine; let it stand six hours, and when given to the patient, give it a slight boiling, so that no time be lost, then strain and let it be given to the sick person as his only drink.

## ANOTHER.

§ 575. Take the surface of new ale in the wort, and administer a good draught to the sick person every three

---

* *Lit.* Lung Pock.      † Typhus.

hours, for twenty four hours; then let him have a slice of wheaten barm bread toasted by the fire, wine being poured upon it whilst hot. This bread and wine should be taken in small portions during four hours. It is proven.

### FOR A BRUISE OF THE EYE.

§ 576. Take parsley and pound well with unsalted butter, then apply it as a plaster to the eye warm.

### FOR SPECKS ON THE CORNEA.

§ 577. Take the juice of celandine, of fennel, and a little honey, let some be dropped into the eye morning, noon, and night, the eye being covered in the mean time so that the light might not affect it. Proven.

### FOR VERTIGO.

§ 578. Take the roots of cowslips, and sage leaves, in equal quantities, boil well, the roots being first pounded. The boiling should be carried on till the herbs are hardly covered, when they should be strained under a press; a good draught thereof should be taken two hours before and two hours after food.

### FOR A SUNBURN.

§ 579. Take the leaves of marsh pennywort rudely pounded with cream, boil them together on a gentle fire so as to form them into an ointment, and anoint the affected part therewith.

### A GOOD EYE SALVE.

§ 580. Take vinegar, white wine, the juice of celandine, and plantain, mix them together in a pan, cover over and let them stand therein three days and three nights, take it hence, keep it in a box, and anoint thine eye therewith.

### THE TREATMENT OF BOILS AN BLEEDDING SORES.

§ 581. Take the fat of an old boar, half as much of virgin* wax, frankincense and mastic, boil together, and when nearly cold, add as much flour of sulphur, as of the frankincense, then mix for an ointment and keep in a box.

* The wax of honey combs, not *brood* combs.

### FOR AN INDOLENT ULCER.

§ 582. Get frankincense, and arnamentum,* grind together in powder, and apply to the ulcer.

### AN USEFUL UNGUENT.

§ 583. Take plantain, pimpernel, and wild tansy, pound well in a mortar with fresh lard, let it ferment for nine days, when it should be boiled and strained through linen, wax, frankincense, and pure rosin being added thereto; when all are molten together, the unguent is ready.

### AN OINTMENT FOR THE HEADACHE.

§ 584. Take the juice of dwarf elder, new wax, and rosin, boil together, and anoint your temple therewith.

### TO PREPARE A GOOD OINTMENT.

§ 585. Get the juice of wild celery, tansy, nightshade, plantain, and marsh pennywort, equal parts of each; also, honey, fine wheaten meal, boar's lard, and sheep's suet, let them be boiled on the fire till the mass becomes thick, then strain through linen. It is useful.

### FOR DEFECTIVE SIGHT.

§ 586. Take the juice of ground ivy, fennel, celandine, sow's lard, honey, a little vinegar, an eel's blood, put the whole in a vessel till it ferments, anoint your eyes therewith, it will restore lost sight. Proven.

### FOR PAIN IN THE EYES.

§ 587. Fill an egg shell with the juice of fennel, and rue, clarified honey, wine, and the urine of a child. Anoint your eye therewith.

### AN EYE OINTMENT.

§ 588. Get a black snail in the month of May and roast on the embers, preserving the oil till required; anoint your eye therewith with a feather.

### FOR A STYE IN THE EYE, OR AN INFLAMMATION.

§ 589. Get the yolk of an egg, wheaten meal, and a little sulphate of copper, let it be applied to the eye when going

---

* A corruption of "Auripigmentum," or yellow sulphate of arsenic. It should be used with great caution.

to sleep, it will produce perspiration during the night. Do this three days and it will cure it.

## FOR DEAFNESS.

§ 590. Get a sow's gall, goat's milk, and clear honey, drop it warm in your ears. It is an unfailing remedy.

## FOR A SLOUGH, BEFORE AND AFTER IT HAS SUPPURATED.

§ 591. Take a good handful of sage, half a handful of plantain, and the same quantity of red fennel, let them be boiled in a quart of water, a quart of honey, (or two quarts of water would be better so that it may stand a longer boiling,) and a pound weight of white frankincense, let it be boiled long and well, so that it be reduced to a third. Let it be kept, and the herbs simply bruised between your hands be left therein, in a vessel. It is a good water to foment any cancer, dead flesh, *(slough,)* painful swelling, or blistered, inflamed, or painful part. By God's help it will cure it.

## FOR AN INDOLENT ULCER OF RÉCENT STANDING, WHEN YOU WISH TO DESTROY THE UNHEALTHY GRANULATIONS.

§ 592. Get honey, treacle, frankincense, sulphur, white-lead, and mercury, make them into a plaster, apply to the part frequently and it will heal it, if not, let a plaster of honey and black soot be applied thereto, and this by the help of God will cure it.

## A SLEEPING POTION.

§ 593. Take the juice of opium, (poppy) and of eringo, or the seed of the latter, compound them into pills with milk, let these be ministered to the patient. One will induce sleep in general, but if not let him take another, and another again if required, taking care that two or three hours should intervene between each dose in order to watch their effect before another is given.

## FOR AN ERUPTION OF TETTERS.*

§ 594. Take lard, black soap, and mercury, rub them together into an ointment, anointing the affected part therewith, and it will be healed.

* Herpes.

### FOR RINGWORM.*

§ 595. Take toadstool,† or (when not to be had) agaric, red alder leaves,‡ and clarified butter; boil them together in sheep's milk and strain through new linen, anoint the part frequently with this, and with God's help you will be cured.

### FOR CRUSTED§ OR HUMID ‖ TETTER.

§ 596. Take the roots of red dock, and boil in sheep's milk for two hours at least, remove from the fire and add some clarified butter thereto, straining it through new linen, anoint the diseased part with this ointment, and it will heal it.

### FOR SCABIES.

§ 597. Take the white of an egg, strained rapidly through linen, the juice of red fennel and celandine, clear honey, a child's urine, and white wine in equal parts ; mix briskly and anoint your body therewith, even your eyes if needful.

### FOR LEPRA.

§ 598. Get the roots of the red dock, the roots of the elecampane, honey-suckle leaves, wild hyacinth, broom sprigs, bugle, violet, heath shieldfern, and avens ; pound them well together in a mortar with unsalted butter, boiling them well, removing from the fire and straining through new linen ; add thereto a portion of flour of brimstone and verdigris. Anoint the diseased part frequently with this ointment, and by God's help it will cure it.

### FOR RINGWORM,¶ BEING A DISEASE SOMEWHAT LIKE HUMID TETTER, ATTENDED WITH MUCH IRRITATION.

§ 599. Take crude honey, a fox's marrow, and rosin, mix well together by pounding them in a mortar till they become an ointment, anoint the disease therewith.

### FOR BOILS.

§ 600. Take the juice of the nightshade,* and of plantain, barley meal, and the white of eggs, make a plaster thereof and apply thereto.

" Favus.        | Doletus.        ‡ When changing their hue in autumn.        § Impetigo.
‖ Eczema.        ¶ Favus.        * *Moriel* in the text must be intended for morella, i. e. nightshade.

3 F

### ANOTHER.

§ 601. Take feverfew, knapweed, mugwort, bugle, devil's bit, and daisy; wash clean, and pound with old ale; a spoonful at a time should be given to the patient, and if given in time it will ever preserve him from the complaint. This is an excellent potion.

### FOR AN INTRACTABLE PAIN.

§ 602. Drink the juice of tansy, pounded carefully with strong old ale, and strained.

### FOR A PAIN OF THE THROAT WHEN THERE IS AN ERUPTION,* OR SUPPURATION IN THE PHARYNX, ATTENDED WITH A FEVER.

§ 603. Boil sage and rue in water, when it has boiled a a little while add vinegar and honey so that it may be somewhat sweet ; then gargle your mouth and throat therewith warm, ejecting the same carefully, so that none be swallowed. When you have gargled well, drink a good draught of the same as a potion; do this for three or four times in the day and night. Take also equal parts of mallows, sage and rue, pounding the same well, and adding thereto sheep's milk, or any other milk covenient, as much as may be needful to give it the consistency of a cataplasm ; let this be applied warm to the throat, changing it as it dries, keep dissolving in your mouth also as much twice in quantity as a nut of pure old honey boiled hard. Do this for three days, and by God's help you will recover.

### ANOTHER.

§ 604. Take sage, rue, and the berries † or flowers of the elder tree (or inner bark when neither can be got,) mallows and feverfew, put them in a mortar mixed with a little honey, white wine, or vinegar, pounding them well together, let a portion of the pounded ingredients be applied warm to the throat as a plaster on flannel, the other portion being strained, two table spoonfuls of the same being taken every two hours, and a spoonful used as a gargle before each dose, this being afteswards carefully ejected, so that none be swal-

---

* Diptheria    † *Lit.* " Gems," a beautiful term for these ruby like berries.

owed, as it would be charged with the poison of the disease. Instead of using the plaster you may foment your throat with the liquid each time you drink. Do this for three days; keeping a flannel about your throat, and with God's help you will recover.

### ANOTHER.

§ 605. Boil rue in white wine, strain and drink four spoonfuls thereof every three hours, fomenting the throat (covering it afterwards with a flannel) at every dose. Before each dose gargle your mouth and throat carefully with the decoction and vinegar, half and half, ejecting the same afterwards. By God's help you will recover in consequence.

### ANOTHER.

§ 606. Take a large apple, extract the eye and core as well as some of the pulp, then take rue, bruise small, filling the apple therewith, and covering it over with the eye first removed, roast the apple before the fire, when sufficiently roasted, pound the whole together, mixing a little honey therewith, also a spoonful of white wine, making a confection thereof; take a spoonful of this every two hours till you have recovered. Before you take it, however, you should wash the mouth and throat with a decoction of rue and vinegar in equal proportions.

### THE FOLLOWING IS A GOOD GARGLE.

§ 607. Take sage, rue, mallows, and elder flowers, either fresh or dry, boil them well in water, then when you have done so for a while, add a spoonful of vinegar, and as much of honey, continuing the boiling some time longer, then strain carefully through a linen cloth and keep; when required for use, warm from two to four spoonfuls, take a mouthful thereof and gargle well as long as you can, taking care not to swallow any, then finally eject it; do this from twice to four times with a spoonful at a time. It is useful for every affection of the mouth and throat, and should be used in all dangerous seasons, when epidemic sore throats prevail, this with God's blessing will preserve you. When you have a sore throat, after gargling, take a draught of the potion, and by God's help it will benefit you.

### FOR INFLAMMATORY FEVER IN A CHILD.

§ 608. Boil a handful of cinquefoil in cow's milk, and administer a spoonful to the child every hour for three days; by God's help it will cure him.

### TO DESTROY UNHEALTHY GRANULATIONS IN AN ULCER RESULTING FROM A WOUND OR BLOW.

§ 609. Take old tallow, stale gander's dung, a crust of rye bread, egg shells, and salt, in equal parts, put them in a pot, calcine and reduce into fine powder, and apply thereto.

### ANOTHER.

§ 610. Take a pound weight of burnt lime, and the same quantity of orpiment, boil in water in a porringer for a great length of time, then remove from the fire and set aside to dry where no dirt can come to it, then when it is perfectly dry let it be reduced to a powder. If some of this is applied to the unhealthy granulations it will destroy them. It should be left upon the part from one to three hours, and then washed away with sheep's milk, or with cow or goat's milk, when that cannot be procured; this should be done once a day till you see that the cancer is destroyed, then dress the part with healing ointment, the patient all the time using no other drink than a decoction of cleavers * and betony, restricting himself to a milk diet, preferring that of goat's, twice a week he should partake of mutton of mature age.

### FOR A WOUND.

§ 611. Take a nettle, roots and all, wash the roots clean, pound it well, then boil in unsalted butter, make an ointment, apply to the wound and it will cure it.

### THE TREATMENT OF WOUNDS.

§ 612. Take lard, honey, wine, and rye meal, boil these ingredients together, and apply to the wound on a cloth, it

---

* This is admirable practice so far as this diet drink is concerned at any rate.

will clear and heal the wound, but should it do so too soon, procure the herb called wild nep,* make a plaster thereof, apply it to the part and it will re-open it.

## ERYSIPELAS.

Erysipelas has divers constitutions even hot and cold, the hot being the most dangerous of the two, and is attended with more extensive ardency,† the cold being less so; in consequence of this they must be treated differently, the hot requiring cold remedies, and the cold hot ones: thus the cold form is treated; this disease being *(lancole?)* take the white of eggs, and rye meal, make a dough of them and leave it on the part till it falls away of itself. Let this be done till the part is healed.

## A MEDICAMENT FOR PUTRID FLESH, ATTENDED WITH LOCAL INFLAMMATION IN AND ABOUT THE ULCERS.

§ 613. Take fine rye meal and clear honey, of which make a dough and apply to the ulceration; when required let it be renewed, and this will restore the patient to health and activity.

### A GENERAL REMEDY FOR ALL KINDS OF ERYSIPELAS.

§ 614. Take tow and cut it fine, wash in lees procured from wheat ale, boil well and apply to the affected part for a night and half a day, let it then be removed and the part washed with male urine; afterwards cover it with a powder thus prepared:—take some wings of geese, pluck off the feathers, calcine them, powder and apply to the disease, this again should be covered with the fat of a wild cat, or pig's lard and a cabbage leaf, then get some good old ale made with wheat unmixed with barley, fill a pitcher therewith, add salt, arfemeint ‡ and pitch in equal parts with more bees wax than either; boil them till they become thick, then remove from the fire and let it cool,

---

* Nep wyllt—Rape, or brassica *napus.* Vide NEPTE, in the list of the medicinal plants at the end.

† i. e. Inflammatory. It may be a question what sense " ffroenau " has in the text, I have assumed it to be derived from " ffro "—ardent, as erysipelas never exhibits any character to which the term " nostrils " (ffroenau) could be applied in any way

‡ A popular corruption of " orpiment," I believe.

this should be applied as a plaster thereto; first the above mentioned powder, then the plaster of fat, and the cabbage leaf upon that; it should be renewed morning and night. Let an infusion or decoction of avens be given the patient, and in the day he drinks thereof, the progress of the disease will be arrested.

### ANOTHER.

§ 615. Take the juice of the avens, of mallows, and lin seed, mix with honey and the milk of a one coloured cow, put in a pitcher, boil it well and apply to the disease as hot as it can be borne.

### ANOTHER.

§ 616. Powder pepper and boil in vinegar till it is quite dried up, then mix powdered frankincense, rosin, verdigris, and honey therewith; incorporate them well in a mortar, and apply on a cloth to the affected part.

### A MEDICINE FOR PAIN IN THE BONES, SOMETIMES ATTENDING ERYSIPELAS.

§ 617. Put the seed of eryngo in an earthen pitcher, cover it over with the embers so that it may roast thoroughly, express carefully through a linen cloth, and with this strained liquid anoint the disease. If you can not get the seed take the entire plant, roots and all, and treat in the same way.

### ANOTHER.

§ 618. Get oil of roses and anoint the part therewith, then infuse sage and hyssop in wine, or mix the juice of these herbs with wine; let the patient drink the same till he recovers.

### ANOTHER.

§ 619. Take white peas and roast them well on the fire, then powder, anoint the part with clear honey, and sprinkle the powder thereon, let it remain till it falls off spontaneously; let this be repeated till the part heals.

### FOR A PAINFUL ERYSIPELAS ATTENDED WITH SWELLING.

§ 620. Take the roots of fern, and pound them in a mortar well, mix carefully with a little warm water, then express through a cloth, and make it into a poultice with barley meal, mixing the white of an egg therewith; spread it thinly on a cloth, and apply it to the affected part.

### AN APPLICATION TO A PAIN, WHICH WILL SHOW WHETHER IT PROCEEDS FROM BRUISED FLESH OR CONTUSION.

§ 621. Anoint the whole of the affected part with honey, and get fresh cheese and rye meal, put these ingredients in the earth for a night, then apply it to the openings in the painful part. When you remove this plaster next day, if there are holes therein, know that there is a worm in the ulcer.

### ANOTHER.

§ 622. Take a black snail and apply to the part, and if you find a portion of the snail eaten next day, know that there is a worm therein.

### THE WAY IN WHICH THE WORM MAY BE DESTROYED.

§ 623. Take the root of the gladwin, and bruise in honey and wine, apply a black snail to the part, and cover it with the above plaster, and it will destroy the worm.

### ANOTHER.

§ 624. Take pepper, rue, linseed, and feverfew, dry these three last, powder and apply to the part; it will destroy the worm.

### AN APPLICATION FOR A BITE, OR A SUPPURATING ULCER, EVEN WHEN IT IS A CANCER.

§ 625. Take marsh pennywort, powder and cover the part therewith.

### ANOTHER,

§ 626. Take old lard, quicksilver, frankincense, mastic, and a little pepper, bruise these ingredients separately, then mix and incorporate with the lard when cold, then rub the quicksilver therewith till it is killed, anoint the part therewith by the fire.

### ANOTHER.

§ 627. Take a little of the juice of the bloody veined dock, the juice of the avens, the juice of the field mint, a little of the juice of the marsh mallow, and the juice of the plantain, put them in a pan on the fire with lard, and form an ointment thereof, anoint the diseased part therewith, it will cure it.

Amongst all dangerous diseases which are to be dreaded, mortified flesh and cancer are the worst, and by careful treatment only can they be cured, not otherwise.

### FOR ALL KINDS OF MORBID FLESH OR ERYSIPELAS EVEN.

§ 628. Take wheat grain, hen's dung, black beans, garlick, salt, goat's dung, horse bones and fragments of blue cloth, put them in a pot, cover carefully, set on the fire and leave there till the whole are calcined, mix it with as much as there is of pepper, of powder of white glass and garlick, wash the part with vinegar and stale urine night and morning, covering it with the powder afterwards. It will heal it.

Cover the powder with goats' dung and butter, also take water-flag and new wax, cover the parts with the powder, and apply the wax over it. When the venom is extracted, dress it with the juice of plantain, honey, white of eggs, and rye meal, drink the juice of plantain, avens, and agrimony.

Let the patient avoid cheese, nuts, and women, then he will recover.

### FOR THE SAME THING.

§ 629. Take a mole and burn it in an earthen pot till it is reduced to powder, powder finely, and cover the part where the mortified flesh is with this powder. Take hartwort and knapweed ground in a mortar carefully, adding some honey and butter, make the whole into a plaster and apply it to the part, it will destroy the dead flesh and the disease.

Sprinkle sage powder thereon, it will bind it and cure it.

### FOR THE SAME THING.

§ 630. Take gum sandarach, frankincense, copperas, natron, and verdigris, powder carefully and sprinkle thereon, leave it there two or three days, then cover the part well with agrimony carefully pounded with honey, clean and dress carefully twice daily and it will cure it.

If you can not get the above, seek some soot, the ashes of old shoes, and stale urine, mix well and apply thereto so that it may remove the disease, then treat it with agrimony and honey as above.

### FOR THE CANCER.

§ 631. Take copperas and pepper, bruise them together, and temper with white of eggs and honey; when it has cleared on the fire, anoint the cancerous part well.

### FOR THE CANCER.

§ 632. Powder white frankincense, and apply thereon.

### FOR A FOUL BREATH.

§ 633. Take the juice of orpine, feverfew, angelica, and pennyroyal, mix with honey, and administer a spoonful to the patient night and morning fasting, and he will recover.

### FOR A PERSON WHO HAS LOST CONSCIOUSNESS OR SPEECH, IN CONSEQUENCE OF ILLNESS.

§ 634. Take pennyroyal gathered on Whit-sunday, or the eve of St. John the Baptist, boil, dry the decoction, and make a powder thereof; let this powder be administered to the patient in some drink, and it will be of benefit.

### FOR AN OFFENSIVE ULCER ON THE LEG.

§ 635. Boil oak leaves in white or red wine, and apply the wine and leaves to the part, and it will be of use.

### ANOTHER.

§ 636. Take oil of olives, and white wine, mix well, anoint the ulcer therewith, it will remove the evil smell, and heal the disease.

### TO HASTEN A TEDIOUS LABOUR.

§ 637. Take the juice of savory, and administer it in water.

### TO RESTRAIN HŒMORRHAGE FROM AN ULCER OR WOUND, OR FROM WHATEVER OTHER CAUSE.

§ 638. Take nettles, pound well, and pour vinegar thereon, apply this to the wound, but beware lest the patient

3 G

should faint; if he does so, anoint his eyebrows with vinegar, and give him some drink.

### FOR UTERINE HŒMORRHAGE.

§ 639. Take nut shells, powder finely, then make a decoction of the inner bark of the black thorn, adding a little honey, mix the powder therewith, and let it be the only drink for a month or two if required.

### FOR A PAINFUL CONDITION OF THE MOUTH.

§ 640. Take a spoonful of the juice of sage, of the juice of rue, of white wine or vinegar, and of honey, and mix them; let the patient first wash his mouth with salt and water, then let him take a spoonful at a time of the above mentioned liquor in his mouth, and gargle it well, but let him have a care not to swallow it, but eject it; then he should take another mouthful and swallow it, and it will cure him; let him repeat this proceeding again and again till he recovers. It is a valuable remedy for dangerous affections (of the mouth and throat.)

### TO PRESERVE FROM DANGEROUS EPIDEMICS.

§ 641. When dangerous epidemics prevail, take the juice of rue, and white wine, or strong old mead in equal parts, and drink a spoonful or two, morning, noon, and night in going to rest, at least an hour before or after food.

### ANOTHER.

§ 642. Take a handful of rue, four heads of garlick, and a handful of sage, pound them together with wine or strong mead, and strain carefully; drink four spoonfulls thereof every morning fasting as long as the epidemic prevails.

### A GOOD CATHARTIC.

§ 643. Take a spoonful of the juice of spurge, mixed with powdered frankincense; it is beneficial to the chest and stomach.

### ANOTHER.

§ 644. Take a spoonful of the juice of hyssop, and boil in a quart of red wine till it is reduced to the half, let the patient drink it warm at night, and cold in the morning.

## PRO MORBO CADENDO, OR EPILEPTIC DISEASE.

§ 645. Take the mistletoe of the oak, and put in an un-glazed earthen pot, cover it well and set it on a slow fire, but not too near, dry the herb till it can be powdered, being care-ful that it does not burn, reduce to powder and give to the patient in every drink and food he partakes of. Make also à mass as big as a pigeon's egg thereof with honey, and give to the patient between his meals, and continue this practice for nine weeks. It is proven.

### ANOTHER.

§ 646. Gather the mistletoe at Christmas, branches, leaves, and berries, make a confection of the berries with honey in equal parts, and keep well covered. The other portion of the plant should be powdered as above mentioned. And when-ever a person is subject to this disease, mix as much of the powdre with the confection as you can, carefully preserving both from mouldiness. Let the sick person eat a good mouth-ful thereof fasting morning, noon, and night. It is proven.

### FOR CARDIALGIA.

§ 648. Take ash keys, linseed, and a pear, pound together well with white wine, and administer the whole lukewarm to the patient mixed with as much wine as will make it drinkable.

### FOR SWELLING OF THE STOMACH.

§ 549. Take the roots of fennel, and the roots of the ash, pound them well, and temper with wine and honey; let the expressed liquor be given to the patient to drink, and he will recover.

### TO KNOW WHETHER A WOUNDED PERSON WILL LIVE OR DIE.

§ 650. Get pimpernel, milkwort, or trefoil, administer to the patient, and if he vomits he will die. The herbs should be pounded with water, and strained.

### TO HEAL WOUNDS.

§ 651. Get hog's lard, melt it with honey, wine, and rye meal, boil carefully, spread on linen, and apply to the wound; it will draw and cleanse the wound, and heal it effectually.

### TO OPEN A WOUND.

§ 652. Take wild turnips, pound to a plaster, and apply to the wound; it will open the wound and heal it. Proven.

### TO HEAL A WOUND.

§ 653. Take the herb called centaury, powder and cast into the wound ; by God's help it will cure it.

### TO RESTRAIN BLEEDING FROM THE NOSE.

§ 654. Get the periwinkle and hang in a bag about the neck of the patient. Proven.

- Many diseases and fevers of all kinds are bred, and affect the body of man in consequence of the scrophulous diathesis, and they can only be avoided by the use of effective remedies.

### FOR SCROPHULA.

§ 655. Take daisy, and plantain, mix with strong drink till it is thickened thereby, and cast some powdered sulphate of copper on the potion. If this is habitually given the patient ere he sleeps, it will cure him.

### FOR SCROPHULA BEFORE SLEEP.

§ 656. Bruise daisy, yellow stone crop, and plantain, and apply it as a plaster to the complaint ; drink the juice also.

### ANOTHER FOR SCROPHULA.

§ 657. Take the flowers or leaves of knapweed, bruise with the yolk of an egg and fine salt; apply to the part.

### ANOTHER FOR SCROPHULA.

§ 658. Take the roots of the red nettle, and the roots of mugwort, when budding; boil in milk and water, and add butter thereto, drink of this night, morning, and noon, and take no other drink till you are well. Proven.

### FOR A SCROPHULOUS ULCER WHEN IT HAS DISCHARGED ITS CONTENTS, AND INFLAMMATION.

§ 659. Take chamomile, and prepared sulphur in powder ; boil in goats' milk and water, till all moisture has evaporated. Dry, and reduce to fine powder, sprinkling it on the ulcer. This will contract all manner of sores.

### FOR SCROPHULOUS SWELLINGS.

§ 660. Take honey, and white rosin, incorporate them together, and apply to the part.

### FOR FRACTUED BONES.

§ 661. To promote the union of fractured bones, take celandine, and boil with wine, pepper, and honey. Use it nine days as drink, and they will unite.

### MEDICINE FOR FRACTURED BONES.

§ 662. First bind the limb, then take roasted acorns, and powder. Put four spoonfuls of the powder in a quart of milk and water, half and half; boil well, and add as much as will render it sweetish of clarified honey. Let the patient have it for his only drink till he recovers. Also take wine, honey, salt, and rye meal in equal parts; mix together for a plaster, and apply to the part. This will unite them. Whoever drinks a decoction of the violet, will greatly promote the extraction of broken bones.

### TO KNOW WHETHER THERE BE LOOSE FRAGMENTS OF BONE IN A MAN'S LIMB OR NOT.

§ 663. Take the white of eggs, linseed, and a woman's milk; make a plaster thereof, and apply to the wound. If the plaster does not dry, know that there is a bone therein; if there is not, it will dry crisp.

### FOR MEN WHO HAVE LOST THEIR REASON.

§ 664. Take daisy, field southernwood, and sage; pound well, and mix with wine. Put it aside well covered for three hours; then strain, and let the patient drink it.

### TO RESTORE SPEECH WHEN LOST FROM DISEASE.

§ 665. Take sage, or pimpernel; extract the juice, and pour it into the patient's mouth. It will restore his speech.

### TO PROCURE SLEEP.

§ 666. Take corn poppy, (for it is better than the foreign poppy) and eringo, or the seed thereof; pound them well in a mortar, and mix with wine. Wash the nostrils, eyes, and ears of the patient frequently therewith, and he will sleep.

### ANOTHER.

§ 667. Take the seed of eringo, and henbane, pound them well in a mortar; mix with milk enough to make them into small pills. Let the patient have one every half hour, till he has taken six or eight if need be, and he will sleep without fail.

### ANOTHER.

§ 668. Boil poppy heads in ale; let the patient drink it, and he will sleep.

### ANOTHER.

§ 669. Boil a goat's horn in water; wash your head therewith when cold, and you will sleep. You should also place the boiled horn under your pillow.

### FOR INFLAMMATION OF THE MAMMÆ.

§ 670. Pound plantain and lard well together, and apply it to the part till it is well.

### FOR A PAINFUL BREAST.

§ 671. Take the roots of wild rape, scrape the outer rind, make a cavity in the top, (of what you scrape) and put a fragment of sulphate of copper therein. Put it in the earth for four or five days, then remove, take what juice there may be therein, and keep in a glass vessel. Anoint the painful breast with this.

### FOR AN ABSCESS OF THE MAMMÆ.

§ 672. Take virgin wax, spread before the fire, and make a mask to cover the breast. This being used to cover the breast will extract the venom therefrom.

### FOR THE SAME.

§ 673. Take the roots of hemlock; pound fine with barley meal, and the milk of a one-coloured cow; make a warm plaster therewith, and apply to the part.

### ANOTHER.

§ 674. Take the sediment of verjuice and new wax ; make a plaster thereof, and apply. You should make the plaster by boiling.

### PAIN IN IN THE MAMMÆ.

§ 675. Pound mint into a plaster, and apply thereto.

### A WORM IN THE MAMMÆ.

§ 676. Burn crow's eggs and powder ; mix with the juice of wood sage, and administer as a drink.

### A MEDICINE TO PRESERVE FROM EPIDEMICS.

§ 677. Take mutton suet, fresh hog's lard, of each equal parts : melt and strain carefully ; then put on the fire again, and add some well pounded rue. Boil briskly for a time, strain, and anoint thy whole body therewith, rubbing it well and soundly as long as the plague continues.

### ANOTHER.

§ 678. Take a spoonful of the juice of rue, and a spoonful of honey every morning fasting, as long as the epidemic lasts. This, as well as the remedy before mentioned, is a good preservative against all sorts of dangerous epidemics, whether the sweating sickness,* eruptive fevers, typhus, or yellow fever.

### A POTION PREPARED BY DIVINE AUTHORITY, FOR THE HELP OF A WOUNDED MAN, WHICH WILL BE DISCHARGED BY THE WOUND, AND HEAL IT FROM WITHIN, WITHOUT FAIL.

§ 679. Take the tansy, sprigs of hemp, red nettles, raspberry, red cabbage, plantain, avens, and madder (of the last as much as of all the rest.) Pound them well in a mortar, boil in strong ale, strain, and let it be drank in the night warm, and in the morning cold. A red cabbage leaf should be applied to the wound, and nothing more, in order

---

* A remarkable epidemic which prevailed in England in the 16th century, and to which those of the English race were said to be subject at home or abroad, and only they. This doubtless was an exaggeration, and we may infer from our text that it was not quite unknown in Wales, though Willan states that it did not affect the Cymry or the Scotch. This authority thinks that some unsoundness in the wheat of the period must have been the cause.

to cure the patient.   If you collect the above ingredients in the month of May, or at furthest at Midsummer, pounding in a mortar, makeing into small pills, and drying without much wind, or sun, you will be able to have them at hand, when they could not otherwise be had.   It is better even to keep what is needful, and then they may be bruised in ale, and used as above directed.

### THIS IS A MODE OF PREPARING MEDICINES FOR FLATULENT DYSPEPSIA.

§ 980. Take spirits of wine, and pour upon a powder composed of the following dry herbs, even dry juniper berries, fennel seed, the seed of wild carrots, parsley seed, and dill seed.   Keep them in a glass bottle, well stoppered, lest the liquor should evaporate.   Let a spoonful or two be taken when the pain is present.

### THE OIL CALLED IN LATIN OLEUM FŒNUM, OR HAY OIL.

§ 681. Get fresh mown grass, of the finest you can get ; cut it small, and fill therewith a two gallon vessel ; then add as much wine as will fill it ; let it putrify for three days and nights, and boil.   Then add hog's lard, boil till the half is evaporated, and strain carefully.   When this is done, boil it again till another half is evaporated, and remove it to cool.   Let it be kept carefully and clean.   It is useful for all sorts of internal complaints, attended with shivering, and also colics.   It is called *oleum fœnum.*

Many dangerous diseases exist, and here are exhibited a variety of medicines to cure them.

### FOR THE ITCH AND SCABIES.

§ 682. Take sulphur, and unburnt lime ; put them in a vessel, and pour thereon a quart of decoction of sage. Cover it well, and set aside for six hours, then decant the clear liquor.   Wash your body therewith before you go to a dangerous house or bed, and you will be preserved from contagion.

ANOTHER.

§ 683. Take the leaves of sage, pound well with vinegar, and strain under a press. Wash your body with this.

ANOTHER.

§ 684. Take spirits of wine, and pour on powdered sage; cover it carefully so that the spirits should not evaporate. Let it stand three hours, and wash your body therewith.

A PROTECTION AGAINST FEVER IN SPRING.

§ 685. Take the inner bark of oak, sage leaves, and valerian; boil in good ale, and drink a good draught thereof in the morning fasting, three times a week, and it will preserve you from disease.

FOR TYPHUS FEVER.

§ 686. Take a handful of rue, sage, and a portion of fennel seed, pound them together; pour two quarts of good bottled wine thereon. Let it stand well covered for three hours, so that the spirits may not evaporate. Drink four spoonfuls in the morning fasting. It is good for all pestilent diseases.

ANOTHER.

§ 687. Take rue, sage, rosemary, and the inner bark of the mountain ash, a handful of each. Take vinegar, mix the lees, and pour upon the herbs in a distillery, so as to extract the spirits by distillation. Drink a spoonful night and morning. Pour some also into your nostrils, and wash your brows, perinœum, loins, wrists, soles, pit of stomach, chest, and neck with the same. This will preserve you from every pestilence.

ANOTHER.

§ 688. Boil some vinegar, put in an earthen jar, and add a portion of spirits. Inhale the vapour into your mouth and nostrils; then drink some of the liquid the first thing in the morning.

ANOTHER.-

§ 689. Bruise the leaves of sage and rue, a handful of each, and put in a glass bottle, with spirits of wine. Let

3 H

it be carefully stoppered, so that the spirits may not evaporate.    Let a spoonful be drank every morning.

### ANOTHER.

§ 690. Take a good handful of rue, sage, and wood sage ; bruise carefully, and put in an unglazed earthen vessel. Pour two quarts of white wine vinegar thereon, cover carefully, and let it stand six hours ; then wash your whole body therewith in the morning when you get up, and drink a spoonful thereof.    This by God's help will preserve you. It is an excellent protection against a pestilence.

### ANOTHER.

§ 691. Wash in sea water, and scrub your whole body well daily.    In addition to this, wash your whole body with wine or vinegar once a day, and drink a spoonful of sea water every hour.

### ANOTHER.

§ 692. Take marigold, pound well with good wine, vinegar, strong mead, or strong old ale.    Strain carefully, and drink a good draught in the morning fasting, whilst the pestilence lasts.    If you are taken ill, you need no other than this as your only drink.    It is a good preservative against the foreign pestilence, called the plague.

### ANOTHER.

§ 693. Gather wood sage, rosmary, sage, red mint, and southernwood.    Dry thoroughly, and fill a mattress therewith, on which sleep an hour every morning, where there may be a person at hand to awake you.    Take care not to sleep thereon for more than an hour, lest the sleep becomes too heavy.    Having risen, wash your hands and face with vinegar, drinking a mouthful thereof also.    You should drink some good wine once a day, avoiding meat, except mutton two or three times a week, with well baked wheaten bread.

### ANOTHER.

§ 694. Take a portion of rue, mint, sage, and rosemary ; pound them well, sprinkling with vinegar, or white wine meanwhile. Then strain under a press, boil till it becomes thick; add a little honey and marigold seed. When cold, make this extract into pills, of the size of peas, and take one every two hours of the day, as long as the pestilence continues, and if the sweating disease be the epidemic, then incorporate as much as you can   *   *   *   [1] instead of the marigold seed, with the extract, when making it into pills.

### FOR PARALYSIS.

§ 695. Rub your whole body with oil of olives once a day, and scrub it well. Then anoint the nape of the neck and spine as far as the sacrum, with warm honey, scrubbing well. The whole body should then be rubbed soundly, and the patient should go to bed, and cover himself well, till he perspires. When the perspiration has ceased, go to the seaside, and wear flannel about your back and chest. This plan, with God's help, will cure you.

### FOR THE MEASLES.

§ 696. Take apples, and cut small; also the same weight of honey, and put in an unglazed earthen pot on the fire, or before the fire, till it is sufficiently baked. Then mix well, and add some fine scrapings of new wax thereto. Boil it so that the whole may be made into a confection. Take a spoonful fasting each day.

### FOR PAIN IN THE JOINTS, FROM COLD, SPRAIN, OR INJURY.

§ 697. Take a cupful of good old ale, some scrapings of wax or honey: boil together till it becomes thick; spread on a cloth, and apply to the painful part.

### A CONFECTION FOR A PESTILENCE.

§ 698. Take rue, sage, and betony; pound well with honey and some vinegar, till they are so thoroughly incorporated, that one cannot be distinguished from another. Take as much as an acorn thereof every two hours, and an hour afterwards take three spoonfuls of strong wine. Take honey

---

[1] Text does not state what.

also, and suet ; incorporate thoroughly in a mortar, and keep as much as an acorn of this confection in your mouth to dissolve gradually. Anoint your whole body also with the same once a week at least.

### COMMON AND ERUPTIVE FEVERS.

§ 699. Take ground ivy, pound well with wine, and strain under a press. Drink a spoonful or two every hour. Drink an infusion of the same herb when thirsty.

### FOR HOARSENESS.

§ 700. Take wood sorrel, or garden sorrel, and garlick ; pound them well till they are thoroughly incorporated ; then take mutton suet, melt, strain, and mix with honey, in equal parts. Let this mixture be incorporated carefully with the pounded herbs, and take a portion of the confection into your mouth, so that it may dissolve gradually, and swallow as it dissolves. When it is done, take some again and again, till the hoarseness is removed.

### ANOTHER.

§ 701. Take the roots of nettles, dry thoroughly, and powder. Let this powder be incorporated with honey and unsalted butter. A spoonful should be taken night and morning.

### SQUAMOUS ERUPTION.*

§ 702. Take the leaves of burdock, pound them well with a little wine, and strain. Take three spoonfuls, night, morning, and noon, and let a decoction of burdock be your only drink. The part should be fomented with the decoction also, as hot as you can bear it, and anoint it afterwards with an unguent composed of wine, olive oil, and honey. Proven.

There are two kinds of painful and dangerous affections ; even wounds inflicted by poisonous reptiles, and poison. To these the human body is subject, and it is needful to avoid them. Thus are they treated.

* Lepra, psoriasis, and pityriasis.

# PHYSICIANS OF MYDDVAI. 421

## FOR THE BITE OF AN ADDER.

§ 703. Take plantain, and knapweed, mix them with water, and let them be your only drink. By God's help it will cure you.

## ANOTHER.

§ 704. Take the juice of plantain, and oil of olives; drink a portion, and anoint the part with the remainder.

## ANOTHER.

§ 705. Drink decoction of mugwort, and foment the part therewith as well.

## ANOTHER.

§ 706. Take the brains of a red cock, the juice of rue, and sweet milk, or butter milk: apply it to the part; or you may apply a raven warm to the part, milk being your only drink or food till you are cured.

## ANOTHER.

§ 707. If the patient is a man, hold a red cock by the anus to the wound, till he dies; if a woman, let the same be done with a hen.

## ANOTHER.

§ 708. Take a thong of buck skin, and bind the limb each side of the wound, then procure a living hen, feather it about the rump, and hold the part to the wound, till you find it swelling; then apply another in the same way, till the poison is extracted, and let the patient drink a decoction of the following herbs, even the elder and knapweed, or centaury; or he may take a decoction of feverfew, and subsist upon milk. This will cure him, be he man or beast.

## FOR THE BITE OF AN ASP.

§ 709. Take bull's dung, and apply thereto warm.

## FOR THE BITE OF A DISEASED DOG.*

§ 710. Take plantain, and agrimony, pound them with white of eggs, honey, and old lard. Prepare an ointment of them, and anoint the part.

* A mad dog.

### ANOTHER.

§ 711. Take leeks, vinegar, the seed of red fennel, and honey ; mix well, and apply as a plaster to the part.

### FOR POISON.

§ 712. Take two nuts, and three dry figs, rue leaves, and thirty-five grains of salt. Let it be administered to the patient fasting, and let him subsist upon milk alone for forty eight hours.

### ANOTHER.

§ 713. Take centaury, betony, sage, fennel, and scentless dame's violet ; pound them well, mix with wine, and express. Let an egg shellful be taken thereof every hour. This is useful for the bite of a mad dog, or an adder, applying also mallow leaves to the bitten part.

### ANOTHER.

§ 714. Take betony, dry and powder ; then take twice as much as you can raise up between your two fingers of this powder, and mix with L L of wine, boiling till it is reduced to a third. This being drank fasting will be of service.

### FOR DISEASE AND PAIN OF THE FEET.*

§ 715. Boil the roots of tutsan, and pour upon curds. Pound the same with old lard, and apply as a plaster. By God's help it will cure it.

### FOR A CONTUSION OF THE NAIL.

§ 716. Apply a mixture of wheaten meal and honey thereto.

### FOR WEARINESS IN WALKING.

§ 717. Drink an egg shellful of the juice of mugwort, and it will remove your weariness.

### TO REDUCE SWELLING IN THE FEET.

§ 718. Take violet, wild campion, sorrel, agrimony, plantain, marigold, daisy, barley meal, unsalted butter, lard, and the white of eggs. Make them into a plaster, and apply

* Chilblains.

thereto, and if it be hot it will reduce it; but if the disease be cold, take water cress, radish, plantain, rue, dittany, and red nettles, boiled in red wine, and apply.

As the nature of many diseases is unknown, and the way in which they should be treated uncertain, unless the internal character of the same be demonstrated, it is herein stated in what way a man's flesh may be layed open whilst the diseases are being relieved.

THE FOLLOWING IS A POTION WHICH WILL INDUCE SLEEP, WHILST ANY DISEASED PART IS BEING OPENED.

§ 719. Drink the juice of orpine, eringo, poppy, mandrake, ground ivy, hemlock, and lettuce, of each equal parts. Let clean earth be mixed with them, and a potion prepared, then without doubt the patient will sleep. When you are prepared to operate upon the patient, direct that he should avoid sleep as long as he can, and then let some of the potion be poured into his nostrils, and he will sleep without fail.

When you wish to awake him, let a sponge be pounded in vinegar, and put in his nostrils.

If you wish that he should not awake for four days, get a pennyweight of the wax from a dog's ear, and the same quantity of pitch; administer it to the patient, and he will sleep.

When you would that he should awake, take an onion, compounded with vinegar, and pour some into his mouth, and he will awake. Take care that you keep him quiet, and warned of the operation, lest he should be disturbed.

SOME PRECIOUS UNGUENTS.

§ 720. As to bites and contusions (noxious potions and all medicaments, other than precious unguents being excepted,) that wise man, Tholomeus testifies thus :—

When the moon is in the ascendant in scorpio, or cancer, or pisces, they being influenced by the sign of the sun, the moon being obscured by the earth, these are favourable aspects for administering fluid medicines. If the moon should be high in the sky, it is said that such medicaments will turn aside excessive oppression and anger, on which account see that you order such as take a fluid medicine, to walk, and inhale the eastern air. But when he is confined to his room, let him prefer a western aspect, and use it. The lord of this sign will not continue to govern the signs, save for the first two days in each of the twelve; and when those two days are passed, let the physician exercise his craft and skill as may be most proper.

The following is a most notable unguent, useful for a variety of bodily disturbances, that is to say; it is useful for all abscesses and impostumes and diseases, every kind of erysipelas, and cancer, even when extending from one rib to another. It will cleanse every part within and without a man's body, whether a child or a man, so that he will not require a second remedy, whatever be the nature or extent of the wound, or the amount of constitutional irritation present.

Take the following herbs; bugle, hound's tongue, brookweed, cleere eye, agrimony, scurvy grass, ribwort, plantain, chamomile, wild clary, strawberry leaves, white ox eye, daisy, wood sorrel, avens, herb Robert, a handful of each; honeywort, as much as all the herbs together, and half as much as the weight of the herbs of clarified butter; then pound the butter and the herbs together, and let it stand for five days. In five days boil the mass, and strain through a fine linen cloth, just washed. Keep it in a safe vessel, and when you desire to cure some patient of the above disease, let him swallow or eat as much as a nut of the above unguent, with some white wine, and the same should be done at night till he is well. This is termed edible ointment.

The following is an infallible remedy, called THE GRACE OF GOD, and this name it obtained in consequence of its unfailing effects, upon any wound, old or recent. In one night it will heal more safely and perfectly than all other ointments and plasters in a month; by doing more to cleanse ulcers, ll intractable diseases, or morbid granulations, unaided, wherever it is used. It will restore any ruptured or swollen tendons, veins, or joints, into as sound a condition as they ever were in. It is a powerful remedy for any great swelling, whether an inflamed or a white swelling.

It should be prepared in the following manner. Take a pound weight of tormentil, fine rosin four drams, as much of virgin wax, and of a certain shrub, similar to the broom, called maglys and in Latin *maglisse*,* three handfuls. Take as much also of the following herbs, betony, brook weed, wild clary, vervain, and calamint, the blessed rosin,† or *strepuledium*, and a product or sort of wine, called *balm balsami*.‡ Boil them together in a gallon of white wine, till they are reduced to the half; then incorporate and mix them again, when mastic, virgin wax, and a small quantity of woman's milk, who suckles a boy, should be added. And thus should it be mixed and stirred without ceasing; then removed from the fire again, the tormentil, fine rosin, and balsam being added previously. When cooled, it should be kept in a clean vessel. Thus is the "GRACE OF GOD" prepared. The weight of the *strepuledium* should be that of two wheat grains.

### THUS IS A STIMULATING UNGUENT PREPARED.

§ 721. Take the plant called chaste tree, or red vitex, agrimony, and dwarf elder; pound them well, and set them on the fire with butter, and     *     *     *     *     *§ and strain through a linen cloth; applying it to the head warm as a plaster.

### AN EFFECTIVE OINTMENT FOR ANY PAIN OF A COLD NATURE.

§ 722. Take sage, birthwort, ambrosia,‖ wood sage, broom flowers, agrimony, the roots of the cinquefoil, dwarf elder, and heath. Pound them well in a mortar, and put them in a little wine, and a quantity of oil of olives, then let them

---

* Medicago.
† Frankincense in all probability.
‡ Balm of Gilead, or Balsamum Gileadense.
§ Corner of MSS. torn. ‖ Atriplex olida.

digest for seven days,    After that let them be boiled, mixed
with lard, goat's suet, unsalted butter, mutton suet, and wax.
Strain well through a cloth, and add *godarsin*† and rosin
thereto.

### A PRECIOUS OINTMENT FOR ANY KIND OF SORE.

§ 723. Take mutton suet, a he-goat's suet, old lard, bitter
ladies' smock, avens, wood sage, and brook weed, or when
not to be had, privet.   Pound, and boil together, straining
through linen.   Keep it carefully, as it is truly useful.

### THE FOLLOWING IS AN OINTMENT PREPARED BY HIPPOCRATES, FOR PARALYSIS, OR SUCH ACHES.

§ 724. Get a fat gander, and extract the fat, also twice as
much of the fat of a tom cat, and as much of that of a wild
cat, the fat of a fox, a quantity of pepper, a hen's fat,
rosin, two onions, a pennyweight of new wax, bitter ladies'
smock, avens, hyssop, privet, and hemp agrimony; pound
them all, and stuff the gander therewith, roasting it before the
fire as long as any thing exudes.   Take them from the
gander, and boil afterwards in butter and rosin, olibanum
being added.   Strain through linen, and keep well and carefully.   Anoint any such cold ache well by the fire.

### AN OINTMENT TO HEAL WOUNDS.

§ 725. Take old lard, frankincense, and wax; put them
on the fire to melt, and strain through linen, then when cold,
spread with a spatula on linen.   Remove it from the part
twice a day, then warm, and re-apply.   Each time it is
warmed, run the spatula all over it.

### ANOTHER.

§ 726. Take the juice of nettles, the juice or powder of
valerian, the juice of dwarf elder, clear honey, the white of
an egg, and wine in equal parts.   Add some wheat flour
thereto, and incorporate them as a plaster.   It should be
spread on linen, and applied to the wound night and morning,
till it is cured.

---

* Goudron de bordeaux, French tar prepared from the Pinus maritimus.

### FOR SCROPHULA.

§ 727. Take plantain, clary, elder leaves, agrimony, cud-weed, knapweed, strawberry leaves and orpine, with unsalted butter: express through clean linen, and keep for the pur-pose of fomenting the part. Prepare a potion for the patient also, with strawberry leaves, orpine, and the vervain, pound-ing them with wine or ale, or boiling them in water. Let the patient have this for his only drink, for it is truly useful.

### THE FOLLOWING IS A HEALING SALVE.

§ 728. Take the male speedwell, violet, borage, ribwort, plantain, betony, pimpernel, and hyssop, in equal parts. Pound, and add butter thereto, being first thoroughly clar-ified before it is added to the herbs. Boil the herbs with the butter as long as you would boil lamb, or salmon, straining it through a new cloth, and keeping.

### ANOTHER.

§ 729. Take two pennyworth of rosin, a cupful of mutton suet, and twice as much of new wax. Melt them together, remove from the fire, and strain. Divide the molten matter into two parts; colour one part with three obolus weight of verdigris, leaving the other simply coloured by the herbs.

### THUS IS A YELLOW SALVE PREPARED.

§ 730. A couple* of rosin, twice as much of tallow, half as much of wax, and half a cupful of clarified butter: boil and strain through linen. Colour half with verdigris, and boil a little honey with the remainder, leaving it yellow.

### TO PREPARE A YELLOW UNGUENT.

§ 731. Take new wax, yellow rosin, clarified butter, and more mutton suet than the whole together. Boil them to-gether for a while, remove from the fire, and strain through linen.

* Cwpl in Cardiganshire signifies a small quantity.

## TO PREPARE A GREEN HEALING SALVE.

§ 732. Take wax, rosin, clarified honey, betony, violet, borage, and ribwort plantain. Let the meltable articles be molten, and the herbs pounded well and boiled therewith, Let them be on the fire for a short while, then remove, strain through a clean cloth, and let it cool, when it should be kept.

## TO DESTROY A CANCER.

§ 733. Take mastic,* camphor, and frankincense, in equal parts : bruise, and incorporate in a clean vessel, then keep it in a clean bladder. When you proceed to treat the disease, get a shovelful of burning oak, cast a silver spoonful of the powder thereon, and hold the cancer over it. This, if continued, will destroy it.

## TO PREPARE A ROLL OF PLASTER.

§ 734. Take six egg shellfuls of oil of olives, and twice as much of red lead. Grind the lead with the oil, and put on the fire in a brass vessel, mixing it well with a stick. Take a pewter plate in your hand, and strike the stick thereon from time to time, till you find the plaster becoming black. Then remove it, and let it stand till it begins to cool, when you should make it in rolls, covering it with paper before it is quite cool. Let it cool fully, then keep.

## TO PREPARE A DRAWING PLASTER.

§ 735. Take wax, rosin, tar, and lard, and place them on the fire. There should be equal parts of the wax and rosin, the proportion of the tar being a pennyweight. Let the whole be boiled to the hardness of wax.

## A CATAPLASM FOR A SPRAIN, SWELLING, OR THORN.

§ 736. Take biting stone crop, and butter, pound them together, warm a short while by the fire, and apply three or four times to the swelling.

---

* " Tastic " must be a corruption of mastic.

### TO PREPARE A DRY PLASTER.

§ 737. Take the roots of elecampane, bruise and boil well :
add the milk of a one coloured cow; mix well, then reject
the roots, and mix fine wheat meal, or barley meal with
the decoction. Honey, and a little rosin should also be
added, the whole being boiled till thick ; then remove from
the fire, and keep in a clean vessel. When you apply it to
the diseased part, mix some lard therewith, so that it might
not be too dry.

### TO MAKE A POWDER OF THE WHITE OF EGGS.

§ 738. Take a broad baking stone, and lay on the fire,
lay white of eggs thereon till it becomes black, then scrape
it off, and keep carefully.

### FOR PHAGEDENIC ULCERATION ;
BEING A DISEASED OR CANCER-LIKE CONDITION OF THE FLESH, SOMETIMES
SPREADING INTO THE THROAT. AND ABOUT THE LIPS, PHARYNX, OR ROOT OF
THE TONGUE.

§ 739. Take a cupful of vinegar, the same of the juice of
parsley, half a cupful of honey, and as much of treacle ; mix
powdered frankincense therewith, till it is of the thickness
of pap. Let it be applied till a cure takes place. It is the
best application, if continued without interruption till the
sore is well.

### HEALING OINTMENT.

§ 740. Take avens, violet, daisy, bugle, ribwort plantain,
and feverfew ; pound, and boil them well with fresh butter,
and strain. Keep it, for it is useful.

### AN UNGUENT FOR SCROPHULOUS SORES.

§ 741. Take bay leaves, violet, daisy, knapweed, milfoil,
the powder of marsh mallows, and the marrow of an aged
ox ; compound, boil, and strain.

### A HEALING SALVE WHEN THE SKIN IS WOUNDED.

§ 742. Take unsalted butter, and set on the fire, skimming
the surface as it forms ; then take male speedwell, and
bugle, in equal parts, (or milfoil, if bugle is not at hand,)
and boil them well with the butter. If you add bur-reed, the

ointment will be no worse.   Let them be on the fire, adding a
portion of the above herbs, so that the ointment may be of
adequate thickness.   Let it boil as long as lamb; add a little
new wax, mixing it thoroughly.   Boil a while again : when
removing from the fire, add a spoonful of clarified honey,
carefully mixing the whole, and warming it thoroughly.
Remove, stir well, strain through a coarse linen, and keep.
If you wish to prepare some that will act as an escharotic,
get some alum or sulphate of copper in powder, sprinkle
some therof on the surface of the salve in a box, or a wide
shallow dish, stir it well till it cools.   This is useful as an
escharotic for the destruction of proud flesh.

### THUS IS A YELLOW SALVE PREPARED.

§ 743. Take a bottle of rosin, twice as much of mutton
suet, as much of wax, and half a cupful of clarified butter ;
boil together, remove from the fire, and strain.   Colour half
of this salve with verdigris, and mix a little honey with the
other, boiling it longer, so that it may retain its yellow
colour.   It should be kept carefully in a clean vessel for use.

### A LOTION TO HEAL A WOUND OF THE INTEGUMENTS, BONES, OR WHATEVER OTHER PARTS MAY REQUIRE THE USE OF AN ESCHAROTIC.

§ 744. Take plantain, daisy, ribwort plantain, and a gallon
of cold spring water; pound the herbs, and boil in water.
Add a pound of alum thereto, and let it boil down to a third.
The lotion is then ready.

### A FOMENTATION OR WASH FOR A BURNING OR RED INFLAMMATION, THE RESULT OF DROPSY, FIRE, OR SUN HEAT, A BRUISE, OR HURTFUL DISEASE AFFECTING THE PART.

§ 745. Take equal parts of milk and water, mallow
flowers, the berries, or middle bark of elder, pennywort, and
(when obtainable) wood sorrel, common sorrel, or French
(garden) sorrel; boil in the milk and water, and anoint the
part therewith somewhat briskly.   Then apply as much as
may be required of the boiled herbs to the part, as a poultice,
changing it every six hours.

### FOR ERYSIPELAS.

§ 746. Take fumitory, stone crop, house leek, yellow stone crop, Jew's ear, grown on the elder, a glove full of each, or of as many as you can obtain ; pound well in a mortar, boil in unsalted butter, and strain through a cloth. This will quench, and cause it to fade away, so-that it will cure it, if it is applied in the morning frequently.

### FOR AN ABSCESS.

§ 747. Take mutton suet, oatmeal, foxglove, and maiden hair ; boil them till they become a thick mass. Apply it to the part, and it will draw it.

### FOR WEAK WATERY EYES.

§ 748. Take an earthenware vessel, and melt brimstone therein, till two or three times the thickness of your nail covers it. When you go to bed at night, make water in the same vessel, and in the morning wash your eyes therewith ; then pour it off, and make your morning water, therein. Let this stand therein till night, washing your eyes therewith in going to bed. The morning water is best, being stronger than the evening one. If your hearing is hard, dip some black wool therein, and put it in your ears at night in going to bed.

### FOR THE STOMACH ACHE OR COLIC.

§ 749. Take mugwort, plantain, and red nettle; boil in goat's whey, strain through linen, and administer to the patient.

### FOR A SWELLING FROM A BLOW.

§ 750. Take water pimpernel, plantain, and fennel, in equal parts; pound them with rye meal, honey, and the white of eggs. Apply it as a plaster, and the swelling will be healed.

### FOR IRRITATION AND CLOUDINESS OF THE EYE.

§ 751. Take the juice of celandine, pound the herb well with breast milk, whereon a male child is nursed, or the urine of a yearling child. Strain through a press, and apply the juice on a feather to your eye.

### ANOTHER.

§ 752. Pound celandine with goat's milk, and strain through a press. Mix with a little honey, and apply to your eye with a feather, three times a day.

### FOR JAUNDICE.

§ 753. Take dandelion, corn blue bottle, and garden parsley; then pound them well with good strong old ale, and keep it carefully in a narrow mouthed water bottle. Let it be used the first thing in the morning an hour before food, and the last thing an hour at night after food. The dose should be from four egg shellfuls to a pint.

### ANOTHER.

§ 754. Take the sprigs of barbary, and the leaves if obtainable; bruise, and boil well in sound strong ale, till it is reduced to a third, and let it be your only drink.

### FOR EXANTHEMATOUS CONTAMINATION OF THE HUMORS.

§ 755. Take the roots and seed of nettles; pound well, then boil in good cider of half a year or a year old. Let this be your only drink. The best cider is that made with good sour winter apples.

### ANOTHER.

§ 756. Take apples, and bake or boil them; mix them with kine or goat's milk, and let it be your only food or drink for a month or nine weeks, according to the strength of the disease. This food is exceedingly good for lung pock,* or blood pock,† and it will also neutralize the poison of scrophula. It was by means of this treatment that Hywel Feddyg, of Llangynwyd, cured Edward the Confessor, when there was not a physician in Christendom who would promise him an hour of life in consequence of the violence of the lung disease. The Emperor Antonius also made use of it at every spring, and the fall of the leaf, and was thereby preserved

---

* Inflammation or tubercles of the lung.
† Scurvy.

from every eruptive poison of the blood and humors, which is the active cause of all eruptive and suppurative diseases incident to a man's body.

### FOR BLEEDING AT THE NOSE.

§ 757. Take a nettle, pound it well, and fill your nostrils therewith.

### TO DESTROY PARASITES.

§ 758. Take milfoil, pound them well, and apply to the part affected.

### FOR PAIN IN THE EYE.

§ 759. Apply the yolk of eggs and wheat meal over each brow, and it will heal them.

### FOR HEMORRHOIDES.

§ 760. Take lime, and the roots of fern; pound them together, apply to the part, and they will cure it.

### ANOTHER.

§ 761. Boil the roots of fern in spring water till it is reduced to the half, and pour upon a small lump of quick lime. When it has settled, pour off the clean liquor, and wash the piles.

### TO KNOW WHETHER THE PATIENT WILL LIVE OR DIE.

§ 762. Bruise violets, apply to the patient's eyebrows; if he sleep, he will live, if not, he will die.

### TO DESTROY WARTS.

§ 763. Pound willow bark with verjuice or vinegar, and apply them.

### TO EASE HEAT AND PAIN IN WOUNDS.

§ 764. Take the roots of marsh mallows, and the middle bark of elder, equal parts of each, add thereto an equal quantity of white wine, and boil well till it becomes thick; then spread this on a well stretched linen cloth as a poultice, and apply to the wound. If the wound closes

3 K

# 434 PHYSICIANS OF MYDDVAI.

into a plaster, apply thereto, and it will open it.

## FOR DIARHŒA.

§ 765. Take the yolk of seven eggs, twice as much of
clarified honey, the medullary portion of a wheaten loaf reduced to fine crumbs, and a pennyworth of powdered pepper;
boil them together, and eat warm, refraining from drinking
subsequently as long as you can. Use this food till you
recover, for it is the most salutary article of diet in the
world.

There is a variety of chronic diseases which oppress the
heart of man, producing faintness, difficulty of breathing,
and heat in the cardiac region. It is only by much studious
and diligent science, aided by effective medicines that they
can be cured.

## FOR DISEASE OF THE HEART.

§ 766. Take the centaury, boil in good old ale, then pound
the herbs, and boil again in the same liquor. After this
strain it through a clean cloth, add a spoonful of clarified
honey, and boil again. Let it be kept in a covered pot, and
three spoonfuls given daily to the patient whilst fasting.
This will indeed remove the oppression from the heart, and
restore the desire for food and drink, if God will.

## THE OPPRESSION OF THE HEART.

§ 767. Take the juice of fennel and honey; boil together
till they become hard, and eat a portion of the same the
first thing in the morning before food, and the last thing in
the evening after food. It will cure you by God's help.

## TO PREPARE A GARGLE.

§ 768. Take rosemary, sage, hyssop, alum, and good ale;
set on the fire, and boil till the quart is reduced to a pint.
Having boiled it, let it be used warm, and that daily for a
week.

THE FOLLOWING IS THE TREATMENT EMPLOYED BY RHIW-
ALLON FEDDYG FOR THE RELIEF OF CONSTIPATION.

§ 769. Take small beer, unsalted butter, and wheat bran ;
boil them well, strain, and pour into a bladder, in which insert a quill, firmly binding the bladder about it. This pipe
should be passed into the patient's rectum, his head being as
low, and his *pelvis* as high as can conveniently be. The
bladder should then be compressed, and the fluid forced into
the body.

### AN EMETIC.

§ 770. Take the seed of asarabacca, boil in good ale, and
strain. Let this be given to the patient.

### A SALVE TO RELIEVE PAIN, AND CURE A CONTUSED WOUND,

§ 771. Take the flesh of a fat sow of ripe age, and melt the
fat, letting it stand till the salt falls to the bottom. Take
as much of new wax, and boil therewith, adding powdered
mastic, and frankincense thereto, incorporating them well, till
the mass becomes thick as honey. It should be spread with
a spatula, on cloth or leather, and applied to the affected
part twice daily. It will heal it, and remove the pain.

### FOR THE COLIC.

§ 772. Pound watercress well, adding soft spring water
thereto, and oat groats, boiling both to a gruel, straining
carefully. Let it be taken an hour before or after food, the
first thing and the last thing for three succeeding days.

### TO PROCURE SLEEP.

§ 773. Cut the lily whilst the sun is in Leo, and mix the
juice of the shrub called laurel, or in Latin *laurus*,* therewith ; put them in a heap of manure, covering them with
plenty of the same, and they will generate worms. Take
these worms and powder, then put the powder about the
patient's throat, or in his clothes, and he will sleep till it is
removed.

* Laurus.

### TO KNOW WHETHER A MAN WHO HAS BEEN SEVERELY BEATEN WILL RECOVER OR NOT.

§ 774. Take the juice of mouse ear hawk weed, mixed with white wine, and let the patient drink it. If he vomits, he will live, if not, he will die.

### ANOTHER METHOD OF PROGNOSIS.

§ 776. Bruise some violets, and apply to the eyebrows of the patient; if he sleep, he will live, if not, he will die.

### ANOTHER PROGNOSIS.

§ 777. Take the violet, bruise and bind about the forefinger; if he sleep, he will live, if not, he will die. You should accertain this before you interfere with the case.

### FOR THE CARBUNCLE.*

§ 778. Take the roots of the lily, wash carefully, bruise well, and boil in white wine, till it is reduced to the half, straining through new linen. Let it be administered to the patient; it will break the carbuncle, and cure the patient.

### FOR BOILS.

§ 779. Take musk mallow, lard, and earthworms; bruise together, and apply to the affected part.

### ANOTHER.

§ 780. Take the yolk of an egg, and salt; pound into a plaster, and apply thereto.

### WHEN A MAN IS AFFECTED WITH PLAGUE, OR BLACK POCK.†

§ 781. Take white ox eye, (when the centre has become black) tormentil, rue, and if you like add a leaf of bay; wash these carefully, bruise with water, and administer to the patient in strong ale as hot as he can take it. Let this be done whilst the patient is in bed between sheets, and near a good fire, so that he may perspire freely. By God's help, the eruption will be transferred to the sheets.

---

* Plague.
† Malignant small pox, mostly in cachectic subjects, the pustules being black from effused blood.

### FOR A THORN WOUND.

§ 782. Take lard, and the roots of red nettles; pound well, and apply thereto nine times. With God's help it will cure it.

### FOR SEMINAL WEAKNESS.

§ 783. Take powdered pennyroyal, and powdered aniseseed, and administer them to the patient in soup, or sauce. This will prevent the flux by God's help.

### FOR SCABIES.

§ 784. Take the roots of the archangel, boil well, and boil a portion of garlick in another water. Take a good draught of the decoction, and wash your whole body therewith every morning. Boil the residue of the archangel and garlick in unsalted butter, make into an ointment, and anoint your whole body therewith for nine mornings.

The following are the virtues and properties of various medicinal herbs useful to man.

### THE VIRTUES OF SAGE.

§ 785. They are useful when boiled to strengthen the nerves. If an infusion sweetened with honey is drank, it is useful for the lungs. If the fœtus in utero is dead, let the woman boil sage with white wine, strain it carefully, and she will be delivered of the same with safety to her life. Also pound this herb, apply to a poisoned wound, and it will extract the venom; though the wound be full of corruption, it will be cleansed to the very bottom, if dressed with this herb. Let some thereof be taken, pounded small, and the juice mixed with white wine, or the pounded herb macerated in white wine, strong wort, or old mead for a night and strained, then drank fasting. By God's help it will cure the patient. It is a good thing for those in health to drink half a draught in the morning fasting of this potion, in order to preserve health, and prolong life.

### THE VIRTUE OF THE IRIS.

§ 786. The iris is a herb, having a white flower, and its virtues are, that its juice, mixed with honey and wine will dissolve urinary calculus. It will also cure the ague and jaundice, as well as nervousness. When you have no wine, take the juice in strong sound mead, or strong malt wort. It is hot and dry.

### THE FOLLOWING ARE THE VIRTUES OF THE NETTLE.

§ 787. Take the juice of this herb mixed with white wine, strain carefully, and let it cool. Drink some thereof night and morning; it will cure you of the jaundice, renovate the blood, and remove any disease existing therein. If the juice is taken, mixed half and half with barley wort, it will cure the pleurisy in the side, and will renovate and invigorate an aged man in body and mind. If the seed of the nettle in powder is taken, mixed with wine, it is very useful for wind colic, strangury, or a chronic cough, and will reduce a swelling, producing a flow of urine without harm to the bladder.

### THESE ARE THE VIRTUES OF THE BETONY.

§ 788. He who will habituate himself to drink the juice, will escape the strangury. If it is boiled in white wine, and drank, it will cure the colic, and swelling of the stomach. Pounding it small, expressing the juice and applying it with a feather to the eye of a man, will clear and strengthen his sight, and remove specks from the eye. The juice is a good thing to drop into the ears of those who are deaf. The powder mixed with honey is useful for those who cough; it will remove the cough and benefit many diseases of the lungs. It is good for the ague when it comes, and if taken in its absence, it will not attack a man that year. If boiled with leek seed, it will cure the eye, and brighten as well as strengthen the sight. And a wise man has said that if reduced to powder, a snake would rather be broken to pieces, than pass through the powder; and should there be swelling in the stomach, it will reduce it, if boiled with wine and figs, and then given the patient in bed. It is a good thing

to mix it with the juice of red fennel, and clear honey, for
it will certainly clear the eyes; curing them if diseased, and
strengthening the five senses wonderfully.

THE FOLLOWING ARE THE VIRTUES OF PARSLEY, CALLED
*PETROSILIWM** IN LATIN.

§ 789. The parsley is a good herb of a warm hot nature,
and moist in the third degree.   It is useful in all food as a
generator of blood.   It will remove obstructions of the veins
and arteries in a man's body, so that the humors may cir-
culate properly as they should.   This it will certainly do.

It is also well to employ parsley for the relief of fainting,
tertian ague, pleurisy, and dropsy, the juice being taken
for three days successively, without any other drink,   It
will stimulate the spirits greatly, and strengthen the stomach.

There is a kind of parsley called in Welsh perllys yr hel,
because it grows in such places as are occasionally overflowed
by the tide, and is of a salt nature.   In Latin it is called
*petroselinwm marinwm*, and is good in all obstructions of
the urine and humors of the body, as well as colic and
strangury, the juice being taken.   The juice is useful
to destroy unhealthy granulations in a wound.   It will grow
in gardens, where it should be kept wherever the sea is
distant.

THE VIRTUES OF THE FENNEL, CALLED *FUNICULWM*† IN
LATIN.

§ 790. The fennel is warm and dry in the second degree,
and is useful for diseases of the eye.   It is good for every
kind of poison in a man's body, being drank in the form of
powder mixed with white wine or strong old mead.   It is useful for tertian ague, and inflammatory fever ; and if the
seed or herb is boiled in water, till it is strong of the virtues
of the herb, and the head, when subject to the headache,
washed therewith, it will greatly benefit and cure the same,
when the headache is occasioned by cold or fever.   It will
remove the headache very quickly.

* Petroselinum.      † Funiculum.

THE FOLLOWING ARE THE VIRTUES OF ROSEMARY, CALLED
*YSBWYNWYDD*, AND *ROSA MARINA* * IN LATIN.

§ 791. Rosemary is warm and dry in the third degree,
and it is termed a shrub, because it is of a kind between a
herb and a tree.

Take the flowers of rosemary, mix with honey, and eat
them daily fasting. You will not suffer from nausea, or any
other noxious condition, as long as you use this remedy.

The flowers also are specially useful, being boiled with
honey, or white wine to the half, and strained carefully. A
spoonful or two should be drank cold in the morning, a little
honey being taken with it. A small quantity taken when
one is attacked by the colic, will remove it in three hours.
If you wish to apply it to your stomach externally, no
honey should be added thereto.

Take also the leaves of rosemary, and wood sage ; making
them into a potion, and adding honey in the same way. It
is an excellent remedy for the strangury, stone, and catarrh.
It will disintegrate and expel it in the water.

Also, put their flowers or leaves under your head in bed,
and you will not be troubled with disagreeable dreams, or
oppressed with anxiety of mind.

Also, if you carry a stick or fragment of this shrub, no
evil spirit can come near you, or any one do you any harm.

The rosemary has all the virtues of the stone, called jet.

Also, if you procure a spoon made of the stock or root of
this shrub, in the day you drink some broth with it, you will
not receive harm from poison, and you will be preserved all
that day from thunder and lightning, as well as all injurious
assaults.

Also, gather the leaves of the rosemary, pound them
small, strain, and drink the juice ; it will remove all phlegm
from the head and lungs, curing it with all certainty.

Also, if a man has an urinary obstruction; let him seek the
flower or leaves, boiling them with white wine, and drink
thereof as a potion, the first thing in the morning, and the
last at night.

* Rosa Maria.

Also, if the flowers are put with white wine in a distillery, and distilled, the product will be equal to spirits of wine, and will prove a fit substitute in all cases. It is useful as a lotion for the head when affected with a headache from cold or fever, or when a man is threatened with insanity. A spoonful of this liquid with a spoonful of honey, and a spoonful of melted butter, or thick fresh cream is useful for a cough, or the expulsion of phlegm from the lungs.

Also, a decoction thereof is helpful to an insane person, or one threatened with delirium ; indeed it is good for every disorder which can exist in the human body.

It is also well to boil the flowers and leaves in water, and to wash yourself well therewith every morning, omitting to dry it with a cloth, but leaving it to do so naturally. By washing thus with perseverance, the aged will retain a youthful look as long as they live. This water will expel phlegm from the brain, and restrain griping in the use of purgatives. It will expel dropsy, cure the liver, bring warmth to the nerves and veins, disperse an impostume, elevate the spirits, strengthen the bones, and increase the quantity, and improve the quality of the marrow therein. It improves the sight, and constipates the bowels, when boiled in vinegar, and applied to the stomach of the patient. It will promote the formation of blood, and cure the tertian ague. Should a man have debilitated himself by venery, he will be restored to his usual strength, if he confines himself to this as his only drink for nine days.

It will also cure impotence, in either sex, if used with food. When a couple are childless, let the wife, if young, use rosemary.

Also, if a man has a cold attended with fever, let him take rosemary, burn it, and convey the smoke into his nostrils. It will cure him perfectly.

Let him also take the water in which the flowers and leaves shall have been boiled, adding a little honey and pepper, drinking it warm. It is useful for all kinds of coughs ; this is true. Also, take the roots of the shrub, roast

3 L

them till they become a powder, then put *Əᵽu 6 Ə6 ƏⱰpⱵ₣*

*Əₐ(6766 ₣z zᵽ Ə6ᵽƏ6z6 (4z6* in truth.

The bark is useful for intolerable cutaneous irritation, in consequence of a deteriorated condition of the blood.

Its root also boiled in vinegar is good to foment painful joints with. Also rosemary and betony pounded and mixed with pure water, is a good wash for all venomous bites, whether animal or reptile. It will cure them without the help of any other ointment.

### THE FOLLOWING ARE THE VIRTUES OF THE SAGE, WHICH IS CALLED *SALVIA** IN LATIN.

§ 792. The sage is a herb of a hot and dry nature. Boiled in all kinds of food and drink it is useful in nervous cases. It is well to take a decoction thereof as the sole drink; honey being added renders it more useful for the stomach. If a woman has a dead fœtus in utero, let her boil sage in white wine, and drink it cold; she will be safely delivered of her burden. When carefully bruised, and applied to a poisoned wound, it will extract the poison, and heal the wound.

If a wound also be full of blood, let it be applied well bruised to the same, and it will cleanse it.

When a man also has pain under his rib, let him obtain some sage, boil it on the fire as hot as he can drink it, and it will cure him.

Also the decoction in water, or a potion prepared with wine, mead, or ale, is a very excellent drink for the cure of dropsy, whooping cough, or headache.

### HERE FOLLOW THE VIRTUES OF THE NETTLE.

§ 793. The nettle is a very hot and dry herb. If it is boiled in white wine, and strained carefully through linen, left to cool, and drank in the morning and night, it will help a man in the jaundice.

Take the seed of nettles, make into a powder, and boil well in spring water, goat's milk, good white wine, or strong

* Salvia.

old mead. This potion is good for an old cough, and the colic. It will also strengthen the absorbent, and circulating vessels, if salt be added thereto.

Also, take the seed of the nettle, mix with pepper, and temper with wine and honey. Let it be given as a potion, and however untamed the body may be, it will completely subdue it.

### THE VIRTUES OF THE BLESSED THISTLE.*

§ 794. The blessed thistle is an aperient; being eaten it will benefit headache, and the midriff, also, strengthen the hearing. It strengthens the brain and sight, not only by eating it, but also when the juice is applied to the eye. When juice cannot be obtained, let the powder be taken in water, the juice being dropped into the eye. This is good for the removal of extravasation of blood in the eyes. This herb is also a strengthener of the intellect and memory. It is also good for vertigo, and bleeding from the nose and mouth. The powder mixed with honey, will promote the expectoration of phlegm, strengthen the digestion, restore the appetite, ease nausea, and renovate the blood. If the herb is boiled in water and drank, it will prevent deterioration of the blood, and preserve it in a healthy condition. If it is eaten it will strengthen members that are weakened by paralysis, as well as the spinal marrow and brain. It will expel the cold humour which weakens the power of the mind, and the strength of the body. It will also ease painful bowels, and boiled or drank with wine, it will destroy the stone. Whoever will drink it in a male child's urine, will be cured of the plague and dropsy. It will mature the carbuncles, cure cancer and hysteria. The powder will cure hysteria in twelve hours, and if applied to a wound, it will heal it painlessly. If the herb is masticated, it will strengthen the breath. It will cure ague if it is boiled in wine, and drank warm a quarter of an hour before the paroxysm, the patient being covered well with clothes, so that he may perspire. This

* Cardus Benedictus.

will also cure intermittent, inflammatory, and rheumatic fevers. The powder also taken on warm wine, or some of the distilled water of the herb, will quickly deliver the patient from every poison affecting the nerves. If the decoction, juice, or distilled water is drank, and the patient perspires for three hours subsequently, it will cure the patient. The powder of the herb, eaten or drank, will ease pain in the sides and chest. These are the virtues of the blessed thistle.

## THE FOLLOWING ARE THE VIRTUES OF CLEAVERS, OR GOOSE GRASS.

§ 795. The juice taken in spring and summer as the only drink, will expel and completely destroy eruptive poison from the blood and humors. This virus is the cause of all eruptions, boils, scalds, scrophula, lepra, cancer, erysepelas, pneumonia, dropsy, rheumatism, gout, strangury, all sorts of fevers, pocks of flesh and skin, all watery diseases of the eye, all phlegm of the head or stomach, all white swellings of joints or other parts, every inflamed condition of the blood and humors, every headache attended with fever, every oppression of the chest and stomach, or submamary region, every swelling of the legs, feet, or other parts of the body, for there is hardly a disease affecting the human body, but that it is occasioned by an eruptive poison in the blood and humors.

Their juice is thus obtained. Take the whole herb, leaves, blossoms, and seed included, (as the season may be,) and pound them together well: then put in an unglazed earthenware vessel, and fill it up without pressing them; then pour thereon as much as it will admit of pure spring water, and let it stand a night. Some say that it is best that a quarter of it should be sea water, or water salted as much as sea water, for the first week of drinking; then ceasing from the salt water, it should be taken fresh as the only drink for nine weeks. It is wonderful how strong and healthy you will become in that time.

Gather the herbs in spring and summer, and dry well by the morning sun, turning them about so that the sun may dry them completely; doing this during the day, and bringing them under cover at night. If not dry enough, do this another day, and another again, if in consequence of rain and fog they are not dry enough. Take care not to leave them out in foggy muggy weather, as the whole virtue of the herbs will be destroyed thereby. Gather the leaves, flowers, and seed, and dry them separately, keeping them in an oak chest, or a basket of wheaten straw, covered over well. When required, take the leaves, make an infusion thereof, and drink for three weeks; after that make an infusion of the blossoms, and drink for three weeks; then make an infusion of the seed, and drink for three weeks. Thus you will proceed in God's order, the consistency of nature, and in accord with the constitution and season of the year.

This is the way in which an infusion is made of these herbs; bruise them small with your hands, and fill up an unglazed earthen vessel therewith, covering it with running water boiled. Before you do this, cover the herbs with the hair-bottom of a milk strainer, so that the herbs may not get over the edge of the vessel when the water is poured thereon. Let the vessel stand well covered for six hours, and use the infusion for your sole drink. The herbs should be expressed at night under a press, and the decoction received through a strainer into a clean vessel. It should be drank warm in going to bed. Should there be any sort of eruption, boil, impostume, ringworm, scab, itching, burning, wound, ulcer, or contusion on your body, wash it with a lotion of the herbs, either juice or decoction. If the disease be considerable, apply the herbs bruised thereto. This treatment with potions and local applications has healed the scrophula, the skin disease called in Latin *lepra*, and the cancer, when it had destroyed the flesh to the bones.

Take also the seed of the herbs when ripe, and dry in an oven after baking two or three times. When dry enough, powder them in a stone mortar, keeping the powder in a glass bottle, well covered; carry this with you on a journey, and take a spoonful on clear water three times a day. It will preserve you from all kinds of complaints, and will serve instead of food in case of necessity. It is well to do the same with mallow seed, and to use it in the same way.

### THE FOLLOWING ARE THE VIRTUES OF THE MISTLETOE.

§ 796. The mistletoe most frequently grows on the apple tree, or the hawthorn, and occasionally on the oak, which should be preferred, though it is a most excellent plant wherever it grows. Its property is to strengthen the body, more than any other plant. Gather it in Christmas time, when the berries are quite ripe, and pick the berries from the branches; pour boiling water thereon, covering the vessel in which they are contained, and setting it to stand near the fire, so that it may simmer a night and a day. It should be then strained to a clean vessel, through a hair cloth. Let the leaves and sprigs of the plant be bruised small, and laid on a hot baking stone, where they should be thoroughly roasted, being stirred about meanwhile so that they may not be burned. When roasted enough, they should be powdered, the half thereof being used for that purpose, and the remainder burnt to fine ashes. The powder and the ashes should be carefully preserved in separate glass vials.

In any case of bodily debility, whether in the nerves, joints, back, head or brain, stomach, heart, lungs, or kidneys, take three spoonfuls of the decoction, and mix with boiling water, ale, mead, or milk; then add to a good draught thereof a spoonful of the powder, which should be drank in the morning fasting. Half as much should be taken the last thing at night. It is good for any kind of disease of the brain, nerves, and back, epilepsia, mania, or mental infirmity of any kind, paralysis, all weakness of joints, sight, hearing, or senses. It will promote fruitfulness, the begetting of children, and restrain seminal flux. The man who takes a spoonful thereof daily in his drink will enjoy uninterrupted health, strength of body, and manly vigour.

* i.e. Misseltoe.

The same result will follow if he takes a spoonful of the decoction in his drink daily.

If a patient is ill of strangury, flatulent dyspepsia, or dropsy, let him take a spoonful of the ashes on drink three times a day, and when practicable let him drink an infusion of the plant, either fresh gathered or dry. It will preserve and cure him.

When the plant grows near at hand, he need only gather the berries fresh daily as wanted, for a decoction, and the plant fresh for an infusion. But when it can only be had far off, let it be used as directed, the plants being kept dry in the house all through the year, gathering them summer, winter, and spring, as they can be procured.

The best places to procure them is Monmouthshire, Somersetshire, Brecknockshire, and Shropshire. The best time to gather them is in the depth of winter, from the feast of St. Andrews to Candlemas; and it is also well to gather the green herb from the feast of St. James to the Calends of November. In order to procure their ashes, it is best that they should be burnt green before they have lost their sap.

THE FOLLOWING ARE THE VIRTUES OF THE OAK.

§ 797. The oak will supply a variety of remedies, for all diseases proceeding from weakness in the nerves, spinal marrow, and brain. Remedies are procured from the oak in a variety of ways.

Take fresh chips of oak, and macerate in running water, till their virtues be extracted; then take them out and put in some fresh chips, treating them as before. This being done nine times, boil the liquor to the half, put in a pound of honey to each two gallons, and ferment. A quantity equal to the honey, or any less quantity of the decoction of the mistletoe, may be added if there is any at hand; but if not, it will be a very excellent drink nevertheless, and is called OAK BEER. It is the best drink of any to strengthen the body, constitution, nerves, brain, and spinal marrow. It will also cure the diseases which proceed from weakness, a good draught being drank every morning fasting.

The inner bark of the oak is an excellent tonic. It should be kept, dried and powdered, as well as simply well dried, so that it may be at hand when needed, in either form. It is excellent when taken in ale, or as a decoction in all cases of debility, in all fevers, whether continued or inflammatory, in tertian or quartan intermittants, or when eruptive poison is present in the blood or humors. A decoction of the fresh bark boiled in ale, or the milk of kine or goats, is very good in the same diseases.

Take ripe acorns, let them be very crisply roasted, and kept in a well covered oak vessel. Take a spoonful on your drink night and morning. Whenever a man or woman is the subject of functional or seminal weakness, three table spoonfuls of this powder should be boiled in a good draught of goat's or kine's milk, then drank mixed with honey night and morning, for it will remove the complaint. It is useful for all the before mentioned diseases, for uterine hemorrhage in women, for eruptions in all manner of men, and for diseased lungs. It is an excellent ordinary diet, (mixed with well baked wheaten bread) for all weak persons, or those subject to affections of the lungs, or bodily or constitutional debility of any kind.

Malt some acorns and make ale therewith. It is the best and most healthy of any, and an excellent tonic in cases of debility, or diseases proceeding therefrom.

Gather the leaves of the oak in August or September, dry well, and keep covered. If applied to any contused integument, or watery excoriation, they will heal it.

Take roasted acorns, or the inner bark roasted, ground with bread corn, and make bread therewith. This bread is the best of any to strengthen a man's body, and to remove all complaints resulting from the winter cold or humidity.

THE FOLLOWING ARE THE VIRTUES OF THE VERVAIN.

§ 798. Should you be affected with scrophula, take a decoction or infusion of vervain, gathering the entire plant when in seed ; roast it well and powder. Keep this very carefully in a well covered vessel; mix it with your ordinary drink for habitual use. Boil the entire plant, root and seed included, in ale, mead, goat's or kine's milk, and let it be your habitual drink. Mix the powder also with your bread, and let it be your habitual diet, with goat's milk, or with cow's milk, when you have no goat's. If one is affected with running sores, the powder should be sprinkled thereon; and take the plant, root and all, pound, and boil with fresh butter, and a little wax, strain well, and apply it; and take the juice of the entire plant, and rub it on your chest daily, as long as the plants can be procured. In Winter mix the powder with honey, and anoint in the same way. The whole plant is good for all diseases proceeding from the poison of scrophula, whether affecting the lungs, liver, kidneys, brain, eyes, or any other part. Gather this, and every other herb in the name of God, and give no heed to those who say that it should be gathered in the name of the devil, as the devil has nothing to do with goodness.

THE FOLLOWING IS AN EXPOSITION OF THE FOUR ELEMENTS OF MAN; WHENCE PROCEED THE FOUR CONSTITUTIONS OR TEMPERAMENTS OF MAN, VIZ., THE SANGUINEOUS, THE CHOLERIC, THE PHLEGMATIC, AND THE MELANCHOLIC.

§ 799. To recognise persons of a sanguineous constitution. A person of sanguineous constitution will be naturally fat, but he is not simply fat, as that would show a cold nature; for as Avicenna* says, an abundance of flesh indicates a hot nature; and plenty of flesh is the result of an abundance of blood, as Avicenna says. Every ruddy red haired spare man, is of a sanguine temperament, as Galen says. Sanguineous men will be merry, and fond of listening to tales and merriment, and for the same cause they are incontinent, and apt to give way to their animal propensities. They will

* Avicenna, or *Abou-Ali-Alhussein-Ben-Abdallah-Ebn-Sina*, the Prince of Arabian Philosophers and Physicians, was born in the neighbourhood of Bokhara, in 910, and died of intemperance, A.D. 1038, after having experienced the vicissitudes of fortune, and being reduced from the post of Grand Vizier to the Sultan Mahmoud to the condition of a fugitive. He wrote "Canorum Medicinæ"; " De Medicinis Cordialibus "; " Cantica " " Opera Philosophica " &c., of which different versions have been made in Hebrew and Latin. ED.

also drink wine jovially. A sanguineous man will have his food of the best kind, for sanguineous people will seek that which corresponds mostly with their nature. A sanguineous man will also be apt to play, for his blood will have merriment. He will also be fair, from the nature of his constitution, eloquent of speech, apt to acquire all knowledge, arts, and deep systems. He will be poetically inclined, and will delight in imagination, and ambitious projects. He will not easily be instigated to anger; will be of a generous disposition, not covetous, amiable, of an affectionate behaviour, and kindly conduct. He will be of ruddy complexion, for as Avicenna observes, a ruddy complexion of the skin indicates an abundance of blood. It should be of a clear transparent red, not livid red, as is the case with those whose countenances are florid in consequence of drinking to excess, or subsisting upon a vegetable diet; for such a complexion indicates lepra, scurvy, excess of humour and blood. He will sing sweetly and amiably with his voice, he will delight in music, and social intercourse with singers, and with the merry and poetical. He will delight in the harp, and all instrumental music; will be quick and industrious in work, or on errand; he will also be brave and confident from heat of blood, and will be gentlemanly in his deportment from activity of circulation. When uneducated, he will be apt to become conceited of his own parts, as well as cross grained, impertinent and disagreeable, in consequence of the over excited state of the blood. He will be more disposed to fix his mind, and act upon the near than the distant. He will also learn from genius rather than study, and will be satirical and curt in what he says or does. He is apt to laugh and be jolly without reason, save the excited and untameable tendency of the sanguineous temperament.

## TO RECOGNISE THE PHLEGMATIC TEMPERAMENT.

§ 800. One who is of a phlegmatic temperament will have brown hair, because his constitution is but weak. In the second place, phlegmatic persons will be short and fat, as their natural strength is not such as to permit them to continue growing. They will be also less energetic than persons of the other temperaments, in consequence of their coldness, which will render them more sleepy also. They will be a prudent people. They will be also idle, and that in consequence of cold, for as heat renders a man light and brisk, so cold makes him heavy and idle; phlegmatic people will also be fat in consequence of bodily impurity. They will also be sluggish in mind, or sleepy, or given to much sleep. If instructed they will be intelligent, and will acquire what will be expected of them; but in consequence of their sluggishness, they will come off but indifferently in all competitive efforts, and will soon succumb. The memory will be bad, and they will not love, but from selfish motives. They will not seek merriment, song, or jollity, and when possessing knowledge, they will be found wanting in genius. But when there is a mixture of the sanguineous in the constitution, then we may often find him a man wise in knowledge, and of strong genius; being patient, long suffering, and discreet. He will not love contention, mimicry, nor flippancy, because he will not love, save what is seemly and substantial.

## TO RECOGNISE THE VAPOURISH CONSTITUTION, AND THE PERSONS WHO ARE OF THAT TEMPERAMENT.

§ 801. He who is of a vapourish or choleric constitution, will be impatient, in consequence of a superfluity of heat, disposing him to precipitancy. One of this constitution will be very ambitious of obtaining superiority, dignity, and authority over others, in as much as natural heat disposes the mind of the man to folly. Vapourish persons will also have a facility of acquiring learning in consequence of the heat of bile, but they will not retain what they have learnt. They will also be high spirited, that is, they will not patiently suffer injustice, in consequence of their heat. They will aspire to great eminence, official position, and social elevation. A choleric man will be as voluptuous as a goat, and passion, rather than love, will direct him in every thing. He will be a deceiver, and will be soon angry on account of trifles, exhibiting in this the heat of vapour, and sanguineous ebullition about the heart. He will be cunning, quick, and imprudent in his policy and plans; being more distinguished for violence than constancy in what he does and thinks. He will be slender in his limbs, ungracious in his address, and yellow as saffron in his complexion. As Avicenna says, this complexion indicates haughtiness, one of slender body and limbs, and one who sees a fault in others where it does not exist, and is blind to his own imperfections. He will be kind to those who honour him, cold and haughty to those who do not, and revengeful towards those who wrongly and falsely injure him. The phlegmatic character cannot be commingled with this constitution; and if it could, a sanguineous temperament will be unfaithful and capricious. Of the four constitutions of man, this is the least capable of amelioration and improvement. Rhys the Physician has termed this the vapourish temperament, as it is occasioned by cardiac ebullition, and the bitterness of the bile in man.

THE FOLLOWING ARE INSTRUCTIONS FOR THE RECOGNITION OF THE NATURE AND CONSTITUTION OF MELANCHOLY, AND OF THE TEMPERAMENT OF THE PERSONS WHO ARE MELANCHOLIC.

§ 802. He who is of a melancholic constitution, will be surly and unmanly, as if at war with himself. Most melancholic people will be also sad and unsociable in consequence of their coldness. They will be also studious, meditative, and thoughtful, as well as disposed to seek solitude. In consequence of the dryness of the brain, their sleep will not be sound, being broken and disturbed with dreams. Of studious minds, their memory will be good. They will be difficult to please, envious, covetous, apt to evil from moral weakness, little able to follow up their good intentions, consequently bad paymasters and cheats. A melancholic man will be a great reader, abstemious, fearful, and his complexion will be earthlike, which, if it has a shade of green, will indicate dignity, as the wise Cassius says. All men of this sort will be exposed to extremes in all things; if sad and sorrowful they will be exceedingly so; if joyful, there will be no limit to their jollity. They love singing in solitude, and from a solitary place, to listen to song and harp. They like to say their minds of others, but in no manner to reveal their own internal feelings. They are lovers of song and curious research, but do not much care to show it. They are apt to cultivate the arts and sciences, taking care to understand what they are about, and to be careful as to what they say and do. If there is a mixture of the sanguineous, they will be found a superior class of men. If choleric be the mixture, they will be bitter, surly, and most disagreeable men. If there is a phlegmatic admixture, there will be a tendency to insanity, and mental strife. This class of men will be slender of body and limbs. Many a poet will be found of this constitution, and often will they exhibit inordinate love, and excessive hate.

Here are recorded the following charms and medical feats discovered through the grace of God, and the intelligence of the sages and saints of olden times.

### TO OBLIGE A MAN TO CONFESS WHAT HE HAS DONE.

§ 803. Take a frog alive from the water, extract his tongue, and put him again in the water. Lay this same tongue upon the heart of a sleeping man, and he will confess his deeds in his sleep.

### FOR THE TOOTHACHE; A CHARM.

§ 804. Saint Mary sat on a stone, the stone being near her hermitage, when the Holy Ghost came to her, she being sad. Why art thou sad, mother of my Lord, and what pain tormenteth thee? My teeth are painful, a worm called megrim has penetrated them, and I have masticated, and swallowed it. I adjure thee daffin o negrbina by the Father, and the Son, and the Holy Ghost, the Virgin Mary, and God, the munificent Physician, that thou dost not permit any disease, dolour, or molestation to affect this servant of

God here present, either in tooth, eye, head, or in the whole of her teeth together.  So be it.  Amen.

### A CHARM FOR UTERINE DISEASE WHICH WAS GIVEN BY RHIWALLON THE PHYSICIAN TO GWYRVYL, THE DAUGHTER OF GRUFFYDD AP TEWDWR.

§ 805.  I adjure thee, thou diseased *uterus*, by the Father, the Son, and the Holy Ghost, so that thou mightest not inflict pain, nor have power (for evil) in me Gwyrvyl, the daughter of Rhys, the servant of God, either in the head, breast, stomach, or any other part of my body.  Let God the Father prevail, let God the Son prevail, and let God the Holy Ghost prevail.  Even so be it.  Amen.

### FOR THE TOOTHACHE.

§ 806.  Get an iron nail, and engrave the following words thereon, -|- agla -|- Sabaoth -|- athanatos -|- and insert the nail under the affected tooth.  Then drive it into an oak tree, and whilst it remains there the toothache will not return.  But you should carve on the tree with the nail the name of the man affected with toothache, repeating the following :  By the power of the Father and these consecrated words, as thou enterest into this wood, so let the pain and disease depart from the tooth of the sufferer.  Even so be it.  Amen.

### THUS DID RHIWALLON THE PHYSICIAN RESTRAIN A BLEEDING IN THE CASE OF THE KNIGHT LOGRANIUS.  SANGUIS THE KNIGHT PIERCED THE SIDE OF CHRIST, THE SON OF THE VIRGIN MARY, AND IN CONSEQUENCE THERE ISSUED THE BLOOD AND WATER.

-|- Stay thou blood -|- in the name of the Father, stay thou blood -|- in the name of the Son, stay thou blood -|- in the name of the Holy Ghost, rest thou blood -|- in the name of the blessed Trinity, thou wound bleed not -|-.

Vnnûth Dews Patris, Vnnûth Dews Filius, Vnnûth Dews Spiritus Sanctus -|- Christi Amen -|- Amen -|- Amen -|- Amen -|- so be it.

### TO PRODUCE SLEEP.

§ 807.  Take a goat's horn, and carve the name of the seven sleepers thereon, making a knife haft of it.  The writing should begin at the blade, and these are their names, Anaxeimeys, Malchus, Marsianus, Denys, Thon, Serapion, Constantynn. When the names are inscribed, lay the knife under the sick man's head unknown to him, and he will sleep.

𝔓𝔯𝔬 𝔪𝔬𝔯𝔟𝔬 𝔨𝔞𝔡𝔢𝔫𝔡𝔬, OR EPILEPTIC DISEASE, WHICH CASTS A MAN DOWN IN AN INSENSIBLE STATE.

§ 808. Set thy mind upon God, and say these words three times in the patient's ear, 𝔄𝔫𝔞𝔪𝔷𝔞𝔭𝔱𝔞, and when he is restored from the fit administer him some dog's gall. The gall bladder should be hung in the house where the sick man dwells, for three days, in a place where it may be exposed to the wind ; then it should be boiled in a quart of ale, till it is reduced to a pint, and given to the patient to drink in the intervals of the fit.

The following is a charm which was made by the Lord Jesus Christ Himself, and shown to the three brethren, asking them where they went ; we go said they to the mount of Olives, to gather herbs to heal wounds and contusions. Then said He, return again and take some oil of olives, the white of eggs, and black wool, applying them to the injured parts, saying thus: I adjure thee, O wound, by the grace and power of the eight wounds which were in the true God, and true Man, which He received in His most holy body in order to our redemption, by that which Thou, Jesus Christ, didst Thyself desire, by the weariness which Thou didst suffer, and the atonement which Thou didst Thyself make, that this wound shall neither pain, nor smell, nor putrify, in the name of the Father, the Son, and the Holy Ghost ; let it be so. Amen.

FOR AN AGUE ; A CHARM.

§ 809. Put the following writing on the sick man's stomach, hanging it about his neck.

When our Lord Jesus Christ beheld the cross which was prepared for Him, He trembled greatly, and the Jews asked Him thus, dost Thou fear this cross, or is it the ague that affects Thee? Jesus answered them thus, I fear not this cross, nor am I yet affected with the ague, but I tremble before my Heavenly Father, in contemplating what He prepares for those who shall crucify Me; and for a truth to you I speak, that whatsoever man shall hear the words I say, and shall believe them, and shall do all that I have commanded therein, prostrating himself before his Heavenly Father, he shall never suffer from the ague, nor shall he have any fear. And now, O Lord Jesus Christ, grant that of thy mercy, the ague may not afflict or trouble thy servant, and the servant of God the Father from Heaven, neither now at present, nor at any other time during his life and existence in this world, in the name of the Father, and the Son, and the Holy Ghost. So be it. Ever Amen.

### TO KNOW WHETHER A SICK MAN SHALL LIVE OR DIE.

§ 810. Take an egg layed on Thursday, in the house in which the sick man dwells, and write the following thereon : *F G O G Y L O Y S*, and put it in a safe place, outside the house. On the following morning break the egg, if blood comes out of it, he will die, if not, he will live.

### FOR THE DROPSY, OR HYDROPS.

§ 811. Rub young swallows with saffron, and in a short time the old swallows will bring them a stone; with this stone the patient will be cured of the *hydrops*.

### HOW TO LET BLOOD SO AS TO PRESERVE A MAN'S SIGHT.

§ 812. Whosoever is bled in the right arm on the eighteenth day of March, and the 20th day of the month of April, in the left arm, will never be blind, for it has been often proved.

### FOR WARTS.

§ 813. Wash the warts with the water from a font in which the seventh son of the same man and wife is baptized.

### A WAY IN WHICH A THING CAN BE SEEN, WHICH IS INVISIBLE TO OTHERS.

§ 814. Take the gall of a cat, and a hen's fat, mixing them together. Put this in your eyes, and you will see things which are invisible to others.

## TO ENABLE A MAN TO HOLD FIRE IN HIS HAND.

§ 815. Take marsh mallows, and the white of two eggs, anoint your hands therewith, mixed together ; then cover your hands with powdered alum, and you may handle fire without harm, or hold fire and hot iron in your hand without fear.

## A SNAKE'S SKIN.

The following are the twelve characteristics of a snake's skin, which Alphibam testifies of, and states to be true and effectual to those that use it. I have translated them out of the Arabic to Latin, and from Latin to Cymraeg also.

When the moon is in her first increase, under the sign called Aries, or the Ram, which falls about the middle of the month of March, on the third day of the Calends of April, when the first seed under this sign are formed, then burn the skin of a snake, which has been cast in the time of harvest. Take the ashes, and keep them carefully, for they are the most precious application which any human tongue can order. Let the first instance at hand suffice : whosoever has a fresh wound, let him cover it with a little of this ash, and it will heal it in three days.

---

Here follows a list of the names of the herbs, fruits, and vegetable substances, which every Physician ought to know and use, in order to heal wounds and diseases in the human body.*

The above herbs and plants, that is to say, as many as possible of them, ought to be grown by every Physician in his garden and orchards, in a plot of good land, sheltered, and facing the sun, that they might be at hand when there is need and occasion for them.

---

* As the names are also given in Latin, and the English Synonymes are not properly translations of the Welsh terms, it has not been considered necessary to insert the list in this place. The reader is referred to page 281.

## WEIGHTS AND MEASURES.

The following exhibits the weights and measures, which every Physician should employ, so that he may know certainly what proportions to use, when necessary.

Weights and measures of proportion.

xx grains of wheat make one scruple.

iii scruples make one dram.

iiij drams make one ounce.

xij ounces make one pound.

And thus are they written in the Books of Physicians.*

A grain thus ꝯ

A scruple thus Э

A dram thus Ϩ

An ounce thus ℥

A pound thus S

And thus are they arranged in accordance with these characters.

| xx | ꝯ | to | Э |
| iij | Э | to | Ϩ |
| ɪiij | Ϩ | to | ℥ |
| xij | ℥ | to | S |

Fluid or liquid measures are arranged thus.

Four podfulls make one spoonful.
Four spoonfulls make one eggshellful.
Four eggshellfulls make one cupful.

Four cupfulls make one quart.
Four quarts make one gallon.
Four gallons make one pailful.
Four pailfulls make one grenn.†
Four grenns make one mydd.
Four mydds make one myddi (or hogshead.)

Even so are fluid and liquid measures arranged.

The following are other measures noted by Physicians :—

Two eggshellfulls make half a pan.
Two halfpans, a pan.
Two pans, a phioled.
Two phioleds, a cupful.
Two cupfulls, a quart.

All the measures of solids and fluids should be of warranted weight and measure, so that they may afford warranted and just information, in order that the medicines administered to the sick may neither be ineffective nor poisonous, and that every dose may be of the proportion intended.

The following are conjectural measures, dependent upon the Physician's judgment.

Four grains of wheat, one pea.
Four peas, one acorn.
Four acorns, one pigeon's egg.
Four pigeon's eggs, one hen's egg.
Four hen's eggs, one goose's egg.
Four goose's eggs, one swan's egg.

---

* Those signs are now thus written : Grain *gr.*   Scruple Э.   Dram ℈. Ounce ℥.   Pound *lb.*

† "A large earthen vessel." W. O. P.

These proportions cannot be warranted farther than the Physician's judgment.

———

There are four principal exciting causes of fever and disease in the human body, even :—

i. Fever, excited by an excess of heat or cold.

ij. Eruptive poison in the blood or humors, produced by irregularities in eating and drinking.

iij. Obstructions in the stomach, veins, or other hollow vessels of the body, so that the food, drink, blood or humors, cannot pass on as usual.

iiij. A boil, carbuncle, or plague, and they are occasioned by the entrance of poison into the system. From these four proceed all fevers and diseases incident to the human body, and by the aid of active remedies are they cured.

## USEFUL THINGS.

The following are things useful to be known by every Physician, and head of a family even :—

INFUSION. Pouring water or other fluid in a boiling state upon herbs, or whatever other ingredient that may be required.

DECOCTION. Boiling the herbs or ingredients in the water or fluid required.

POTTAGE OR PORRIDGE. Pouring boiling or cold water, or other fluid such as may be required upon the herbs or other ingredients, leaving them to stand, then straining under a press.

SOAKAGE. Pouring cold or boiling water, or other fluid on any substance capable of being influenced thereby, so as to become incorporated with what is poured thereupon.

CONFECTION. Fluids mixed with powders or other substances capable of being administered as a draught.

POTION. A draught or fluid prepared according to art.

ESSENCE. An amorphous or odoriferous substance, which may be taken in a draught by mouth, or injected into the nostrils, head,* rectum, or other part.

ELECTUARY. Substances incorporated into a dough so as to be eaten.

CONSTITUTION. The disposition which is in a man, or other living being, or herb, or other matter; being their virtue, inherent property, or nature.

PILLS. Incorporated medical substances, formed into small balls so as to be taken at a gulp.

BATH.† An infusion or decoction in which the patient or his limb is to be put.

FOMENTATION. To be applied as a wash to a hurt, whether hot or cold, as may be wanted.

REGIMEN. The food and drink as regulated by medical advice.

———

* External ear.

† This word (ennaint) is improperly rendered "ointment" in the Mabinogi of Geraint ab Erbin.

### THE ESSENTIALS OF A PHYSICIAN.

These things should be in the possession of a Physician: and then follow the characteristics which should distinguish him, which are called the Essentials of a Physician.

i. A lancet to bleed or open an abscess, also a knife somewhat larger.

ij. A steel or silver spatula to spread plaster.

iij. A pipe and bladder in order to inject to the urinary organs or rectum.

iiij. His plasters, his ointments, his pills, his powders, his potions, carefully preserved to meet any demand and occasion.

II. A garden of trees and herbs, where such herbs, shrubs, and trees, as do not everywhere grow naturally, may be kept cultivated, and where foreign trees and plants, which require shelter and culture before they will thrive in Wales, may be grown.

ij. He should also have his dry herbs, roots, seeds, and barks kept at hand, so that they may be had in winter, and other times when they are not to be obtained growing, or above ground.

iij. He should also have at hand, his honey, his wax, his pitch, his rosin, his gums, his oil, his tallow, his grease, his lard, his marble slab, his ale, his wine, his mead, his distillations, and other articles as may be required.

iiij. He should also have at hand his mortars, his strainer, his press, his stone ware, his glass ware, his wooden vessels, his fire utensils, and his vessels for keeping articles, whether of glass, earthen, or silver, with good covers, so that the drugs may not become inert, or poisonous from want of keeping, carelessness, or ignorance.

ii. He should also have weights and balances at hand, either of silver or tin, so that nothing deleterious might get into the drugs. All his liquid or fluid measures should also be made of silver or tin, for the same reason. Likewise his surgical instruments generally, with the exception of lancets, cutting scalpels, and probing needles.

i. All his weights and measures, whether of solids or of liquids, should be of warranted weight and capacity, that he may be certain of the proportions of all ingredients, so that he may neither exceed or come short of the quantity required, as this would render the remedy either inert or poisonous.

ij. He should also have his warranted Books of Art authorized by a master, so that he may be cunning in the judgment and science of the wise and skilful Physicians who have preceded him, and who have written with authority in the Cymraeg, the Latin, and the Arabic.

iij. He should be also declared competent to practice by authority of the wise and learned masters of the art.

iiij. He should be a kind man, gentle, mild, meek, intelligent, wise, and gentlemanly in act and deed, in word and conduct, being careful not to shame those whom he has to examine, particularly when he has to examine women.

īīīj. He should be skilled in all professional acquirements, and should know the complexion and sign of every feminine disease. He should be able to examine the sick, whether man, woman, boy or girl, in regard to age, constitution, sex, and that in a mild, gentlemanly way, both as to address and voice.

īīī. He should carefully keep all professional secrets, nor should he divulge them on any account, to any man, nor on any consideration.

īīīj. He should most carefully avoid intoxication, tippling, or incontinence in any shape, as there can be no trust or dependance upon those Physicians who are addicted to such evil deeds, nor can that respect, which learning and professional intelligence are entitled to be accorded them.

īīīj. He should be a faithful subject, lest he should practice treachery or treason in the exercise of his profession, on native or foreigner, friend or foe ; for the office of a Physician is not to slay, but to preserve from what would slay, and to be in accord with God and His peace, and not with the rage and enmity of man to his fellow man.

īīīīj. He should always have his case of instruments, his emetics and antidotes about him, in case of need.

īīī. He should keep about home as much as he can, so that he may be found when wanted.

īī. He should be constitutionally and habitually devotional, so that the blessing of God may be upon him, and what he does, and that he may be conscientious to do what is right and beneficial in the practice of his art.

And these things are called the Essentials of a Physician.*

* It will be interesting to compare these wise " essentials " with the oath of the Asclepiadæ, in old Greece, being a formula not unlike that in use among the Pythagoreans, and which was in the following words :—

"I swear by Apollo, the Physician, by Æsculapius, by Hygeia, Panacea, and all the gods and goddesses, that, according to my ability and judgment, I will keep-this oath and stipulation, to reckon him, who teaches me this art, equally dear to me as my parents, to share my substances with him, and relieve his necessities if required, to look upon his offspring in the same light as my own brothers, and to teach them this art, if they shall wish to learn it, without fee or stipulation ; and that by precept, lecture, and every other mode of instruction, I will impart a knowledge of this art to my own sons, to those of my teachers, and to disciples bound by a stipulation and oath according to the law of medicine, but to none others. I will follow that system of regimen, which, according to my ability and judgment, I consider for the benefit of my patients ; and abstain from what is deleterious and mischievous. I will give no deadly medicine to any one if asked, nor suggest any such counsel ; and in like manner, I will not give a woman a pessary to produce an abortion. With purity and with holiness I will pass my life, and practice my art. I will not cut persons labouring under the stone, but will leave this to be done by men who are practitioners of the work. Into whatever houses I enter, I will go into them for the benefit of the sick, and will abstain from every voluntary act of mischief or corruption ; and farther, from the seduction of males or females, of freemen or slaves. Whatever in connection with my professional practice, or not in connection with it, I see, or hear, I will not divulge, as reckoning that all such should be kept secret. While I continue to keep this oath inviolate, may it be granted me to enjoy life, and the practice of my art, respected by all men at all times. But should I trespass and violate this oath, may the reverse be my lot."

Adams' Hippocrates, Vol. II. p. 799.

And thus ends this Book of Medicine, and I, Howel the Physician, the son of Rhys, the son of Llywelyn, the son of Philip the Physician, have selected the same from the authorized old books of the original Physicians of Myddvai, even Rhiwallon the Physician, and his three sons, Cadwgan, Gruffudd, and Einion, and the other Physicians, their sons and descendants who succeeded them.

And I, Howel the Physician, am regularly descended in the male line from the said Einion, the son of Rhiwallon the Physician of Myddvai, being resident in Cilgwryd, in Gower. May the grace and blessing of God attend this Book, and him who studies it as a directory of the art, for the love of God, and the health of the diseased and mained.

Amen.　With God's help even so let it be.

I, William Bona have transcribed this Work from the Book of John Jones, the Physician, of Myddvai, who was the last of the descendants of the Physicians of Myddvai, Anno Christi, 1743.

And I, Iolo Morganwg have re-written the same carefully from the Book of the above William Bona, now in the possession of Thomas Bona, Physician, of the Parish of Llanfihangel Iorwerth, in the County of Carmarthen, in the year 1801; and with old Howel the Physician I say,

The grace of God attend it.

I, John Pughe, Fellow of the Royal College of Surgeons, of Penhelyg House, near Aberdovey, Merionethshire, have finished translating the same into English, this 12th day of February, 1861.

# INDEX.

D. J. RODERIC, PRINTER, LLANDOVERY.